REDESIGNING
THE COMMUNIST ECONOMY:

THE POLITICS OF ECONOMIC
REFORM IN EASTERN EUROPE

PAUL M. JOHNSON

EAST EUROPEAN MONOGRAPHS, BOULDER
DISTRIBUTED BY COLUMBIA UNIVERSITY PRESS, NEW YORK

1989

EAST EUROPEAN MONOGRAPHS, NO. CCLXX

**for my children,
Charles and Laura**

CONTENTS

Acknowledgements

The intellectual debts I have amassed in this undertaking are so numerous as to defy all accounting. This study began as a doctoral dissertation at Stanford University in the mid-1970s, and, although the original manuscript has been extensively revised, updated and expanded since they last laid eyes on it, the advice and helpful suggestions of my principal advisor, Jan Triska, and the other members of my committee, Gabriel Almond and Robert North, did much during the formative stages to improve the final product. I also want to register my special gratitude to several people whose comments in conversations or written notes at one time or another helped me to clarify important points — Valerie Bunce, Cal Clark, Paul Cocks, Ellen Comisso, Peter Hardi, Janos Kornai, Andrzej Korbonski, John Michael Montias, the late Raymond Powell, Alex Pravda, Stephen Sachs, Maurice Simon, and Wayne Vucinich. I would also like to acknowledge gratefully, even if necessarily anonymously, the assistance of Polish, Czech, Hungarian, Romanian and East German scholars whose willingness to recount personal experiences in promoting new economic practices and policies proved invaluable to my understanding of the politics of economic reform. My research was greatly facilitated by a grant for summer language study from Stanford's Committee on Russian and East European Studies and by my participation in the Stanford University/-Warsaw University Exchange Program during 1973-1974. Even though my memory fails me when I try to recall all their names, I am grateful indeed to the small army of specialized staff research librarians whose professional skills I have tapped over the years in my fumbling efforts to exploit the Russian and East European holdings of Stanford Library, the Hoover Institution, the Library of Congress, and the Yale University libraries. My thanks also go to Mary Schneider, who handled the word processing chores for the final manuscript with patience and unfailing good humor, and to Aie Rie Lee and Paul Hanna, who assisted in the production of the graphic illustrations.

This book is very much the better for all these people's help, and I pray that my gentle readers will hold none of them too harshly to account for any remaining errors or shortcomings they may negligently have allowed the author to perpetrate.

INTRODUCTION

Periodic conflicts over issues of economic policy and even over the basic legitimacy or effectiveness of economic institutions are characteristic of the politics of our age, and countries governed by Communist parties exhibit no special immunity to this consequence of modernity and a rapidly changing environment. If anything, economic matters are much more readily politicized in Communist systems than is normally the case in Western-style liberal democracies (although, to be sure, the political processes by which economic issues are resolved differ radically in the respective systems). Because Communist revolutions seek systematically to abolish the "bourgeois-liberal" distinction between separate "economic," "social," and "political" spheres of human activity and to integrate them into a single rationalized and · consciously controlled structure, "economic" decision-making and the exercise of authority in "economic" organizations are generally understood to constitute "political" activity in a very immediate and practical sense. In an order where state ownership of the means of production and the systematic penetration of secondary groups and associations by agencies of central control give the same relatively small group of leaders the ultimate powers of decision and supervision over almost all forms of organized human activity, the distinction between economic, social, and political authority becomes largely abstract. Not only "macroeconomic" decisions but also "microeconomic" ones involve the application of political criteria as well as economic criteria, and the authority to decide such matters at any level derives its legitimacy from delegation through hierarchies by the top leadership of the Party and state. Dealing with economic questions occupies the time and attention of state and Party officialdom to an extent unparalleled in Western capitalist states.

The decade of the 1960's was a period in which the long-established verities of economic policy and the basic institutions of socialist economic planning and administration were called in question by the increasingly disappointing performance of a number of the East European economies. It was also a period of rather intense political conflict in many of these same countries, and one of the most important sources of both intra-elite and elite-mass tensions was precisely the changed economic situation. Given the attenuated boundaries between the economic and the political systems in East European countries, the inevitable disruptions and conflicts of interest attendant upon efforts to adapt economic institutions and practices manifested themselves almost immediately in political form. At issue in the struggles over economic reform were not only the question of how best to ensure the future prosperity and development of the nation but also which mechanism should govern the social distribution of material wealth, social status, and political power — issues with crucial implications for virtually every important segment of the population and for powerful actors abroad as well. The ability and inclination of the top East European political leadership groups to adopt and successfully to implement major changes in their approaches to economic planning and management were in all cases seriously constrained by political considerations. In a very real sense, to examine the politics of economic reform during the 1960's is to probe many of the mechanisms and processes by which the basic values and structures of politics are maintained and transformed in industrialized Communist states.

Chapter I explores the various concepts of "correct" socialist economic organization which have historically had an impact on East European practice. It examines the evolution of Soviet and East European economic thought that made it possible for alternatives to the previously established "Stalinist" model of planning and management to be elaborated by East European economists and to be brought forward in the 1960's as serious and concrete proposals for the consideration of policy-makers. The focus here is on the realm of ideas and how "reformist" proposals for decentralization of economic decision-making and greater reliance upon market mechanisms were legitimated and made to seem compatible with the official ideology, thus greatly enhancing the possibilities for their practical adoption as policy innovations.

Chapter II examines the period of the early and middle 1960's, when most of the East European countries undertook concrete programs of economic reform. In this chapter, an effort is made to account for the varying degrees of "radicalism" exhibited by the programs adopted in the different countries. The analysis is carried out at a "macro" level, and the basic approach is to treat economic reform as an adaptive response of a self-maintaining system to a persistent decline in the economic subsystem's performance below acceptable levels. As a first approximation, the top national leadership of each country is treated as a single decision-making unit, and the degree of reform is explained as a function of the magnitude of the economic performance gap, the "openness" of the decision-making process to informational inputs from outside the narrow economic administrative elite, and the degree of constraint on national policy-making imposed from outside by actors in the international environment (principally by the leaders of the U.S.S.R.).

Chapter III relaxes the assumption of a unitary decision-maker implicit in the analysis of Chapter II and investigates the actual processes by which the issues of economic reform were decided in those countries where they came in for serious elite consideration. In general, the adoption (and especially the implementation) of substantial economic reform programs involved a considerable degree of conflict among the policy-making elites. System adaptation is seen to be governed in part by the approaches taken to contain and resolve elite conflict. The role of the Communist Party's first secretary in the initiation of the economic reforms and his ability and willingness to mobilize support for them to overcome institutionally-based sources of opposition are examined as important determinants of adaptability in economic institutions.

Chapter IV considers the impact of market-oriented, decentralizing economic reforms on the broader public and the kinds of reactions that were most significant for the evolution of elite-mass political relationships. The main focus is on the experiences of the countries which went the farthest in implementing "radical" economic reforms in the 1960's — Czechoslovakia and Hungary. Given particular attention are the implications for the interests of middle-level Party and state officials, enterprise managers, and industrial manual workers, especially the ways in which the economic reforms brought (or threatened to bring) changes in the social allocation of wealth, status, power, and security. Of particular interest is the way in which the actual and threatened responses of these sizable groups within the population imposed severe constraints upon the leadership's freedom of action in carrying out their initial policy initiatives and led to the creation of more regularized channels for the expression (and "taming") of the particularized group interests of those who otherwise threatened to thwart the reform's successful functioning and even to precipitate a possible political crisis.

Chapter V summarizes the main findings and conclusions derived from the study of the East European economic reform movements of the 1960s.

The "Afterword" is appended to provide an overview of developments in the region since the early 1970s, including the current revival of economic reformism that began in 1978-1979 and greatly accelerated with the accession of Mikhail Gorbachev to leadership in the Kremlin. The prospects for successful implementation of this latest round of economic reforms are then discussed in the light of the experiences of the 1960s.

CHAPTER 1

PREVIOUS MODELS OF SOCIALIST ECONOMIC ORGANIZATION

The proposals for restructuring the systems of economic planning and management that proliferated in most of the East European Communist countries during the 1960's seemed to represent rather radical innovations in Marxist-Leninist economic thought and practice. Certainly they stood in sharp contrast to the established official wisdom and to the institutions that had dominated economic life in these countries almost since the foundation of their post-World War II Communist regimes. But the economic reform proposals were not simply improvised out of thin air to meet the exigencies of the moment. The sheer longevity of the economic model created under Stalin and transferred almost intact to East Europe, coupled with the assiduous efforts of several generations of Soviet propagandists, had fostered excessively narrow conceptions (both in the East and in the West) of the economic arrangements compatible with the continuing domination of economic, political, social, and cultural life by a Leninist party. Nevertheless, the Marxist heritage has long contained elements dissonant with the highly-centralized, administrative-authoritarian model rendered sacrosanct as the only "true socialism" by the 1940's. The gradual retrieval from the memory hole of the history of Soviet economic thought in the 1920's, the re-examination of the various East European experiences with more heterodox forms of economic planning during the period 1944-1947, and the renewal of intellectual contacts with Western economists (socialist and non-socialist) concerned with the theory and practice of economic planning and management — all these byproducts of the thawing process following the death of Stalin contributed to a growing awareness by East European economists of the startling variety of arrangements that have been devised at one time or another to organize economic activity on the basis of public ownership of the means of production. A more critical and instrumental attitude toward the design of economic institutions in turn made possible the revival of theoretical economics as an intellectually and politically respectable discipline in many parts of the Soviet bloc (most notably in Poland and Hungary) and even in the Soviet Union itself.

The vigorous development of theoretical and applied economics in the Soviet bloc during the late 1950's and early 1960's significantly expanded the repertory of specific techniques for planning and managing a socialist economy as professional economists of several nationalities reacted to the particular problems of their own countries. But the economic reform movement was very much a transnational phenomenon, rooted in a common intellectual tradition and reacting against similar established verities. The similarities of the proposals advanced in the various countries derived partly from borrowing from a common storehouse of historical experiences and theoretical knowledge and partly from the fact that many of the key reformist economists kept in touch with each other's economies. Diffusion of reformist proposals took place rather rapidly across national borders, mediated by technical journals, international congresses, informal interactions between individual scholars, and contacts between professional delegations involved in the permanent commissions of the Council for Mutual Economic Assistance (COMECON).

In order to render comprehensible the basic issues and options involved in the various debates over reforming economic planning and management, it is useful to begin by reviewing some of the more important varieties of socialist economic models with which East European economists were familiar in the early 1960's.

Earlier Soviet Models of the Socialist Economy

Leninists and other Marxists have always concurred that the attainment of the "socialist" society necessarily involves the radical transformation of the economic institutions and processes that are the legacy of the capitalist past. The basic premise of historical materialism holds that the character of the relations of production determines (or at least decisively conditions) the development of the political, social, and cultural spheres of human existence. So the task of outlining the appropriate organization of the socialist economy must logically constitute the core of any Marxist theory of the transition to socialism and the building of "communism."

Yet Marxist economic analysis before 1917 was concerned almost entirely with developing and applying a comprehensive critical theory of the capitalist order, with special attention to the internal dynamics that would lead to its inevitable overthrow. Marxist notions about the future economic order of socialism were by no means lacking, but, beyond the elementary imperatives for the abolition of private property in the means of production and the organization of production on a rationally planned basis for the satisfaction of human needs, the prescriptions remained quite remarkably vague and abstract even on the eve of the first successful socialist revolution. Little had been done beyond eclectic repetitions of the small number of passages in the writings of Marx and Engels dealing with the post-revolutionary order (most of which were expressed only negatively, in the context of ridiculing the speculations of their rivals for the leadership of the broader socialist movement). Moreover, the leading Bolshevik theorists had never been much involved with such speculative theorizing on the socialist economy as had taken place, preferring to concentrate quite singlemindedly on the problem of seizing power instead. Apart from the scattered passages in the writings of Marx and Engels, virtually the only major pre-1917 orthodox Marxist treatment of the subject (and the one most familiar to Lenin and his associates) was Kautsky's sketchy outline in his 1906 pamphlet *The Social Revolution*, which was only a slightly revised version of a speech hastily prepared for delivery in Delft in April of 1902.[1]

The most persistently asserted theme in early Marxist and Leninist treatments of the future socialist economy was the necessity to transcend the "spontaneous" regulation of economic processes by an impersonal market mechanism and instead to subordinate economic activity to the conscious, rational control of human subjects disposing collectively of the socialized means of production in the interests of the working class. The replacement of spontaneous economic forces ("the anarchy of the market") by Human Reason (as embodied in an all-embracing economic plan) would, it was assumed, entail not only the abolition of commodity production but also the elimination of money as a circulating medium. Economic calculations necessary for rational plan construction would be carried out in physical rather than value units. With the elimination of the money economy, such economic categories as value, price, profit, rent, interest, wages, etc. would also become obsolete and irrelevant to the conduct of socialist investment, production, and distribution. It was also taken for granted that eliminating the massive waste of resources seen as characteristic of capitalism (embodied above all in unemployment and periodic depression, but as well in the diversion of resources into parasitical and repressive uses instead of production) and the removal of monopolists' self-interested restrictions on the exploitation of scientific-technical progress, would make possible a substantial acceleration of the rate of economic growth as well as a more equitable distribution of material benefits. Moreover, the transition to such arrangements following the seizure of power was expected to be rather rapid.[2]

The task of designing and setting up a system of concrete economic institutions that would be both practically workable and certifiably socialist proved, as is well known, to be much more difficult than was anticipated by the pre-October conventional wisdom of organized Marxism. That the Marxist classics provided but limited authoritative guidance is strikingly apparent from the fact that the first fifteen years of the Soviet state were to witness the elaboration and concrete implementation on a national scale of no fewer than *three* radically different systems of economic planning and management: War Communism, the N.E.P., and the emergent Stalinist system of the early five-year plans. And in their respective periods of ascendancy, each of these systems was elaborately and vehemently defended in sophisticated ideological terms by major Bolshevik leaders as the *only* "objectively correct" (i.e., Marxist) approach to socialist economic administration. (Arguably there was also a fourth embryonic model that received some degree of Bolshevik support briefly: the semi-syndicalist seizure and operation of the factories by their own autonomous workers collectives, with coordination at the regional or national level by an autonomous trade union apparatus. This set-up was endorsed for tactical reasons in the 1919 Bolshevik Program but was soon abandoned in practice. It was never seriously defended by Lenin or any other top Bolshevik as genuinely Marxist, but the intense struggles over the "anarcho-syndicalist deviation" in the Party Congress until 1921 show clearly that such ideas had wide appeal among certain middle-ranking Bolshevik leaders.)

During the period of "War Communism" (roughly from mid-1918 to early 1921) earlier, more millennial Marxist conceptions of socialist economic organization combined with the perceived necessity for maximum mobilization of men and resources to fight the civil war to produce a degree of suppression of market forms and forces never since attained again in any socialist country (with the possible exception of Pol Pot's Cambodia in the late 1970's). "War Communism" is of only limited interest as a functioning model of economic life because in fact almost the exclusive achievements attained were in the field of distribution, while production declined nearly to the vanishing point. War Communism was a method of securing necessary military supplies and maintaining the critical elements of the civilian population at a subsistence level in the midst of economic chaos: it was not primarily a method of producing economic well-being. It involved massive nationalization of large- and small-scale industry and handicrafts, the forced assignment of labor, the administrative allocation of virtually all industrial machinery and supplies, the centralized direction and control of the operative management of production, the effective abolition of the role of money in the economy (through hyperinflationary policies), and the distribution of food and other consumer goods according to a rationing scheme incorporating deliberate class and political discrimination. State enterprises still able to produce did so on the basis of administrative transfers of materials for which no payment was required. Their output similarly was placed immediately at the disposal of the state authorities without compensation, since the enterprises had no effective legal identity separate from that of the state as a whole and were administered very much along the lines of any other more conventional government bureau or office. While workers and employees generally continued to receive monetary wages, paper currency was in fact worthless, and employees' real compensation consisted of payment in kind from the factory's own output (which could be bartered) and rationed foodstuffs distributed through the factories. Under such circumstances, *ex ante* economic calculation for the rational selection of alternative actions and policies was not possible and hence economic planning in the normal sense of the word was precluded. The activities of the central economic bodies are better regarded as *ad hoc* reactions to continually intensifying crises than as "scientific" socialist planning.

The model of socialist organization that was devised during the period of the New Economic Policy (roughly 1921 to 1928) involved a much more substantial role for the "spontaneous" forces of the market. The Soviet government, in the interests of economic recovery and social peace, greatly contracted the sphere in which administrative decisions of state bodies were to be the basis for economic decision-making. Acquisition of agricultural products from the peasantry no longer depended upon forced requisition but was based on a combination of cash purchase by the state and regularized taxation in kind. The value of the currency was stabilized, and monetary exchanges and financial calculation came to have an important role in economic life once again. Retail trade and small-time manufacturing on a private basis was revived, while the state reserved the "commanding heights" of industry and transportation unto itself.

The mode of organizing the state sector under N.E.P. was itself substantially different from that under War Communism. Industrial activity was based on large industrial units or associations operating under the principles of *khozraschet* (or "economic accounting") on a more or less free market (ignoring the Soviet state's penchant for price controls and occasional *ad hoc* interventions). Under *khozraschet*, the finances of the enterprise were no longer absorbed directly into the state budget, and the

enterprise itself possessed a separate legal "personality." Enterprises purchased their materials and machinery and hired their labor forces on the
(regulated) market and disposed of their output on the same basis. Except
in special cases, enterprises were expected to turn a profit or at least break
even. Managers were appointed from above and removable on demand,
but the higher state authorities did not normally engage in the detailed dic-
tation of production and marketing decisions. The enterprise manager
determined his own production plan (subject to ratification by *Vesenkha*)
and decided upon the composition of output, the acquisition of various
types of materials. Prices were mainly determined by free contract
between the state enterprises concerned (subject to increasingly numerous
price controls) in the light of market conditions. Wages and working conditions were regulated by collective agreements with the trade unions.
Enterprises could even finance their own investment projects on the basis
of loans from *Gosbank*. They could sell operating or working capital to
other enterprises or individuals, but they could not legally alienate fixed
capital assets.

Although the degree of formal centralization of economic power in the
state planning and administrative organs under N.E.P. was far lower than
during the period of War Communism, the government's effective power
to plan and to select the general direction of economic growth was in
practice much enhanced. The central leadership, freed from dealing with
constant crises and the minutia of day-to-day production decisions, were
able to devote their limited manpower and intellectual energies to more
fundamental problems and to planning with a longer time-horizon,
particularly the planning of new investment in infrastructure and the
expansion of key branches of industry. Nor were they helpless in regulating important aspects of current operations, since they had potent policy
instruments available to them in the form of price regulations, subsidies
and grants, taxation, credit allocation, creation of new enterprises, foreign
exchange controls, and, when all else failed, the retained legal right to
intervene administratively to secure desired actions from managerial personnel in the employ of the state.

The most durable of the Soviet models for economic planning and
administration was, of course, the dialectical "synthesis" of the proposals
of the Bolshevik "left" and "right" that is associated with the rule of
Joseph Stalin, who presided over agricultural collectivization and the first
five-year plans. By the time that Communist parties came to power in
East Europe, the version of socialist economic organization that had
evolved in the U.S.S.R. in the 1930's and 1940's had become sanctified
as the only genuinely socialist *modus operandi*. After several years of

rather innovative experimentation during Eastern Europe's post-war period of coalition government and economic reconstruction, Stalin's decision to inaugurate the full-scale building of socialism in that region led to the rapid installation of Soviet-style economic planning and management after 1947-48. While the "Stalinist" economic model underwent important modifications after Stalin's death and especially after the upheavals of 1956, nevertheless its basic institutions and assumptions remained substantially intact in nearly all of the European people's democracies at the end of the 1950's. The Stalinist legacy in economic organization (as in politics) was the basic institutional framework against which the advocates of economic reform were reacting during the 1960's, and to understand the substance of their proposals it is necessary to examine that legacy somewhat closely.

The Stalinist Model, East European Version

The underlying conception (or, rather, aspiration) of the classical Soviet-type system of economic planning and management is fairly clear and can be succinctly stated, although the reality nowhere ever quite measured up to the theoretical standard. Under the close supervision of the top Party organs, the State Planning Office constructed a fully detailed national plan for the entire economy, covering quantitative targets for production and distribution of virtually all goods and services. The plan was presumed to be both internally consistent and optimum from the perspective of the values and priorities of the top political leadership, which defined the national interest with "scientific" precision. Secondly, after the plan had been enacted into law, the economic administration ensured the fulfillment of the plan by issuing legally binding, detailed, operational instructions to every economic agent, whose only function was to obey the instructions given to the letter. (Obviously this is an unrealistic description of actual economic processes, yet it was characteristic of the Stalinist period that it was officially held to be "essentially" valid as an abstract representation of life, and this conception was rather firmly embodied in the legal theory underlying those portions of public law pertaining to economic administration as both a convenient legal fiction and as a symbolic affirmation of the socialist character of the state and economy and of the supremacy of plan over market.)

A somewhat more realistic description of the operational model of the 1950's requires more detail.

(1) Although the direct administrative allocation of economic goods through the physical plan was indeed extremely detailed in content and broad in scope, market forces and money-mediated transactions also played

a very real (though restricted) role and had important consequences. Market forces were particularly operative (and often troublesome) in the sphere of labor allocations, since (unlike under War Communism and Maoism in its more leftist variants) workers were normally free to change jobs at will in response to variations in wage rates and the availability of job-related material compensation in kind. The direct allocation of labor was mainly manifest in military conscription and the use of penal camps for certain kinds of extremely dangerous or unpleasant economic activity like swamp drainage, canal building, road or dam construction, and the famous "salt mines." While the state had a (formal) near-monopsonistic position in the labor market by virtue of state ownership of the means of production and could thus exercise a great degree of control over total and relative wages paid, nevertheless a monopsonistic market position is neither theoretically nor (still less) practically equivalent to direct administrative control of labor migration. Reallocation of the labor force among enterprises, industries, or sectors of the economy required the economic decision-makers to "bid away" the necessary workers by adjustments in relative and absolute wages to conform roughly with the preferences of the workers.

Market relations also were very important in the distribution of consumer goods to the population, which was handled largely through cash purchase from retail outlets, in which households were free to allocate their monetary incomes according to personal preferences (subject of course to the physical availability of the various items in inventory). Rationing (except for "rationing by quieu") was largely a wartime and early reconstruction phenomenon, although certain other forms of direct administrative allocation of consumer goods continued to have considerable importance, especially for higher-status people and the politically well-connected, who often enjoyed special preferences in the opportunity to purchase extremely scarce or high quality items and who also might benefit from such "perks" as a chauffeured official car, free theater tickets, access to special clinics and spas, and the like. On a more modest scale, many members of the general population were eligible to receive a variety of goods and services either without charge or at heavily subsidized prices: free public education, health insurance, rent subsidies, cheap staple foods, factory-issued work clothing, and so on, much of which was administratively allocated to a greater degree than market-allocated.

The market also played a major role in the sphere of agricultural production. Although the collective farms were required to conform their production patterns to the demands of the state plan by means of a "compulsory delivery" quota with only token compensation, generally any surpluses could be disposed of through more market-like procedures, and hence agricultural output was very substantially dependent upon the incentive effects of both official procurement prices and private market prices. Apart from these (important) exceptions where market forces were permitted to operate in a restricted fashion (they did not operate even here during the Soviet experience of War Communism), administrative allocation through the planning process was in general the norm. Perhaps most importantly, there was no place for market forces to operate (legitimately) in transactions between state enterprises. Although enterprises operated under *khozraschet* and transfers of materials or output (but not capital goods) always involved an entry in the books of the state banking system, such financial methods were necessary mainly as a convenient method of summing up heterogeneous physical units for purposes of recording and checking up on transactions. In general, the financial results of enterprise activities had little or no bearing on determining which transfers would take place, since this function was governed by the administrative directives deriving from the physical plan rather than the financial plan that was its pale and imperfect shadow. Since managerial performance was judged almost entirely on fulfillment of the most important physical output targets, managers had little or no incentive to take financial results into consideration in making decisions within their (circumscribed) discretionary sphere of decision. Prices were fixed arbitrarily and remained unchanged for many years at a time.

(2)   There was in practice a very high degree of centralization of economic decisions, although, of course, it was not absolute. The national plan was worked out in an extremely detailed manner and was comprehensive in its coverage of production, distribution, labor force, wages, foreign trade, investment projects, and so on. Plan targets were broken down in two or three stages. The Planning Office assigned plan directives to the economic ministries, which in turn disaggregated them for assignment to their subordinated production units (enterprises) directly or to branch directorates that repeated the process for their own subordinated enterprises. Wherever possible targets were expressed in physical rather than value units, with detailed output targets being supplemented by direct administrative disposition of producers goods, materials, permissible size and composition of labor force, wage scales payable for the various categories of workers, technical processes to be employed, required delivery dates, prices of commodities produced — nearly all thought to be "managerial" decisions in less centralized systems.

(3)   The plan did not simply spring forth from the brow of an all-knowing leader fully elaborated and consistent. The plan (actually, plans —

elaborated for varying planning periods, but with the one-year plan being
the really operative one) grew out of a long, slow, and cumbersome succession of steps. The process would begin with the elaboration of a first
draft by the Planning Office. On the basis of the draft, the top Party and
governmental leaders would discuss the principal policies embodied therein
and develop their own ideas as to the suitability of the proposals. The
plan would then be appropriately modified to conform to the resulting
policy decisions. This would involve discussions between the Planning
Office and the ministerial officials about the feasibility of the draft plan's
various sectoral targets. Because the ministries were in possession of better information about their own capabilities than was available to the less
specialized staff of the Planning Office, the setting of targets for the ministries emerged from a complex process of bargaining and bureaucratic
compromise. Subordinates had an interest in being assigned an "easy"
plan (low output targets, generous allowances for machinery, materials,
and labor) because their competence was assessed by their success in fulfilling or overfulfilling the plan targets assigned them. The disaggregation
of the agreed plan targets by the ministry and the issuance of the
corresponding directives to the branch directorates or enterprises involved
a similar process of bargaining, this time with the ministerial representatives in the position of wanting to impose the highest feasible targets
(to ensure their own fulfillment of the plan) and the enterprises or branch
directorate having every incentive to conceal capacity and exaggerate
requirements. After necessary adjustments were made and the "final"
plan was approved by the leadership (and enacted into law by the pro
forma action of the Parliament), the final details of delivery schedules and
concrete allocation of enterprises' output to particular consignees were
nailed down through the conclusion of delivery "contracts" between the
enterprises involved. (These were not contracts in the more conventional
sense of the term, since neither enterprise party to such an agreement had
significant discretion in determining either the most important provisions
or whether to sign at all or even with whom to deal.)

The plan in its final version was supposed to be completed and its contents disseminated before the beginning of the plan period. In practice,
enterprises frequently had to work on the basis of temporary or *ad hoc*
directives for the first few months due to delays in the negotiating process.
Even with the final plan in place on time, the correspondence of the actual
economic process with the plan's provisions was highly imperfect. Time
constraints and the strategic distortion of information during the bargaining process constantly resulted in unanticipated shortfalls in deliveries of
necessary materials and components, resulting thereafter in secondary and

tertiary shortfalls in other enterprises or sectors. Such phenomena led to the necessity of modification in the plan at all levels, continually reopened the bureaucratic bargaining process, and virtually assured that the burdens of the disruptions would be borne by those sectors of the economy with the least bargaining power and the lowest political priority (typically the consumer goods and residential construction sectors, since reduction of their outputs did not directly involve a consequent reduction of inputs for any other sector).

(4) The process by which planned economic activity was administered and supervised did not conform to the simple linear chain of command from Planning Office to ministry to branch directorate to enterprise. The control of the top political authorities over economic activity was not confined simply to presiding over the single bureaucratic hierarchy of the state administration. Because of the fusion of economic, political, and social power in the Communist political order, the top leaders had available to them a variety of organizations outside that hierarchy which were regularly mobilized to control it, and thus the coordination of political and economic authority could be accomplished through the complex system of "dual" (or, better, "multiple") subordination. Economic administrators and managers were subject not only to the legitimate control of their hierarchical superiors but also to the *equally legitimate* (but not usually equally powerful) control of political and socio-political organizations operating from "outside" the state apparatus but parallel to and penetrating it at virtually every level. The most important such external control groups licensed to "meddle" (as the Weberian tradition would have it) in economic administration have normally been the specialized commissions and local officials of the Communist Party, local or regional governing councils and their bureaus,[3] the military procurement organization, trade union bodies, special citizens' control groups of part-time activists, and, on occasion, the state security apparatus. While the basic function of these instruments of political control from the point of view of the top leadership was to provide information about violations of planners' preferences and policies and to exert pressure for more obedient behavior by managers and administrators, these other organizations too were not without their own special interests and concerns, and in their activities related to economic administration, those who were charged with such responsibilities could be expected to promote these interests along with (or even in opposition to) those of the political leadership. Thus despite their best efforts to devise multiple controls, the top leadership could not really be certain that regulating the economy on the basis of detailed administrative directives

would actually insure that economic decisions would always conform to
their preferences.

The Market Socialism Alternative

As has already been described in the first section of this chapter, a very
strong antagonism toward the market mechanism as such has been a
persistent theme in socialist thought generally and Marxist thought in particular since the 19th century. As early as the writing of the *Economic
and Philosophical Manuscripts* of 1844, Marx identified the subjugation
of human productive activity to the blind forces of the market, the mys-
tification of social relations through the uses of money, and the associated
compartmentalization of the human spirit as fundamental elements in
mankind's alienated condition under the capitalist order that should be
overcome through the socialist revolution. The young Marx fitted rather
easily into the romantic tradition of social thought that saw markets as
fostering avarice, egoism, the denigration of aesthetic and expressive
values, the erosion of the intrinsic satisfactions of productive activity, the
destruction of ethical values, the impairment of man's capacity to achieve
psychological security through the formation of strong personal ties with
either individuals or the larger community, and so on. The more "scientific" writings of the mature Marx, such as *Capital*, present an analysis of
the capitalist order and the central role of money, commodity relations,
and markets which complements rather than contradicts his earlier
philosophical analysis and which leads him to the clear conclusion that the
market mechanism is not only aesthetically or morally undesirable but also
doomed to inevitable destruction with the fulfillment of the proletarian
revolution.

These general preconceptions about the character and consequences of
the market mechanism lie very close to the core of Marxist (and, especially,
Marxist-Leninist) ideology. Although post-1917 experiences in the Soviet
Union rather quickly led to the acceptance of some practical compromises
(rationalized as attributable to the temporary difficulties of the transition
period and to the still-insufficient development of the material forces of
production), the strongest possible conviction remained among committed
Bolsheviks that full attainment of socialism involves the progressive
reduction of "spontaneous" economic phenomena by means of ever more
comprehensive and "scientific" central planning and direction. In this
intellectual tradition, which was transplanted as orthodoxy in East Europe
along with the institutions of Soviet-style economic planning and
administration, the very concept of "market socialism" seemed to be a
contradiction in terms, save perhaps as a (misleading) label for such rather

primitive transitional arrangements as might be dictated by unfavorable circumstances. (Comparisons of Eastern Europe's pre-1948 "indicative" economic planning for postwar reconstruction with the Soviet N.E.P. were not uncommon among Party theorists at the time.)

Nevertheless, the idea of "market socialism" as a full-fledged and progressive model of a socialist economy suitable for an economically advanced country eventually entered the mainstream of East European economic thought and proved to be quite influential in laying the theoretical base of the reform movements of the 1960's. The elaboration and dissemination of this body of theory derived from two principal sources: (1) heterodox socialist theory that arose out of the so-called "socialist calculation debate" in Western Europe during the pre-World War II period, and (2) the theoretical gloss produced for defending, describing, and (increasingly) guiding the evolution of Yugoslav economic institutions and practices following the break with the Soviet Union in 1948. (The writings of Nikolai Bukharin and other Soviet theoreticians of the N.E.P. might have constituted a third source of market socialist ideas. However, the thoroughness with which Stalin suppressed the ideas (and physically liquidated the persons) of the Bolshevik "right deviationists" in the 1930's seems to have largely prevented East European and Soviet economists from acquiring much knowledge of such material until quite recently. In any case, because of continuing Soviet historical dogmas about the guilt of Bukharin and his associates in anti-Soviet plotting, it would have been highly impolitic for reformists of the 1950's and 1960's to refer openly to these writings in any way.)

Impact of the Socialist Calculation Debate

The "socialist calculation debate" was mainly a continental European enterprise that spread to English-language journals only in its later stages. The opening gun was fired by the Austrian economist Ludwig von Mises in 1920, with the publication of his influential article on "Economic Calculation in the Socialist Commonwealth."[4] Mises discovered some intrinsic practical barriers affecting any attempt to establish or operate a socialist economy that does not provide for markets trading in the means of production.

Mises' most unnerving contribution to socialist thought was his definitive debunking of the pervasive conception of global economic planning as essentially an exercise in scientific or technical-engineering calculation from the availabilities of the forces of production and objective human needs "without the intervention of the famous 'value'" (Engels' phrase in *Anti-Duhring*). The Marxist vision of socialism as the triumph of human rationality over the wasteful and dehumanizing "anarchy" of the market failed utterly to take into account the essential preconditions for rational economic calculation.   It is not a sufficient condition for maximizing human well-being that the administration know precisely what physical products are needed most urgently in what amounts (although this assumption itself raises immense epistemological and methodological questions). It is necessary to choose the means by which available labor, machinery, and materials can best be deployed for the maximum aggregate satisfaction of these needs.   In modern industrialized societies, productive resources are of millions of different kinds and can be employed in a great variety of technologically possible combinations to produce many different kinds of output.   Choosing the least wasteful method of producing even a predetermined quantity of a single good necessitates calculations comparing the varying production processes' total social costs, which in turn requires assimilation of the physically disparate means of production to a common value denominator.

In a capitalist system, the common denominator that makes economic calculation possible is, of course, monetary prices attached to the means of production by virtue of their character as commodities produced for, and traded on, the market.   Since socialism as then understood by all socialist spokesmen involved the concentration of ownership of all these means of production in the hands of the state, they would not be traded on competitive markets, and hence market forces of supply and demand would not be operative in setting prices for them.   It was therefore incumbent upon those advocating socialism as a means of economic rationalization to develop some alternative and non-arbitrary solution to the fundamental problem of valuation of the means of production once capital markets have been abolished.   This no socialist theorist had ever seriously attempted, and Mises' careful analysis offered rather strong arguments that the task was in fact impossible, except in the special case of a technologically and demographically static society with zero economic growth and unchanging needs-cum-social-preferences.

The debate which followed Mises' opening salvo was intense, detailed, and protracted and eventually included contributions by many of the most distinguished economists of the 1920's and 1930's, including Max Weber, Karl Polanyi, Jakob Marschak, Oskar Neurath, Lionel Robbins, F.M. Taylor, Abba Lerner, Maurice Dobb, Oskar Lange, A.C. Pigou, and F.A. von Hayek.[5]   Although some of the Soviet economists of the early and middle 1920's attempted to deal with the problem raised by Mises (most notably S.G. Strumilin's dogged attempts to elaborate a workable method of calculation based on Engel's offhanded remarks about the direct computation of direct and indirect labor inputs), such theorizing increasingly became politically dangerous, and with the ascendancy of Stalin, theoretical economics largely ceased to exist as a discipline in the U.S.S.R. With "orthodox" Marxist-Leninists largely out of the debate (except for occasional polemical pieces denouncing all such inquiry as bourgeois propaganda), the defense of the ideal of socialist planning fell by default to Social Democrats and independent socialist economists trained in both Marxist and neo-classical analysis. The most noteworthy of these (from the point of view of subsequent influence in East Europe) was the distinguished Polish Marxist Oskar Lange, who spent most of the 1930's and the war years in Western Europe and the United States.

Lange's response to von Mises' critique (as subsequently elaborated and refined by Friedrich Hayek and Lionel Robbins in the course of the debate) was first published in 1936-37 and built upon earlier rebuttal by Fred M. Taylor and H.D. Dickenson.[6] Lange's attempt at a solution in effect conceded that rational calculation for the optimal allocation of economic resources did indeed require monetary pricing and that planning *in natura* was highly wasteful (or even unworkable) in a complex modern economy. However, Lange denied that state ownership of the means of production was incompatible with the sort of determinate marginal cost pricing system familiar to Western "bourgeois" economists as the outcome of perfect competition in Walrasian general equilibrium. The Lange-Taylor-Dickenson model which he proceeded to propose was the prototypical version of "market socialism" as a coherent program.

Oskar Lange returned to Poland after World War II and held a variety of influential state, academic, and advisory posts until his death in the 1960's. Since his works were widely translated in the other developed East European people's democracies (and even on occasion in the U.S.S.R.) after 1956, and since many of the more radical proponents of economic reform were his former students or close associates, the ideas expressed in his major published work prior to assuming the inhibitions of political office are of more than antiquarian interest.

Lange's version of the socialist economy was one in which the individual citizen's choice of occupation would be free and labor allocation would be regulated principally by the relative wages of various occupations (i.e., by the price mechanism). Consumers would be at liberty to dispose of their money incomes by purchasing the consumer goods (but not producers' goods) of their choice at the going price. The means of production would be in the hands of the state and organized in the familiar hierarchical fashion of Central Planning Board-Ministry-Branch-Enterprise. The principal task and policy instrument of the Central Planning Board would be the setting of legally obligatory prices (including interest and ground rents—another significant departure from Marxist conventional wisdom, but consistent with Lange's concern for marginalist "optimal allocation of productive resources"). The purpose of the CPB was to discover and enact general equilibrium prices, not only for wages and articles of consumption, but most especially for productive resources. This would be accomplished by a process of trial-and-error in which the appearance of shortages and gluts in the inventories of various goods would signal to the CPB the necessity of raising or lowering the corresponding prices in order to bring demand and supply into equilibrium. Socialist managers at the enterprise and branch level would be administratively directed to follow two general rules to guide their otherwise autonomous decision-making: "Use always the method of production which minimizes average unit costs calculated by the centrally-set prices for inputs" and "Produce as much of each service or commodity as will equalize marginal cost and the set price for the product, acquiring additional materials, labor and capital goods as necessary at the going rates." The resulting equilibrium solution, Lange argued, is formally equivalent to the allocative process of a perfectly functioning competitive market economy of the capitalist type— but substantively better in actual allocations, since the CPB could take better account of externalities in its accounting process and since income distributions among the population could be more equitable by virtue of the fact that interest, rents, and profits would accrue to the state (for possible redistribution as a "social dividend" along egalitarian lines) rather than to a small privileged elite of capitalists and rentiers. Lange also asserted (without demonstration) that such a system would be immune from the fluctuations of the business cycle.

It should be noted that Lange's principal model as just described was essentially one of "consumer sovereignty." Preferences of the general population as demonstrated in their purchasing decisions affect the relative prices of the various goods and services in the consumption sector, which in turn (via Rule # 2) affect the pattern of investment and materials allocation among product lines and even whole industries. Demand for the various capital goods, materials, and worker skill categories in turn would derive from the structure of demand for final outputs, and would be reflected in wages and in the prices of producers' goods. In this model, the Central Planning Board's chief role is to predict the outcome that would be eventually brought about by an idealized market and then to bring it about more quickly and with less wasteful fluctuations than would occur if left to spontaneous pricing decisions on a decentralized basis. The only truly autonomous decision of the CPB in which planners' preferences would be sovereign would be the overall social rate of savings/investment (determined in the annual decision as to how much of the revenues from profits, rents, and interest on socially owned land and capital should be distributed to the population as a "social dividend" and how much should be retained for reinvestment.)

While Lange clearly found "consumer sovereignty" an attractive feature of his model, he recognized that his insights into the functions of a price mechanism in a socialist economic order were capable of generalization to other applications in which the mix of consumer's preferences and planners' preferences might vary considerably. The price system might be based entirely on consumer preferences, or the price system might be based entirely on planner preferences (the latter would require abolishing the free choice of employment and eliminating the free selection of individual consumption mixes). Or there might be a *dual* price system in which every item is associated with two prices: one applicable to purchases by the general public, and the other used by the state for internal accounting purposes and transfers between state enterprises. Thus, for example, it would be abstractly conceivable to construct a scheme in which production decisions and the allocation of non-labor productive resources would derive from cost/revenue calculations based on planner sovereignty prices, while sales prices of the final goods to consumers could be based on whatever prices are necessary to clear the market. Thereby physical rationing of consumer goods could be avoided and free choice in consumption preserved, but without allowing consumer preferences to have any impact on investment policies or even on the output of particular items. Other variations and combinations based on a dual price system might, of course, be devised.

The critique of Lange's theoretical model, either analytically or with respect to its plausibility as a guide to real world institution-building, need not concern us here. Although Lange's ingenious intellectual construction proved to be an enormous morale-booster for Western socialists concerned about retaining their scholarly credentials as members in good standing of the broader community of professional economists (and thereby earned Lange considerable acclaim), the trenchant criticisms by Maurice Dobb (from the left)[7] and F.A. von Hayek (from the right)[8] seem to have convinced Lange to abandon any plans he may have had to lead a continuing crusade for its literal implementation, even before the political realities of post-war Poland would have made such an effort self-evidently doomed to defeat. The significance of Lange's ideas for future East European economic thought was not so much his specific prescriptions for carrying out socialist economic calculations as it was his full acknowledgement of the existence of the problem (which orthodox "Stalinist" economic thought never really did) and his demonstration that market-like phenomena within the state sector itself might be positively beneficial for attaining the principal advantages of economic planning and centralized control. Lange in effect rehabilitated the price system as an "active" rather than a "passive" (and subordinate) element in the planned economy. And indeed, although Lange largely disassociated himself from the specifics of the model that bears his name once he became politically active in post-war Poland, he never abandoned the more fundamental insights that underlay it, and he devoted much of his professional career to their legitimation and incorporation in "mainstream" East European Marxist economics.[9] Thus, even though Lange's personal role in the economic reform movement of the 1960's was a relatively modest and moderate one when viewed in terms of his direct political activity, the intellectual climate which he had done so much to foster within the community of professional economists must be accounted one of the critical preconditions for the emergence of more radical reformist proposals throughout the region.

Impact of the Yugoslav Economic Model

Gregory Grossman, in his early survey of the economic reform of the 1960's, proffered the opinion that "the importance of the Yugoslav example . . . can hardly be exaggerated" in the rise of the reform movement.[10] In retrospect, it now seems that that importance *can* be (and has been) somewhat exaggerated, particularly in many of the more journalistic treatments of the subject. The Yugoslav model seems to have evolved in response to quite different political and economic circumstances from those pertaining to the East European people's democracies, and seems to have been perceived by most East European economists[11] as having only limited relevance to their own problems, at least when viewed as a whole. Because of the international situation and the Soviet leadership's on-again-off-again attitude toward Tito and his associates, as well as for reasons of their own, the East European policy-makers found direct emulation of Yugoslav innovations still less palatable.

Nevertheless, information on the organizational and functioning aspects of the Yugoslav economy did become more readily available in some East European countries during the *rapprochement* between the U.S.S.R. and Yugoslavia of 1954-1956, and it became politically acceptable for economists to study the details of this system (somewhat cautiously) as a genuinely socialist but somewhat misguided development. Scholarly interest was most marked in Poland and, to a somewhat lesser degree, in Hungary[12]—not coincidentally, the two countries in which the period of the New Course had brought about the most sizable shifts in economic policy and the most far-reaching re-examinations of the Stalinist economic model itself.

Apart from the direct influence of Yugoslav economic *theorists*, which seems to have been minimal (except possibly in Poland, where a collection of essays by Yugoslav economists[13] was published in translation as part of the general public discussions on the reformist theses of Oskar Lange's Economic Council in 1957), Yugoslavia's economic model proved to be influential in another, less "logical" and more "psychological," way. The facts that a recognized Marxist-Leninist party was presiding over an economy with very strong "market socialist" elements in it and that this economy seemed to be performing very well indeed during the 1950's and early 1960's lent a certain concreteness and added credibility to what had heretofore been only an abstract theoretical model. However much the actual operation of the Yugoslav system of economic planning and management might deviate both from the Yugoslav economists' and ideologists' theoretical models and from the rather different models being advocated abroad (and both kinds of divergences were quite substantial in the early 1960's[14]), reformers in all socialist countries were more than happy to credit the "correct" market socialist elements of the system with Yugoslav successes, while blaming residual "bureaucratic" or "administrative" elements for practical shortcomings.

The principal elements of the Yugoslav economic model as it stood in the early 1960's were as follows. Within the socialist sector were included all enterprises employing more than a few workers. Enterprises were largely free to determine the composition of their output, the scale of their production, the technical variants to be used in production, the size and the composition of the work force. The enterprise was free to sell its products to any interested purchaser at the best prices it could negotiate with that purchaser (subject to price controls on certain key commodities) and on mutually agreeable terms. Similarly, the enterprise purchased its raw materials and machinery on the market within the constraints of its financial resources (including the possibility of borrowing from state banks operating on commercial principles and charging interest).

The receipts of the enterprise, after payment for the costs of materials and interest on outstanding loans, were subject to a variety of compulsory deductions mandated by the state: (1) estimated depreciation of fixed assets in the custody of the enterprise; (2) an "interest" tax on the net value of fixed and working capital in the custody of the enterprise; and (3) sales taxes and certain other miscellaneous taxes, as well as membership fees designated for the support of industrial associations. The rationale of the foregoing deductions was that the means of production remained the property of society as a whole rather than of the individual enterprise itself and that therefore it was necessary that the enterprise should compensate the remainder of society for appropriating the social property to its exclusive use. (Thus, enterprise management would have an incentive to retain only so much capital and use only so many resources as could not be used more profitably elsewhere by another enterprise.) What was left of the receipts of the enterprise after deductions constituted "profits" (and was subject to a kind of corporate income tax). Net income after the profits tax remained at the disposal of the enterprise for flexible allocation between two sets of purposes: (1) business funds for financing new investment, and (2) personal incomes of the workers (either paid out in the current year or contributed to a reserve fund used to even out fluctuations in living standard that might otherwise result from financial difficulties in the enterprise from time to time). Net enterprise income allocated to personal income rather than investment was subject to an additional tax, to encourage enterprises to invest at the higher rates demanded by central policies.

A unique feature of the Yugoslav model was the character of managerial authority within the enterprise, designated in law and ideology as "workers' self-management" and identified with the Marxian concept of an "association of free producers." While the means of production were considered to be in social ownership, the *management* of social property in the enterprise was legally entrusted, not to a Soviet-style, state-appointed director, but to the entire labor collective of the enterprise as represented by a freely elected workers' council. Day to day operations were supervised by a smaller executive board (elected by the workers' council) and by a Director appointed jointly by the workers' council and the council of the commune in which the enterprise was located. (After 1965, appointment and removal of enterprise directors became the sole prerogative of the workers' councils, thereby greatly enhancing effective control by the workers' council and diminishing the ability of local political figures to intervene in enterprise decision-making.)

The role of the central planning authorities in the Yugoslav model of the early 1960's was quite limited by comparison to the Stalinist model, yet still quite large compared to even the more *dirigiste* Western market economies. Operating mainly through measures of fiscal and credit policy (and, to a diminishing but still quite substantial extent, through direct administrative intervention), the center could control the allocation of national products between saving and consumption (Yugoslav investment rates through the 1950's were among the highest in the world), the geographical direction and product structure of foreign trade, and the general distribution of the national income among the various groups and strata in the population and among the various kinds and levels of public authority. While enterprise decisions at the "micro" level were normally supposed to be left to the determination of the enterprise (there were no legally binding, externally imposed plan targets), in practice the policy-makers were able to exert very substantial influence on the enterprise through legal restrictions on profit distributions, selective taxation, subsidies, preferential foreign exchange and credit allocations, manipulation of interest rates, price controls and rationing for selected commodities. The enterprise's need for cooperation from local and republican government in a wide range of matters, the penetration of enterprises by external hierarchical organizations such as the League of Communists and the trade union apparatus, and the personal dependence of enterprise directors on "connections" to gain future employment and honors—all these acted to modify the tendencies for enterprises to behave as purely self-interested creatures of the market. While Adam Smith's "invisible hand" of the market was indeed widely relied upon to bring about optimal allocation of productive resources, Yugoslav theory and practice retained the Marxian conviction that (collective) Human Reason must consciously assign it the basic values and long range goals to be served.

Some Developments in Soviet Economic Thought

Because of the Soviet Union's claims to primacy in the field of ideology and because of the great emphasis traditionally accorded the planned character of the economy as an essential aspect of the broader system of socialism, any modification in East European economic institutions was inherently a somewhat touchy matter with possible international repercussions (quite apart from domestic political considerations, which were also quite significant). A necessary precondition for the reinvigoration of East European economic thought and the development of reform proposals was either an attenuation of Soviet control over matters ideological in East Europe and/or the attainment of a greater measure of autonomy and flexibility for theoretical economics within the Soviet Union itself. Both of these occurred to a significant degree over the course of the 1950's. The general tendency toward Soviet leaders' accepting a somewhat greater range of variation in the institutional arrangements of other communist states after the upheavals of 1956 is fairly well known and need not be discussed here, except to note that it had important effects in the realm of economic theory and practice by its legitimation of experimentation in those countries where the local Party leadership was willing to encourage (and control) it. Certain technical developments within Soviet economic theory, however, are less widely known, yet had an important impact on the general ideological respectability of what were to become key elements in East European reform proposals in the 1960's. These technical developments provided a kind of ideological bridge between the verities of the Stalinist economic model and the new emphasis on value categories and the beneficial uses of the price system in the regulation of production.

Lange's idea of centralized coordination of socialist production and distribution almost exclusively by means of price manipulations, his embrace of "marginalist" theories of optimal resource allocation, and his insistence upon the necessity of interest and ground rents as an element of economic calculation in the planning process all had a distinctly "unsocialist" odor, to say the least. The concept of enterprises in the state sector being guided by their own calculations of costs and benefits rather than by administrative directive seemed inconsistent with the notion of state ownership, since the traditional concept of ownership entails the right of direct disposal and direction. The imputation of interest and ground rents to non-labor factors of production was common-sensically regarded as incompatible with the nature of the socialist order (in which "exploitation" of living labor was supposed to have been abolished) and in any case inconsistent with the labor theory of value (which, according to the Stalinist formulation, continued to operate in a "limited sphere" during the transition to communism but could *not* be a "regulator of production"). Since commodity production and the money economy were officially regarded as destined for the dust bin of history with the further development of socialist relations toward the more mature stage, the attempt to re-emphasize monetary and financial indicators in the planning process could easily be made to seem retrogressive and unsound to Marxist-Leninist fundamentalists.

At a more sophisticated level of evaluation, such proposals as Lange's were objectionable because they seemed to be in conflict with some of the basic epistemological, methodological, and theoretic-axiomatic tenets of classical Marxian political economy. Indeed, they appeared to repeat many of the shortcomings of "bourgeois" political economy pilloried by Marx in *The Critique of Political Economy*, *Theories of Surplus Value*, and *Capital*. Marx was convinced that social science (and, if we accept Engel's word for his views, *any* science) had to provide explanations for human activity in terms of a single objective universal and that any "explanatory" factor not ultimately reducible to matter in motion did not adequately reveal the underlying reality of things as they are. The proper task of the economist, therefore, was to discover how objective material relationships shape economic life. The familiar "economic" phenomena of prices, markets, supply, and demand represented only the superficial manifestations of more fundamental underlying processes, and theories which were grounded in such categories were inadequate because they failed to "get behind" the *apparent* determination of market variables by people's subjective evaluations of benefits and costs. Marx went to considerable lengths in his economic writings to argue that such "subjective" factors are *really* themselves ultimately determined by the available material means of production and the technology of their use, as constrained by the concrete relations of production within which the exploited classes labor. Accordingly, Marx's economic theory concerned itself almost entirely with "supply" factors rather than "demand" factors as the real regulators of production, regarded supply as wholly determined by the (average socially-necessary) costs of production, and interpreted "costs" in a radically materialist way as being the determinate result of current technology and as being measurable quantitatively by the necessary direct and indirect inputs of physical labor per unit.[15]

The fundamental problem was that Marxian economic theory was rooted in classical political economy and had already essentially reached "closure" before the major conceptual breakthroughs of Menger, Marshall, and Walras transformed the intellectual landscape with the "marginalist revolution" and the subjective theory of value. The basic interests of classical political economy had been in the phenomena of economic growth and the distribution of incomes among occupational categories or classes. Neo-classical economics came to see the subject matter of economic science as primarily the process of optimal allocation of resources and the workings of the price system in its allocative function. Since the formal logic of the optimal allocation of scarce resources had only barely begun to be elaborated by the time of Marx's death, and since in any case this was not Marx's principal intellectual focus in the field of economics, it is not surprising that the corpus of his work contains little that would be of any use in devising a methodology for actually constructing the scientific plan he foresaw as governing the future socialist economy. Whatever Marx's reaction might have been had he lived to see the marginalist revolution, his Soviet heirs rejected it root and branch,[16] thereby foreclosing for several generations the ability of Soviet scholarship to come to terms with many of the central problems of plan construction.

Given the Marxian insistence on the epiphenomenal character of the pricing system, and given the firm conviction that socialist ownership of the means of production made practical their direct allocation without monetary calculation, it is not very surprising that Soviet and East

European economic authorities were predisposed to dismiss as "unscientific," "idealist," and "inconsistent with historical materialism" any models of allegedly socialist planning and management whose central categories and indices were expressed in financial value terms based on mere "preferences" rather than being directly and "scientifically" calculated from the "objective laws of socialist development" (as apprehended by the Party's top leadership) and from the "objective technological coefficients" already employed in the Stalinist system of planning by material balances.

The development which did more than anything else to break up this intellectual/ideological log-jam was the post-1957 revival of abstract mathematical economics as a semi-approved academic enterprise in the Soviet Union, which also coincided with a relatively low-key and abstruse debate on the role of the "law of value" in the Soviet economy.[17] The main accomplishment of this new wave, from our perspective, was not so much the practical contributions of mathematical economics to everyday planning operations (although there were some) as the fact that these discussions provided an appropriately "materialist" theoretical rationale for "marginalist" methodologies of resource allocation and held out the promise that appropriate financial "shadow prices" could at least in principle be mathematically derived from planners' preferences expressed initially in the familiar physical units and material balances. The two chief innovations that led to these conclusions were input-output analysis and linear programming techniques, and their chief advocates and popularizers in the East European scholarly community were the Soviet economists L.V. Kantorovich, V.V. Novozhilov, and V.S. Nemchinov, along with the ubiquitous Pole, Oskar Lange.

Input-output analysis lent itself most readily to legitimation in Soviet-type economies because its pretensions were exceedingly modest and because its adoption did not seem to require extensive changes in the existing organization of the administrative apparatus. Input-output analysis is essentially a balancing technique for clarifying in a systematic way what are the required output levels of intermediate products (raw materials, semi-finished parts, etc.) that will be necessary for producing a desired assortment of final products using a fixed and predetermined technology of production for each final and intermediate product. Supporters of the method could assure skeptics that input-output was merely a useful formalization and simplification of the existing system of planning by "material balances" without all the laborious trial-and-error that formerly was necessary to arrive at the same result.[18] There was no possibility that input-output analysis could define an "optimal" plan by itself, and the existing preferences of the top- and even middle-level administrators and political authorities as to technological variants (and, of course, structure of final output) would be in no way undermined. The chief advantage would be that internally consistent plans could be produced both more rapidly and more reliably than by the older *ad hoc* method because formalization of the method made it amenable to the exploitation of modern high-speed electronic computers, which were just beginning to become available to Soviet Bloc economic planners. The top leaders might even be presented with two or three fully-elaborated plan variants to choose from rather than having to settle for the first feasible and balanced plan that their technicians came up with because of time constraints, thereby enhancing leaders' effective control over the economy rather than diminishing it. Moreover, reactive resistance to the importation of a "foreign" methodology like input-output analysis (it was first employed on a large scale in the United States military) could be defused because of the happy discovery that Wassily Leontief of Harvard University, the principal inventor and developer of the methodology, had first published the basic conceptual framework in the Soviet Union in 1925 (*before* his emigration to the U.S.) while he was engaged in the preparation of an early version of the First Five-Year Plan.[19] By the end of the 1950's, opposition in the U.S.S.R. to the use of input-output analysis (which had been interdicted for years, even after Stalin's death) was principally based on pragmatic doubts as to its practicality rather than on doctrinal or dogmatic grounds.

Input-output analysis turned out to be a foot in the door for "mathematical methods" in general, most notably linear programming and its intellectual descendants, known collectively in the Soviet Union by Kantorovich's expression, "optimal planning."

Whereas the input-output technique assumes the utilization of only a single available technology for the production of each item in the economy, linear programming can take into account the availability of multiple alternative methods of producing any given intermediate or final product with varying kinds and proportions of inputs of labor, materials, and machinery. Linear programming might be used to deal explicitly with the problem of choosing appropriate combinations of technologies and allocations of inputs in order both to achieve previously postulated targets for the final product mix (using minimal outlays of inputs) and to demonstrate how leftover inputs might be used to exceed the initial targets in a variety of ways, if desired. That is to say, the more enthusiastic proponents of linear programming promise the central authorities a framework for explicit optimizing in plan determination in a way that neither input-output analysis nor the "manual" approach of the "method of material balances" can. While the specification of the assortment of final outputs would remain the prerogative of the top political leadership, an enormous sphere of economic decision-making formerly the prerogative of middle-level administrators through bargaining and "rules of thumb" (choosing specific production technologies and allocating investments among the various branches and sectors) would (ideally) be reduced to a purely technical problem of calculating the detailed logical consequences of the planners' preferences for final output.

The obvious implications of such a system for "bureaucratic politics" at the level just below the top would lead one to expect strong resistance to any effort at applying "optimal planning" models to the economy as a whole. However, the "threat" could not materialize for quite practical reasons in any case. "Computopia" is not just around the corner. The technical assumptions of linear programming models are outrageously oversimplified (linearity of all production functions, no provision for changes in production functions due to technological progress). Moreover, the information on which the "objective technological coefficients" are computed has to come from the same lower-echelon administrators and managers with the same interests in distorting it to get an easy plan as was the case before. But the decisive constraint on the field of applicability of "optimal planning models" is the practical limitations imposed by the state of computer technology. An all-national plan would have to incorporate literally millions of discrete products and production variants, and the computer capacity and operating time necessary for the solution of a linear programming problem through iteration both increase *exponentially* with the number of variables. Thus, the practical applications of linear programming techniques in planning have been limited almost entirely to very circumscribed problems of allocation within a single branch where possibilities of substitution of inputs are limited and where technology is expected to remain rather static over long periods (coal mining, fishing, ferrous metallurgy, food processing, and transport).

The chief consequences of the rise of the "optimal planning" school, as previously suggested, were theoretical and ideological. In the first place, it encouraged planners and theorists to raise their aspirations a bit and begin to take seriously the problem of optimizing the central plan rather than simply being satisfied with designing an internally consistent one. Secondly, the discipline of having to formalize models of the planning process led to the discovery of "counter-intuitive" but nonetheless logically entailed insights about the procedures already being employed in practice and encouraged more detailed study of neglected aspects of the planning process that were bound to lead to the discovery of previously unnoticed connections between the basic structure of Stalinist planning and certain perennially recurring adverse phenomena (excessive inventories, chronic shortages of key materials, etc.). Finally, and most importantly, the mathematical logic of linear programming revealed some interesting connections between planning in purely physical quantities and certain numerical "multipliers" derived as a necessary part of the solution process.

It was discovered that every linear programming problem formulated in terms of maximizing selected outputs subject to physical constraints on the availability of the various inputs of labor, capital and land can in principle be rewritten through a mathematical transformation as a problem of solving for a set of coefficients imputing to each one of the various kinds of inputs its full contribution to producing whatever output was previously specified by the planners as the "objective function" to be maximized. These "multipliers" or "objectively-determined coefficients" turned out to be interpretable as "shadow prices" equivalent to those postulated in the "bourgeois" general equilibrium analysis, where prices gravitate toward equality with marginal costs (the identical principle also enshrined in Lange's pre-war model as Rule # 2).[20]

Thus by a roundabout route and under the respected banner of materialism and technological determinism, advocates of linear programming techniques for economic planning smuggled into Soviet and East European Marxist economics the formerly scorned neo-classical preoccupations with the idea of scarcity, the interrelationship of prices to rational economic calculation of allocation decisions, the notion of "opportunity cost," and the conceptualization of value as an outcome of objective scarcity of material means relative to subjective preferences among possible ends to be sought. Among other consequences, the general realization that value is conditioned by scarcity suggests that economic calculation for investment and production decision-making needs to take explicitly into account that *any* input into the production process (and not labor alone) contributes to the value of the product and has an opportunity cost. It was then only a small step to elaborating a rationale for setting an explicit price on the use of socially-owned capital and land (interest and rent) as a means for promoting their efficient utilization. And since *these* kinds of prices were derived from planners' preferences and displayed no taint of consumer sovereignty, the idea of a price system as an effective tool of the plan rather than a passive byproduct useful mainly for accounting purposes took on greater credibility among the central planners, who had in the past almost automatically associated an active or directive role for the price system with the "anarchy of the market."

While the ideas of the mathematical economists remained highly controversial in the early 1960's (and indeed are still controversial today) their
gradual acceptance into the realm of permissible debate in the Soviet Union
provided a foothold of legitimacy for a great variety of other less abstruse
ideas about the theory and practice of planning by bridging the abyss
between micro-economics (derived from the price theories of Western
marginal analysis) and the characteristically Soviet concern for macro-
economic control and the manipulation of physical flows. If scarcity prices
could even theoretically be useful for transmitting plan priorities and a
device for parametrically controlling decentralized marginal decision-
making, then even if the full derivation of such prices from pure
computerized models of the entire economy might be impractical, it was
worth re-examining the older role of the price system and the methods of
price setting with a view toward more fully exploiting some part of the
neglected potential now known to exist. The dichotomous view of plan
versus market was giving ground to a consideration of the possible
complementarities of plan *and* market.

Summary

The proliferation of proposals for the reform of socialist planning and
management in East Europe during the 1960's drew upon an intellectual
storehouse built up over a period of decades during which East European
economists worked through and came better to understand the idea that
the institutional arrangements of the socialist economy were susceptible to
a wide range of variations, no single one of which could be considered
absolutely valid. With the partial relaxations of political controls over
economic science and the improved ability of interested socialist
economists to gain access to each other's work and that of Western
economists, the functioning of the socialist economy once again could
become the focus of serious theoretical analysis and empirical study after
the long period of rigid orthodoxy and thinly disguised apologetics that
passed for academic economics under Stalin. Taking a more instrumental
view of particular economic institutions and arrangements became possible
without subjecting oneself to the charge of attacking socialism itself, and
the making of modest proposals for improvement of the functioning of the
system became a somewhat more important part of the professional role
of the East European socialist economist (always taking care, of course,
not to exceed the boundaries of the currently politically acceptable in one's
speculations by drifting too far into "negativism").

In the quest for alternatives to the status quo, East European economists
turned to a variety of sources for inspiration: historical-theoretical

examinations of historical experiences with other forms of socialist planning and management (the N.E.P. and War Communism in the U.S.S.R., the evolution of their own systems in the brief period between the end of World War II and the imposition of the Soviet model that began in late 1947, Yugoslavia's changing system) and purely theoretical and formal model-building such as the efforts of Oskar Lange in the 1930's and the more congenial perspectives of the Soviet mathematical economists with their up-to-date "scientific" technologies. In addition, concrete studies of particularly successful or unsuccessful enterprises (or even whole industries) proliferated and provided a data base for limited generalization.[21]

By the early 1960's (even earlier in the cases of Hungary and Poland), most of the basic elements of a program for comprehensive reform of the countries' economic institutions had long since been invented. What was essential to being about the practical adoption of such organizational innovations was quite simply this: the acceptance by powerful political leaders of the desirability or the practical necessity of such reforms and the subsequent effective mobilization of their political resources to overcome any important opposition. It is to this process that we now turn.

EASTERN EUROPE'S ECONOMIC DISCUSSIONS OF THE 1960'S AND THE DECISIONS TO UNDERTAKE REFORMS

Development of an Active Economic Reform Constituency

As has already been suggested, the period after the death of Stalin, and especially the period after 1956, saw a revival of innovative thought on the political economy of socialism in Eastern Europe and in the Soviet Union. The greening of the economics profession can largely be interpreted as part of a more general re-examination of the policies and institutions of the Stalinist past cautiously begun in the period of the New Course and then greatly intensified in the wake of Nikita Khrushchev's bloc-wide "destalinization" campaign initiated at the Twentieth Congress of the C.P.S.U. in February of 1956. Khrushchev's "secret speech" revealing the crimes of Stalin against the Party was, of course, the featured attraction of the Congress. This vigorous assault had the indirect effect of calling into question the assumption of the infallibility of the *Vozhd*'s views on other matters besides the value of socialist legality. While Khrushchev's remarks did not deal directly with economic matters, Anastas Mikoyan's speech to the Congress specifically singled out Stalin's *Economic Problems of Socialism in the U.S.S.R.* for harsh criticism,[1] which was highly significant by virtue of the fact that, since 1952, the exegesis of this text had constituted the principal subject matter of what had passed for theoretical economics in Eastern Europe. Mikhail Suslov continued the attack indirectly by vigorously berating the economic profession in the U.S.S.R. for its lack of new ideas, its concentration on superficial descriptive studies, and its substitution of quotations for genuine theoretical analysis.[2] By their remarks, the Soviet leadership had given the go-ahead for wide-ranging discussions of economic policy, and the economists of the more developed people's democracies were quick to take advantage of the opportunity wherever their own regimes did not take strong steps to prevent them.

It was no accident that the earliest and most far-reaching proposals for changes in the system of economic planning and management were elaborated in precisely those countries where destalinization had the most dramatic political effects as well: Hungary and Poland (just as, under very different circumstances, destalinization had earlier led to economic reforms in Yugoslavia as well). A degree of decompression and a certain desanctification of established institutions, as well as at least an indirect invitation from the leadership, was necessary before reformist economic proposals could safely be circulated for discussion among economists and thereby become sufficiently detailed and realistic to be even potentially "considerable" by economic policy-makers in the Party and the government.

Without at least semi-public discussion and criticisms in the light of contemporary elite preferences and policy goals, without being disciplined by the practical and political necessity of confronting concrete dilemmas and opportunities most salient to the political leadership and of incorporating them into the broader theoretical discussions, the insights of even the most brilliant theoreticians of socialist planning and management could scarcely have progressed beyond the stage of abstract "models" to become programmatic proposals. The formation of "expert" Party or Party-state advisory commissions in several countries during 1956-1958 seems to have played a crucial role in the process of crystallizing specific counterproposals to replace the status quo by providing just such opportunities for many of the individuals who were later to become the architects of the economic reforms of the 1960's. The two most important such commissions were the Polish "Economic Council" (chaired by Oskar Lange) and the Hungarian "Committee of Economic Experts" (chaired by Istvan Varga), but a similar though less-publicized body also was set up in Czechoslovakia.[3] (Less formalized and organized involvement of academic economists in somewhat broadened discussions of methods to "perfect" the functioning of the national economies also occurred in the German Democratic Republic,[4] but evidently not to any significant degree in Albania, Bulgaria, or Romania.) Despite the fact that the "market socialism" recommendations of the commissions of experts were nowhere implemented in anything like their original form, the process of formulating the proposals (and especially the contacts made between reformist theoreticians and sympathizers involved more actively in the policy process) provided the opportunity to solidify a kind of informal subculture of pragmatic reformism with a foothold in the Party and government and strong representation in the academic community.[5]

The elaboration of reform blueprints by the commissions of experts in Poland and Hungary also had a certain positive impact abroad. Even though these proposals were not in the end implemented by the regimes which solicited them, they were still allowed to be published and discussed in both technical economic journals and the popular press, which meant that the substance of the debate could be followed by interested economists in other, less open socialist countries.[6] The total long-term effects of diffusing such detailed (and, at the time, quasi-official) proposals for economic reform would be impossible to measure precisely, but they were undoubtedly substantial, judging by the frequency with which knowledgeable references to this literature of the 1957-59 period turned up in the economic literature of the mid-1960's (especially in Czechoslovakia). Unlike Yugoslavia, Poland and Hungary were unquestionably still members of good standing of the Soviet bloc, and consequently what the censors deemed legitimate for discussion there was difficult for the guardians of orthodoxy to proscribe altogether in other, less openly experimental Communist countries. The reformist subculture among professional economists was already well on its way to becoming a transnational one by the end of the 1950's, although its size and, especially, its penetration into the ranks of the policy-making apparatus varied greatly from country to country.

The international factor in the fortunes of the various national reform movements was important in another way. The serious lack of agreement on economic organizational issues prevalent within the top Soviet political leadership[7] from 1954 to 1958 and the intense power struggle for Stalin's succession undoubtedly played a great part in the increased scope for criticism and speculation in the realm of economic theory by fuzzing the boundaries of orthodoxy. In such an international environment, innovative proposals could be voiced where local East European leaders were inclined to allow it or afraid to prevent it. The other side of the coin was, however, that Khrushchev's substantial consolidation of his position and the adoption of specific economic reform measures in the U.S.S.R. in 1958 once again provided a more rigid standard against which East European reform proposals might be gauged and found wanting.

Despite earlier indications that the Soviet leadership had been considering a substantial widening of the autonomy of the enterprise and a greater reliance on financial rather than administrative levers in controlling plan implementation,[8] the actual changes in Soviet economic institutions that went into effect in 1958 concentrated almost entirely on geographical rather than functional decentralization. While former ministerial powers were transferred to a number of new regional economic councils (*sovnarkhozy*), the basic position of the enterprise managers vis-a-vis their new superiors remained one of subjection to the "petty tutelage" and detailed physical directives familiar from the past. The role of "economic levers" and of market-like forces was little enhanced.

The positive impact of the 1958 Soviet reforms was quite limited in Eastern Europe. Although they provided the rationale for a certain strengthening of the economic functions of local and regional government (especially the transfer of certain enterprises working in light industry and food processing from ministerial to local council control), wholesale adoption of the new Soviet scheme for regional economic councils would have been ridiculous because of the immense disparities in the countries' relative sizes. The entire national economy of the average East European people's democracy was already smaller than the regional economies controlled by some of the new Soviet *sovnarkhozy*. Only those most reliable of Soviet allies, the Bulgarians and the East Germans,[9] made major efforts to emulate the regional focus of the new Soviet model of planning and management, and even they seem to have been rather selective in their modifications of the old ministerial system.

The main impact of the 1958 Soviet reforms was a negative or indirect one. The failure of the Soviets to endorse any very great increase in the discretionary authority of enterprise-level management, to abandon many of the former approaches to awarding incentives or measuring enterprise performance, or to introduce a substantially expanded role for financial and market factors in the coordination of economic activity all acted to undercut the legitimacy of the earlier proposals of the reformist economists in Poland, Hungary, and Czechoslovakia. The further deterioration of Soviet bloc relations with Yugoslavia and the renewal of hostile polemics following the Yugoslav's adoption of a new and even more radically "revisionist" Party program in 1958 also left the East European advocates of more enterprise autonomy and a larger role for market forces in a politically exposed position. And while all of this was happening on the international scene, the domestic backlash stimulated by the violence and disorder of 1956 and 1957 was increasingly bringing Party hardliners to the fore and reinforcing the bloc-wide campaign against the threat of "Revisionism." These domestic and international factors combined from 1958 to narrow greatly once again the range of acceptable debate and dissent on the subject of economic planning and management throughout East Europe. The proposals of the Polish, Hungarian, and Czechoslovak reformers were almost entirely discarded by policy makers in 1958 and

1959, although *some* isolated bits and pieces found their way into law, perhaps as a cosmetic gesture to justify all of the hullabaloo which had initially accompanied the appointment of the commissions. The hopes for major institutional reform (other than simply tinkering with the details of the existing highly centralized administrative system) had been effectively dashed by the end of 1958 throughout the region. Indeed, the resumption of the drives to complete agricultural collectivization and the launching of ambitious investment plans emphasizing the growth of heavy industry seemed to foreshadow a return to stalinist orthodoxy in many aspects of economic policy.

New Stimulus for Reform in the 1960's

The history of the 1950's had clearly shown that proposing reforms of the organizational structure and the incentive systems of the socialist economy was a much less difficult process for academic economists caught up in the heady atmosphere of the post-Stalin intellectual renaissance than it was for the harried decision-makers in the Politburo and in the higher state organs who concentrated in their own hands the responsibility for directing not only the national economy but also nearly every other aspect of political and social life as well.

Economists could afford to take a somewhat detached view of "the system of planning and management of the national economy," to think about it principally as an instrument or a mechanism for rationally pursuing the conventional goals of economic policy, and to evaluate its functioning chiefly on the basis of the effectiveness and efficiency with which the given arrangements facilitated the performance of economic functions.

Political leaders had to be concerned with economic performance and, indeed, put a very high priority on certain aspects of economic development. But as political leaders with other responsibilities and interests, they also had to bear in mind certain practical realities. Economic organization in any society plays an important part in structuring the distribution of wealth, power, and status among individuals and groups. In a socialist society of the Soviet type this relationship is vastly magnified by the high degree of interpenetration between the economic and political power structures that was deliberately fostered at all levels as a fundamental component of the Communist revolution. Any large-scale overhauling of the economic mechanism (even one which remains within "socialist" bounds) unavoidably must involve some degree of redistribution of power, status, and wealth. When innovations demand changing the ground-rules under which important categories of people participate in economic life, stresses and conflicts must surely arise. Given the "fused" character of economic and political power under socialism, such personal and group antagonisms can be extremely difficult to compartmentalize or isolate, since many combatants are positioned to mobilize political connections in high places in defense of their interests. Thus, drastic reform of economic planning and management entails risks to the integration of the political elite, the magnitude of which would be hard to calculate in advance but which have to be taken seriously by the leaders of a political order premised on Leninist conceptions of the indispensability of a unified vanguard Party.

Moreover, although top East European political leaders enjoyed considerably more autonomy in formulating domestic policy in the post-1956 period, questions touching upon the proper organizational forms of the socialist economy remained closely linked to fundamental aspects of Marxist-Leninist ideology, and Soviet leaders had by no means abandoned their pretensions to primacy in delineating the permissible range of variation in such matters. Certainly condemnation of "anti-socialist" economic views figures prominently in the Soviet polemics against the dangers of "Revisionism" in the late 1950's. Too innovative an approach to economic institutions could and did lead to strains in intra-bloc relations.[10]

The foregoing considerations about the domestic and political ramifications of far-reaching economic reforms make it clear that there were strong reasons for political leaders to draw back from such undertakings in the late 1950's, despite the urging of many economic experts. Yet only a few years later, in the early 1960's, major economic reform was once again a live issue on the agenda for political discussion throughout most of the region, and this time around, important changes in the planning and management mechanisms (of varying degrees of "radicalism") actually resulted. Why and how did such a turnaround occur?

Many of the factors involved in determining the character and timing of the economic reforms were, of course, specific to the various countries involved. Nevertheless, we may also identify several general factors which affected the process to at least some degree in every country.

International Factors

The first set of common factors facilitating the adoption of innovations in economic planning and management derived from changes in the international environment within which domestic policy-makers operated. These involved both a loosening of externally imposed restraints on East European leaders already predisposed to encourage economic innovations and a positive stimulus toward reform for those whose previous conservatism was derived from a propensity to emulate the Soviet Union.

The launching of the second great destalinization campaign by Khrushchev around the time of the Twenty-Second Congress of the C.P.S.U. (October 1961) may have been motivated primarily by his desire to eliminate his most formidable opponents remaining in the Politburo,[11] but whatever the original motivation may have been, the practical consequences for East Europe were no less profound, both with respect to changes in the composition of the ruling groups that occurred under the rubric of suppressing the last vestiges of the "personality cult" (especially in Bulgaria and Hungary and, somewhat more half-heartedly, in Czechoslovakia)[12] and with respect to the resolution of substantive policy disputes. The general attack on the rigidity of the Stalinist period tended to spill over into the area of economic theory in much the same manner as in 1956-57, further buttressing the defenses of "new wave" economists against the onslaught of their more orthodox colleagues within the profession. Moreover, specific statements made at the Twenty-Second Congress on the subject of the economy seemed to indicate a renewed receptiveness by the Soviet leadership to further organizational innovations. Acceptance in Moscow seemed to mandate a similar open-mindedness by East European authorities also. Khrushchev's own report to the Congress noted:

Our task in the course of building communism is to make ever greater use of and to improve the finance and credit levers, ruble control, prices and profit. . . . It is in the interest of better plan fulfillment that enterprises be given greater opportunity to determine the use of their profits.[13]

The new Party program approved by the Congress supplemented its call for "heightening of the role and responsibility of the local agencies" with a flat declaration that operative independence and initiative of enterprises on the basis of the state plan assignments must be increased in order to mobilize internal reserves and make more effective the use of capital investments, production facilities and funds.[14]

The Twenty-Second Congress was followed by a series of articles in the press and the economic journals, each proposing various concrete steps that might be taken to implement the general principles enunciated at the Congress, beginning with O. Antonov's relatively modest proposals in November 1961.[15] Principal topics of discussion in the spirited exchanges that followed included the relative merits of different types of plan indicators, the desirable degree of autonomy for enterprise managers in various areas, the significance and proper measurement of enterprise efficiency, and the best methods for harnessing individual and group self-interest for the more effective implementation of the plan. In line with the general emphasis of the Congress, proposals focussed on piecemeal improvements at the level of the enterprise and did not take on macroeconomic topics until almost a year later, when *Pravda* featured Professor Yevsei Liberman's now-famous iconoclastic article on "Plan, Profits, Bonuses" and invited the reactions of other Soviet economists.[16] The so-called Liberman discussions that followed displayed a diversity of views among well respected economists and an acknowledgement of fundamental problems in the theory of socialist planning and management that went far beyond anything the Soviet public had seen since the 1920's, and their significance was further underlined by Khrushchev's proposal at the November 1962 plenum of the Central Committee that practical experiments ought to be carried out at selected industrial plants and enterprises to test the workability of some of these new ideas.[17]

The Liberman discussions were followed with great interest among East European economists and economic officials, who either read them in the original Russian or made use of the numerous translations published in the East European press. While the proposals of Liberman and his supporters and allies could not have seemed particularly novel to those who were familiar with the recommendations of the Polish Economic Council or Hungary's "Varga Commission," the fact that they were being given a sympathetic hearing in the Soviet Union was of immense significance. It opened the way to even wider-ranging discussions in the East European press and economic journals.

New Problems with Economic Performance

Substantially diminished Soviet pressures to maintain the established model of economic planning and management throughout the bloc was a necessary but not a sufficient condition for the revival of economic reform as a serious possibility in the more dependent East European countries. More Soviet flexibility in such matters meant that leadership groups in the various countries were more free to respond to their own preferences and to their own perceptions of the political and economic realities specific to the domestic situation. But given the past experiences that had shaped their outlooks and habits and given the balance of forces and interests from which they derived their power within the existing order, it was far from clear that all East European leadership groups would wish to take advantage of their increased autonomy to undertake major reforms. And as it turned out, the variations in the scope and timing of economic reforms discussed, adopted, and implemented were very substantial. How may we explain these variations?

Organization theorists tell us that a stimulus to change organizational arrangements occurs when there *is* a perceived discrepancy between the way the organization *is* performing and the way that decision-makers believe it *ought* to be performing. When such a discrepancy between the criteria of satisfaction with performance and the actually measured performance persists, it becomes likely that those who perceive the "performance gap" will initiate a search for alternative ways of closing the gap.[18] One way that we might account for variations in East European leaders' interest in the economists' proposals for reform would be to show whether it is plausible to believe that they gauged the seriousness of performance gaps in their respective national economies and proceeded accordingly. To establish the magnitude of such a performance gap, one needs to specify the particular measures of organizational performance that are crucial to the leadership group, and one needs some way of gauging the level of expectations according to which the leaders evaluate their relative success or failure.

Whatever may have been the occasional shifts in relative saliency of economic goals in East Europe, there can be little doubt that maintaining high rates of economic growth has characteristically been assigned a very high priority in the policies of the Communist leadership, and measures of this dimension of performance are easily available from the press or statistical yearbooks. The standard according to which leaders form their expectations as to what rates of growth ought to be attained is much more difficult to ascertain, but several intuitively appealing yet simple models of the process can readily be adduced.

The literature of social psychology suggests two common ways in which people form their expectations: (1) they may do so by simple extrapolation of their own past experiences, or (2) they may shape their expectations by the performance of some particularly salient reference group or groups. The first suggests the measurement of expectation levels with some sort of simple moving average of the actual rates of growth achieved during the recent past. The second suggests that one might want to see how each country's growth rates compare with those of at least two categories of "significant others": (a) other fraternal Communist countries, and (b) their most important capitalist rivals.

Figure 2.1 displays yearly rates of growth of national income for the six East European Comecon member-states, as compared with their own respective average rates of growth over the previous five years. Inspection of the graphs reveals generally declining trends in growth rates in most of the region and most obviously in Czechoslovakia and the G.D.R. (the two most economically developed countries). If we take substantial discrepancies between annual rates and five-year average rates as an operational definition of the performance gap, then we can identify unusually sustained or severe performance gaps as having occurred in Poland during 1956-60, in Hungary in 1956 and 1961-65, in Bulgaria during 1960-64, in Czechoslovakia during 1962-64, and in the G.D.R. almost continuously until 1964. While Romania displays a pattern of wildly oscillating annual growth rates, there were *no* periods of two or more years below the previous average prior to 1966-67, but the spectacular one-year bust of 1956 (-7 percent) is perhaps worthy of note. (Although Albania's performance is not displayed because of missing data problems, available information and approximations suggest a very similar pattern to that of Romania, with several isolated disastrous years in 1956, 1960, 1965, and 1967, but with no clearly declining trend or sustained periods of relative depression.)

If we compare the annual growth rates of each country with the overall average rates for all of the East European Communist countries, we derive somewhat similar results. (See Table 2.1.) Countries which had "runs" of three or more consecutive years in which their growth rates were below the bloc average were as follows: Poland during the period 1957-1960; the G.D.R. during the period 1960-1966; Czechoslovakia from 1962 to 1965; and Hungary from 1964 to 1966.

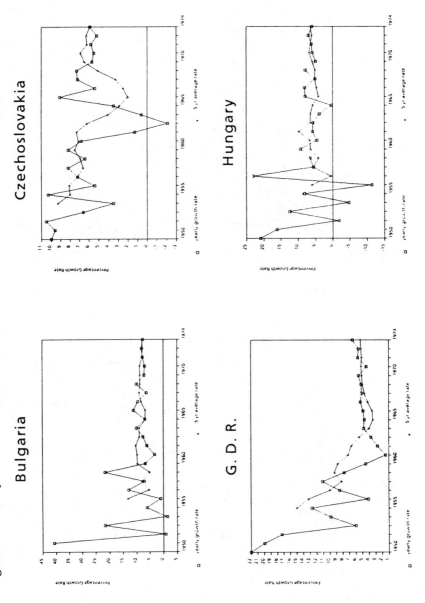

Figure 2.1: Yearly Growth Rates of National Income (Net Material Product at Comparable Prices)

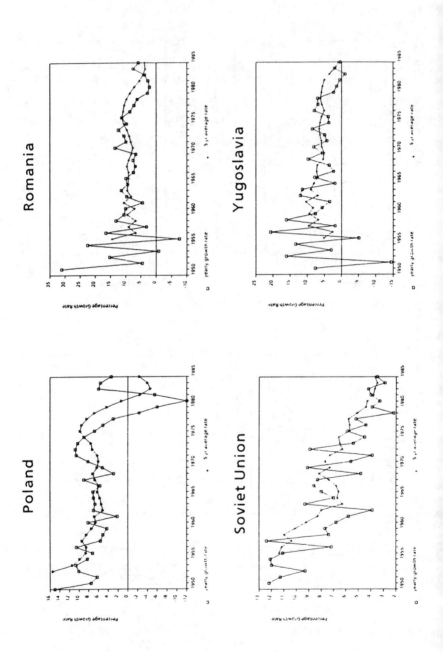

TABLE 2.1

Yearly Growth Rates of National Income (Constant Prices)
(% per annum)

Year	Alb.	Bul.	Hun.	Pol.	GDR	Rom.	Cze.	Ave.
1951		41	16	8	28	31	10	22
1952		- 1	- 2	6	17	5	10	6
1953		22	12	10	7	15	7	12
1954		- 1	- 5	11	10	- 1	4	3
1955		6	8	8	9	22	10	11
1956	1	1	-11	7	5-	7	5	1
1957	14	13	23	11	7	16	7	13
1958	7	7	6	6	19	3	8	7
1959	19	22	7	5	10	13	6	12
1960	- 2	7	9	4	6	11	8	6
1961	7	3	5	8	3	10	7	6
1962	6	6	6	2	2	5	1	4
1963	10	8	6	7	3	10	- 2	6
1964	6	10	4	7	3	12	1	6
1965	14	7	1	7	5	10	3	7
1966	11	11	8	7	5	10	10	9
1967	1	10	8	6	5	7	5	6
1968	5	6	5	9	5	7	7	6
1969	13	10	8	3	5	8	7	8
1970		7	5	5	5	7	6	6
1971		7	6	8	4	14	6	

Sources: National statistical yearbooks and U.N. *Yearbook
of National Accounts Statistics*, various years.

Comparisons between growth rates of Communist and capitalist
economies are somewhat difficult because of the great differences in the
methods and concepts underlying their respective systems of compiling
national income statistics. Table 2.2 presents the results of one group of
Western economists' efforts at recomputing East European official data in
order to render it more nearly comparable to Western G.N.P. growth rates.

It seems reasonable to assume that these figures are at least roughly indicative of whether the growth rates were increasingly or decreasingly disparate, even if the absolute magnitudes of G.N.P. may not be reliably comparable. While West European growth rates slackened somewhat in the early 1960's, East European growth rates decelerated to a greater extent, on the average. Hungary, Romania, and Poland held on to or even improved their growth rates relative to Western Europe, while Czechoslovakia, the German Democratic Republic, and Bulgaria showed marked deterioration in their performances relative to those of Western Europe as a whole and relative to their nearest capitalist neighbors. (One can expect that historical associations and rivalries would make neighboring countries particularly salient "reference groups." If one compares the two Germanies with each other, Czechoslovakia and Hungary with Austria, Poland with Germany and Austria, and Bulgaria and Romania with Greece and Italy, the picture delineated above does not substantially change: Hungary, Poland, and Romania did relatively well by this criterion in the early 1960's, while the G.D.R., Czechoslovakia, and Bulgaria must be adjudged to have done rather poorly.)

TABLE 2.2
Comparison of G.N.P. Growth Rates, East and West

Country	Annual Percentage Increases			
	1951-55	1956-60	1961-64	1951-64
Bulgaria	5.9%	7.3%	4.3%	5.9%
Czechoslovakia	3.6%	6.6%	1.3%	4.0%
G.D.R.	7.2%	4.9%	2.7%	5.1%
Hungary	5.5%	4.2%	4.6%	4.8%
Poland	4.8%	5.0%	5.0%	4.9%
Romania	8.6%	3.5%	4.9%	5.7%
Western Europe Ave.	5.9%	5.2%	5.1%	5.4%
Austria	6.1%	5.2%	4.2%	5.2%
F.R.G.	9.1%	6.2%	4.8%	6.8%
Greece	7.0%	5.6%	8.7%	7.0%
Italy	6.0%	5.9%	5.5%	5.8%

Source:Maurice Ernst, "Postwar Economic Growth in Eastern Europe," in U.S. Congress, Joint Economic Committee, 89th Congress, 2nd Session, *New Directions in the Soviet Economy*, p. 883.

The identification of performance gaps in overall economic growth rates according to the above three criteria is summarized in Table 2.3. It suggests that in the 1960's, the leaders of the G.D.R. and Czechoslovakia had particular reason for dissatisfaction with their economies' respective growth performances on all three counts.   The Hungarians and the Bulgarians must also have been concerned at their relatively poor growth performances based on two of the three criteria during roughly the same period.   After a relatively poor performance in the second half of the 1950's, Polish growth rates underwent relative improvement in the 1960's (except for two particularly disappointing isolated years in 1962 and 1969). Romania's growth rates held up well during most of the 1960's but displayed a bit of a deceleration in 1967-1970.   It would appear that (at least from the point of view of the single but highly salient performance dimension of overall economic growth rates in the early 1960's) the Romanian, Polish, and (probably) Albanian leadership groups had considerably less cause for alarm then their comrades in other European Communist countries.

TABLE 2.3
Occurrence of Performance Gaps in Economic Growth Rates

		Relative to:	
		Other Bloc	
Country	Recent Past	Countries	Capitalists*
Bulgaria	1960-1964		1961-1964
Czechoslovakia	1962-1964	1962-1965	1961-1964
G.D.R.	1951-1957	1961-1970	1961-1964
	1960-1964		
Hungary	1956	1964-1966	
	1961-1965		
Poland	1956-1960	1957-1960	
Romania	1967-1970		

* Data available only through 1964.

Other aspects of economic performance than just overall growth rates were also of concern to East European policy-makers during the 1960's, and a number of chronic problems seemed to be growing worse, especially in the more economically developed countries.   In addition to declining rates of economic growth, the symptoms of the malaise widely discussed in the economic literature and in official pronouncements included the widespread and expensive waste of labor and physical productive resources due to excessive absenteeism, job-hopping, hoarding, and bad planning in the distribution system; the presence of severe shortages of certain goods simultaneously with the rapid expansion of unsalable inventories,[19] due to failures of quality control and simple lack of responsiveness to consumers' preferences; and pronounced sectoral imbalances in the distribution of manpower and capital that were adversely affecting agriculture, construction, transportation, and light industry, in the process creating costly bottlenecks for future industrial development.[20] In addition, Czechoslovakia, Hungary, and the G.D.R. began experiencing increasingly serious international balance-of-trade difficulties, as the less developed Communist countries to the south and east increasingly produced for themselves the capital goods they formerly had to import from their sister states to the north. Efforts to overcome trade difficulties through Comecon specialization agreements were helpful but insufficient to take up the slack. Expansion of trade with the Third World tied up resources over too prolonged a period because of the need to sell on credit. Efforts to break into Western markets were made difficult by trade restrictions of Cold War origin and, especially, by difficulties in responding flexibly to Western customers' demands for higher quality standards, faster deliveries, and better servicing networks.[21]

Most alarming of all, the productivity of new investment seemed to have established a long-term declining trend in Czechoslovakia, the G.D.R., Hungary, and Poland. Although the planners were channeling higher and higher proportions of the national income into investment (that is, the growth rates of investment outlays were increasing more rapidly than the growth of national income), growth rates of output were not only failing to keep pace, but were even actually falling in some cases.[22] This was not merely frustrating to the leadership's desire for sustained high rates of economic growth. It was politically dangerous as well, because the corollary of an ever-increasing share of the national income going into investment (and those burgeoning inventories) was that a declining share of the national income would be available for the consumption of the population. (If capital/output ratios kept rising indefinitely, simple algebra demonstrates that the living standard must slow its rise and ultimately decline absolutely.) Growth rates of real wages were already lagging behind the growth of labor productivity (and to an increasing extent),[23] with obvious adverse consequences for labor morale (high turnover rates, serious absenteeism, diminished efforts on the job). Should such workforce discontents become politicized (as they did in Berlin and Plzn in 1953, and in Poznan and Budapest in 1956), the consequences could potentially be very serious indeed.   In those countries so afflicted, *something* would have to be done: the only question was *what*.

Developing a Rationale for Economic Reform Measures

The discovery by the top Communist leaders in several countries of East Europe that a serious performance gap had developed in the economic sphere was usually enough to convince many of them that remedial action needed to be taken, but such a perception did not in itself indicate unambiguously what the nature of the corrective measures ought to be. The unpleasant symptoms of the economic malaise were evident enough, but a more sophisticated diagnosis would be necessary before a course of therapy could confidently be embarked upon.   As prudent men, the East European Communist leaders were not anxious to accept radical ideological surgery without first being convinced that a bigger dose of the old medicine could not do the job.   However, inasmuch as a good many traditional Stalinist remedies for getting the economy moving again had already been tried in Eastern Europe during 1959-1961 with disappointing results (the massive acceleration of investment outlays, the rapid drive to the completion of agricultural collectivization, the effort to rekindle the ideological fervor of the Party cadres and the masses through the "anti-Revisionist" campaigns, the purging of the Party of "wavering elements"), the leadership of several of the worst-hit countries found themselves rather at a loss.   Feeling a greater-than-usual need for expert advice and less-than-usual confidence in the existing inner circle of economic administrators and planners who seemed to have failed them, the Party leadership in a several countries reached out to a broader cross-section of the economics profession for guidance and concrete advice.   This was the principal function served the by "little Liberman debates" that took place in the press in some (but not all) of the people's democracies.   The depth and intensity of the debates were approximately in proportion to the severity of the countries' respective "performance gaps."

Extensive excerpts from the Soviet Liberman debate that began in *Pravda* in September of 1962 were translated and reprinted in Czechoslovakia, Bulgaria, Hungary, and the G.D.R., but not in Romania or Albania.   In Poland, accounts of the gist of the Soviet discussions were published (and some excerpts), but in general they were given little play, probably because they seemed rather tame in comparison with the Polish debates of only a few years before.   In Hungary, and especially in Czechoslovakia and Bulgaria, the initial publication of the Soviet materials was followed up by vigorous domestic debate in the media by native economic reform advocates and their opponents.   In Czechoslovakia and Bulgaria, the editors even turned up two "Libermans" of their own — relatively unknown and "unconnected" economists whose ideas were too wild to be actually accepted but who were useful in stimulating discussion. Radoslav Selucky's jeremiad against "the cult of the plan"[24] in Czechoslovakia and A. Miloshevsky's gushing endorsement of Yugoslav-style workers' self-management for Bulgaria,[25] by the very fact that they were allowed into print, graphically demonstrated that unconventional and innovative economic thinking was being solicited. In East Germany, the published discussion was quite restrained and largely limited to explicit exegesis of the Soviet discussion — but even here there were important symbolic gestures in the form of the sudden reappearance in print of two formerly-denounced heretics, Jurgen Kuczynski[26] and Fritz Behrens,[27] as well as the widespread citation of Party leader Walter Ulbricht's statement that the "broad public discussion of important economic questions underscores the growing role of economists and planners."[28]

Thus emboldened, reformist economists proceeded in their discussions to elaborate their own theories as to why economic performance (and especially rates of growth in labor productivity) had been deteriorating. While they were far from agreement with each other on a wide range of analytical issues and on the exact prescriptions for improving the situation, nevertheless there developed at least a broad consensus as to what the major problems were. Moreover, they were able to translate their conclusions in such a way as to demonstrate important continuities with more traditional Marxist concepts and habits of thought, even while proposing fairly radical reforms.

Crucial to the reformers' arguments was the acceptance of certain theoretical models of the process of economic growth under socialism which were consistent with the earlier Stalinist conceptions of this process but which could be used to show that the earlier model was really only a special case of the newer, more general model. Instead of placing themselves in the politically untenable position of denouncing the Party's established strategies of economic growth (and the organizational arrangements that went with them) as fundamentally unsound from the beginning, it was safer to argue that Stalinist approaches to economic development were indeed highly appropriate in the past under the special conditions then prevailing but that the successes of wise policies of the past had by now brought about a fundamentally new set of conditions that demanded rather new approaches by the party if this successful record was to continue.

The theoretical work on economic growth under socialism that made this strategy of reform advocacy possible grew very largely from the intellectual influence of Michal Kalecki, another distinguished Polish economist who, like Oscar Lange, had established an international reputation in the West during the 1930's and 1940's before returning to his native country to assist in its post-war socialist reconstruction. The details of Kalecki's model are highly complex and need not be gone into here.[29] The major significance lies in the character of Kalecki's theories as being both certifiably Marxist in orientation and descent and pointedly critical of the overgeneralization of Soviet growth strategies to non-Soviet conditions. His formulations related such variables as national income, investment, the size and distribution of the labor force, capital/output ratios, and consumption levels in sophisticated fashion and provided an ingenious analytical framework within which it became possible to discuss the determination of "optimal" rates of growth of investment and of national income in terms more sophisticated than the Stalinist notion of "the higher, the better." (Among other things, Kalecki demonstrated formally that, beyond a certain level of investment, further increases tended to slow rather than accelerate economic growth, and that consumption foregone in the present for the sake of future consumption beyond a certain point was simply wasted or even counter-productive. He also demonstrated that excessive concentration of investment funds in capital-intensive heavy industry, as Stalinists asserted would be necessary in perpetuity, would in fact have negative consequences for long-term growth rates if continued beyond a specifiable point.)

Aside from demonstrating the "relative" nature of the "absolute" laws of socialist development propounded by Stalin's school, the utility of the new "post-Kaleckian" school of thought to the diagnosis of East Europe's contemporary economic ills was most evident in drawing analytical attention to the fact that the growth rate of national income was not the simple consequences of the rate of investment. Growth was rather the resultant of two quite different kinds of processes. Elaborating on Marx's distinction between "extensive" and "intensive" forms of economic expansion, they became especially interested in analyzing the sources of economic growth in East European historical development, and they came to the conclusion that the more economically advanced socialist states were experiencing the ending of an economic era and the transition to a new one in which rather different institutional arrangements and policies would be necessary.

To oversimplify somewhat, the analysis employed to such excellent political effect by the advocates of economic reform (at least in the more developed people's democracies) was roughly the following. Stalinist theories and strategies of economic development (and the system of planning and management appropriate to their implementation) relied almost entirely on "extensive" sources of growth. Extensive growth is produced by the quantitative expansion of the material means (land, labor, and capital) which the economy is able to devote to "expanded reproduction." Extensive growth strategies concentrate on increasing massively the total quantity of inputs as the principal method of increasing total national output: building more factories, increasing the size and utilization of the labor force, and massive land reclamation projects would be characteristically extensive methods. Such a strategy had great possibilities under the conditions prevailing in Russia during Stalin's time because of the enormous pool of unemployed or underemployed peasants who could be transferred to industrial production at very low social opportunity costs if only the massive investments in building new factories were undertaken. The existence of massive rural underemployment in many East European countries at the end of World War II made this strategy initially viable there as well. So long as the possibilities of massive mobilization of labor were still there, high growth rates could be maintained, even if "intensive" sources of growth were largely neglected.

"Intensive" growth refers to the portion of economic growth that results, not from increases in the sheer quantity of inputs supplied, but from improvements in the efficiency with which these inputs are combined. Technological improvements in production methods are the most obvious intensive growth factors, but there are others: improvements of the techniques of management at the micro-level (to reduce waste of materials, loafing on the job, absenteeism, incompetence, excessive inventories, inefficient assignment of tasks, frequent shut-downs due to poor maintenance, etc.); improvement of the methods of management and organization at the macro-level (so as to bring about more productive allocations of resources among enterprises or among branches, to take advantage of economies of scale, to improve the flow of materials and foresee bottlenecks, to insure the prompt diffusion of new technologies, and in general to avoid the pathologies of bureaucratic rigidity and irrationality); and, finally, participation in the "gains from trade" made possible by a more complex international division of labor with specialization based on the principle of comparative advantage.

The reformist economists diagnosed the increasingly negative phenomena of rising capital/output ratios, declining economic growth rates, and inadequate improvement in the living standard as the predictable consequences of the impending exhaustion of the major extensive factors that had fueled the high growth rates of the 1940's and 1950's. Investments in the immediate post-war reconstruction had largely involved repairs and renovation of war-damaged plant and infrastructure temporarily out of commission, and under these circumstances, the immediate returns to investment were quite disproportionately large. The massive new construction of the first five-year plans nearly maintained this early pace (though at somewhat higher costs) by making possible the massive transfer of the rural underemployed to more productive activities in an industrial setting. The labor force was also massively enlarged by economic and social policies that caused housewives to seek gainful employment outside the home. By the late 1950's and early 1960's, the depletion of these "reserves" for very rapid expansion of the labor force was clearly in sight.[30] The rural exodus was creating problems in agricultural production, as the average age of farm workers rose dangerously high. Female employment ratios were already among the highest in the world and unlikely to increase much further. The natural increase of the labor force was leveling off or declining due to earlier changes in the trend of birth-rates.[31] Moreover, fifteen years of concentrating on building new physical plant and machinery to the neglect of proper maintenance or replacement of existing stocks had by the 1960's resulted in serious problems of technical obsolescence and poor reliability that was a growing drag on productivity.

Since it would no longer be possible to achieve spectacular growth rates by the earlier combination of massive expansions of the industrial labor force through massive investments in new productive plants (except perhaps, for the time being, where rural population "reserves' were still substantial — Poland, Romania, and Albania), policy-makers over the long haul would either have to accept substantially lower rates of growth in national income, or else they would have to concentrate their efforts much more than before on increasing the contribution of intensive factors of growth. The reformers argued that the way out of the impasse would have to be a well-designed set of institutional reforms and policy changes aimed at accelerating scientific-technical innovation, improving the efficiency of planning and management at all levels, upgrading the levels of skill and motivation of the labor force, and turning to much better account the possibilities for a rational division of labor in the area of foreign trade.[32] The reforms would have to be rather radical, they argued, because the existing model of economic planning and management (basically the one inherited from Stalin) was effective in the massive mobilization of men and resources for extensive growth strategies only by means of certain intrinsic features that now stifled innovation, made rational allocation of resources impossible, demoralized the work force, and inhibited successful participation in the international division of labor. Marx might have noted that the relations of production were in danger of becoming "a fetter on the forces of production," but Goldman and Kouba were diplomatic enough to phrase their equally blunt conclusion in less inflammatory terminology:

> The chief obstacle to further progressive advance and a strengthening of socialist production relations is set by a conflict between the present need for economic growth and the out-dated system of management.[33]

Such views were by no means universally accepted within the economics profession, and the debates were long and vigorous. In the end, however, there was widespread agreement that a number of earlier preconceptions *had* been erroneous and harmful and that there was indeed a pressing need to reform economic institutions in order to reinvigorate the economy. The main points of consensus that emerged from the debates throughout the area (excluding Romania and Albania) were these:

(1) The conception that "plan" and "market" are polar and irrecon-cilable opposites should be discarded as simplistic and misleading. Under proper socialist institutional arrangements the operation of market forces need not be an impediment but rather can be an active and positive factor in the achievement of the economic objectives of the top political authorities as formalized in the plan.

(2) It was always necessary for the top political authorities to use both "administrative" (imperative) and "economic" (financial incentives) methods in controlling the economy in accordance with the plan, but in the past, the proper balance had not always been maintained. At higher stages of development, with the growing complexity of the economy, the proper balance shifts in the direction of greater reliance on economic levers and less on administrative ones.

(3) Improvement of financial accounting methodology is indispensable for rational decision making in the planning of investments and becomes increasingly critical as the complexity and differentiation of the economy increases. Where increased participation in international trade is to be pursued as a means of promoting growth, the objective ability of decision-makers to discover their economies' "comparative advantages" through meaningful economic calculation becomes essential. Prices used in such calculations should reflect real costs and real relative scarcities.

(4) It is essential in an advanced industrial economy that the material interests of workers and lower level managers not be set in conflict with the requirements for their effective achievement of planned goals.

Institutional arrangements for the payment of wages and bonuses should be reformed to conform to the principle that

> what is profitable to society as a whole will also be profitable to each production collective and, on the other hand, what is wasteful from the standpoint of public interests will be extremely unprofitable to each enterprise.[34]

(5) While central authorities must retain decisive control over the determination of certain key "proportions" (growth rates of national income, investment, and consumption; the relative growth rates of the various branches and sectors of the national economy; the development of employment; the "main directions" of research and development; the territorial location of investment; and the overall structure of international trade), nevertheless the overall effectiveness of central control is enhanced rather than decreased if the planners are not constantly obliged by the workings of irrational incentive systems to engage in the constant and detailed supervision of operational management decisions at the enterprise level.

(6) Usually enterprise managers should have more authority to take advantage of their unique knowledge of local conditions in order to cut costs and promote efficiency, and they should have a material incentive to use this discretion vigorously and expertly. To this end, it was generally conceded to be desirable to reduce the number and detail of the compulsory plan directives dictated to the enterprise manager and to rely on fewer and more "synthetic" indices in evaluating overall enterprise performance. This generally implied greater emphasis on financial indicators (which could be added and subtracted to provide the basis for "cost-benefit" evaluations) and less emphasis on traditionally favored physical-unit indicators. (If in their pursuit of efficiency and effectiveness the managers are expected to use their own unique knowledge and capacities, then they must necessarily be guided, not by *how* their superiors think they ought to set about it, but rather by the *value* their superiors can be reliably expected to place upon the net results produced.)

(7) It was generally acknowledged that the existing, highly centralized methods of allocating flows of machinery, materials, and semi-fabricates between enterprises (and especially between enterprises subordinated to different ministries) were outdated, inadequate, and a major obstacle to the smooth operation of the enterprise. The necessity of routing all requisitions through the central materials-supply administration and the necessity for the central planners to be constantly rationing out the

inadequate available supplies (on the basis of unmanageable quantities of unreliable information) resulted in delays in production schedules, maintaining by the enterprises of unreasonably large defensive inventories of the most sought-after items, and a large variety of other very expensive pathologies. The situation seemingly could only get worse, by virtue of what might be termed "the square law": the more developed the economy, the more different varieties of final and intermediate goods there will be to be allocated in the production process, and the number of input-out interrelations to be regulated must increase in proportion to the *square* of the number of products. It would plainly be impossible for any hierarchical organization, no matter how large the staff, to keep up with any such exponentially increasing information-and-decision overload. Ways *had* to be found to allow enterprises to deal directly with each other for the vast bulk of their requirements — yet it was also essential that ways be found to avoid aggregate outcomes from such a decentralized process that would violate the "basic proportions" set down by the central authorities in the plan.

Principal Reform Measures Suggested

The specific reforms recommended to the attention of the authorities by the participants in the public debates were quite diverse and often conflicting. A few economists (usually employed in ministerial staff or administrative posts) continued to defend the established system. Many recommended piecemeal changes of an ameliorative character. Still others came to assert the need for the full-scale revamping of fundamental institutions and practices of economic planning and management. While the degree of "radicalism" in the tone of the public debate varied considerably from country to country (being most pronounced in Czechoslovakia, Hungary, and Bulgaria), the underlying issues were familiar ones: the proper balances between plan and market and between centralism and enterprise autonomy in the making of various categories of decisions; the proper role of money and the price system under socialism; and the nature of the institutional requisites for rational micro- and macro-economic calculation to produce socially optimal decisions.

The more radical reformers aimed at a shift in the general direction of "market socialism," and many who did not support so radical a position nevertheless saw the value of adopting a number of features that were originally devised as a part of such a model. These reformers advanced the view that efficiency at the level of the enterprise could be most readily attained by permitting maximum discretion to the management (who alone had the invaluable knowledge of special local conditions, capacities, and opportunities which had to be taken into account if optimal decisions were to be made in the guidance of production).

In order that decentralized managerial decisions should be coordinated and consistent with social-economic priorities, it was necessary to insure that decision-makers at all levels would be provided with the information minimally necessary for making socially-optimal decisions at least *possible*. Moreover there should be appropriate material incentives devised to insure that decisions would in fact be taken on the appropriate basis. The reformers saw the price system as potentially a very efficient transmitter of information about the social costs and benefits of alternative lines of action, and they advocated the use of profits as the best "synthetic" indicator of overall enterprise efficiency — with the proviso that prices should be "correctly" determined. Managers (and the work force generally) should be given material incentives based on enterprise profitability to encourage profit maximization. (If profitability was to be the measure of net social benefit provided, it would be essential that *all* social opportunity costs be deducted, not just the ones traditionally considered under the established system — which meant that there should be instituted financial charges of appropriate magnitude for the use of fixed capital, operating funds, and land sites: "rent" and "interest.")

Moreover, the function of the pricing system should not be limited to the enterprise level of decision-making for current operations. The enterprise should have substantial resources left at its disposal (from depreciation funds, interest-bearing bank loans, or retained profits) to carry out its own discretionary investments for the expansion or diversification of its product line or for improving profitability by means of technological innovation. Ministerial and other central authorities should not fritter away their valuable time and limited manpower in the making of minor investment decisions. These should be left to existing enterprises in interaction with a banking system that also bases its activity on "commercial principles." Rather the central planners should devote their attentions to evaluating the alternatives for major "structure-determining" investments, such as those involving infrastructural improvements or the creation of whole new branches of production. Even the central authorities should take careful account of financial calculations in their decision-making, although the reformers usually conceded that current prices would be a somewhat less adequate guide for making very long-term and large-scale structure-determining investments. (A variety of mathematical formulae were suggested for purposes of facilitating choice between alternative major investment projects.)

Because of the central regulating role assigned to financial calculations in the reformers' models, the question of how "correct" or "economically justified" prices could be generated was absolutely crucial. The degree of decentralization of decision-making power that could safely be allowed depended upon the confidence that could be placed in the adequacy of the price system as a transmitter of planners' preferences and/or consumers' preferences. There were two fundamental alternative approaches to price-creation: either a given price could be determined by autonomous agreement between buyers and sellers (i.e., on the market — whether competitive or monopolistic) or it could be administratively fixed by some third party (or, rather, non-party) to the transaction, such as a central price commission. To the extent that planners' preferences rather than consumers' preferences were to govern economic activity (and political realities dictated that planners' preferences would certainly be accorded deference in many areas), some sort of central price-fixing would be required for at least the "most important" commodities. Reformers generally favored (1) greater scope for market determination of many kinds of prices (i.e., those where the central authorities really have no distinctive or strong preferences at stake, as in much of the consumer goods field) and (2) more "scientific" processes for calculating those prices which would be centrally fixed for one reason or another (so that actors basing their decisions on the information contained in the prices would not be constantly misled as to the planners' true preferences).

At least five major variants in administrative price-setting formulae were debated internationally. It is unnecessary to go into their details, but one may readily discern substantial agreement among reformers that prices would now have to meet certain new criteria. They would have to reflect some practical approximation of marginal costs of production (however "costs of production" might variously be construed), and they would have to be quite frequently updated to reflect changing material costs of production, changing preferences (either of planners or consumers), and the resulting changes in relative scarcities. (In contrast, under the established system, prices for industrial commodities had often remained the same for five to ten years or even longer and had become essentially arbitrary and thus worthless as conveyers of information about current or projected conditions.) Since frequent updating of prices would require much expensive and time-consuming processing of information, it was desirable to limit administrative price setting to a basic minimum of commodities.

A major area in which reformers were active in making recommendations was that of incentive systems within enterprises. As already indicated, the reformers usually advocated some sort of profit-sharing scheme for rank-and-file workers as well as for managers, to encourage solidarity, cooperation, and even mass initiative in the effort to increase enterprise profits. In addition, reformers usually complained that existing wage and bonus structures were radically deficient because they were insufficiently sensitive to actual variations in individual and group contributions to net production. A variety of factors in the overall system of wage regulation tended to encourage featherbedding in some industries while other industries suffered acute labor shortages. It was also alleged that inappropriate wage differentials had created substantial disincentive effects inhibiting workers from increasing their levels of qualification and skill, to the detriment of social productivity. Many reformers emphasized the need to improve the motivation of the work force through a more discriminating and differentiated system of compensation.

It was sometimes suggested that worker productivity might also be considerably enhanced through encouraging a more "participatory" and less "authoritarian" style of decision-making on the shop floor, which would enhance the workers' sense of identification with the enterprise. Greater autonomy for enterprise management could facilitate workers' initiative because the manager would not be prevented from responding to worthwhile suggestions by rigid central regulations. In general, the theme of encouraging greater worker participation in enterprise affairs had to be handled somewhat gingerly because of the politically sensitive resemblance to the Yugoslav advocacy of full "workers' self-management." Although, as we shall see in subsequent chapters, such issues did indeed arise in the struggles over the implementation of the reforms, they were largely avoided in the 1962-1964 discussions. The only major exception to this tendency happened in Bulgaria, where Professor Angel Miloshevsky of the Karl Marx Economic Institute boldly asserted

. . . that, in order to reach a more complete solution to the question of increasing the interest and the activity of the workers in the state enterprises, a form of management must be established which ensures a more immediate participation of the workers in the management of the enterprise. . . . It can be considered that the conditions are already ripe for the creation of such an organ in our state enterprise, through which the workers participate in the solution of many questions of production connected with the organization of labor, with labor remuneration, with the distribution of profit; they have a word to say even in the appointment of the director of the enterprise. . . .[35]

Professor Miloshevsky's over-enthusiastic suggestion was roundly criticized in the Bulgarian press, and no other reformer came to his defense in print.

Reformers' Access to Policy-Makers

The public discussions in the press and the technical journals that took place in 1962-1964 played an important role in mobilizing the broader participation of the economic profession (and others as well) and eliciting a wide range of concrete suggestions for consideration by top policy-makers. It provided a method by which hitherto isolated proponents of reform could come into the open and proselytize, and it decisively altered the general atmosphere within which economic policy decisions were being made. Suggestions which only a few years previously would have been denounced as unacceptably "revisionist" and which might well have cost the author his career, suddenly could now receive at least a thoughtful hearing and substantive criticism rather than *ad hominem* attacks. While many of the more "utopian" schemes put forward had little chance of full acceptance, they still seemed to have a noticeable effect in shifting the political and scholarly definitions of what constituted "moderate" and "realistic" opinion worthy of serious consideration in actual policy-for-mation. A new sense of the "connectedness" of a wide range of problems that had hitherto been perceived in isolation encouraged policy-makers to seek systemic solutions through structural reforms rather than undertake *ad hoc* and isolated remedial measures of an essentially reactive character.

But however great the impact of the broader discussions undoubtedly was in redrawing the mental road-maps to which policy-advisers could refer, the actual policy decisions were not taken on the basis of any majority vote of the professional economists, but at the highest levels of the Communist Party leadership in the various countries. The drafts and proposals which they considered did not come directly out of their morning newspapers but rather were the products of more or less formal technical advisory staffs selected by and responsible to the top political organs of the Party and state. In order for the advocates of radical economic reform to get their proposals adopted, it was necessary for them first to acquire channels of access to the political decision-makers themselves or at least to their close advisers and subordinates.

Opportunities for access by the more committed reformers were in fact being opened up in a number of the East European Communist countries during 1962-1964. In addition to (and, in the G.D.R., almost instead of) the public discussions of the economies' problems, a quieter process of consultation was going on, involving economic experts from outside the planning and administration hierarchy. This process was greatly facilitated in a number of cases by the fact that new, more sympathetic officials (many of them trained formally in economics and having connections in the universities and research institutes) were placed by the Party in positions of leadership in the Party and state committees and commissions most directly concerned with formulating economic policy alternatives for the Politburos. In many cases, the new officials had acceded to their positions as the result of their predecessors' having been personally disgraced or discredited by the evident shortcomings in recent economic performance. They were under pressure to produce results and in many cases already had an explicit mandate from their superiors to devise an innovative response to the previously intractable problems. Such officials were open to suggestions and had strong incentives to go outside established administrative channels to get some of the technical advice they needed.

In the G.D.R., Erich Apel (who had only joined the Party in 1957) became the Central Committee Secretary for Economic Affairs and a candidate member of the Politburo in mid-1961. In mid-1962, he handed over the CC Secretaryship to his protege Gunter Mittag in order to take over the chairmanship of the Planning Commission. Apel and Mittag were the two officials most directly responsible for the drafting of the blueprints for East Germany's "New Economic System," a task in which they enlisted the close cooperation of the Institute of Economics of the Academy of Sciences (a "revisionist" hotbed since 1956), the Rector of the Hochschule fur Okonomie, and respected theorists from several research institutes attached to the Planning Commission.[36]

Hungary's Planning Commission acquired a new, reform-minded chairman in September of 1961 (Miklos Ajtai), and November of 1962 saw the promotion of Rezso Nyers to the position of C.C. Secretary for Economic Affairs (and candidate member of the Politburo), as well as the appointment of a new Minister of Finance (Matyas Timar, later to become an active public advocate of extending the economic reform). Nyers, like Apel, was among the youngest and best educated of the Party's leadership (Minister of Finance in 1960 at the age of 37, a candidate member of the Politburo at 39, holder of a degree from Hungary's most prestigious school of economics). Nyers took the initiative in getting the Politburo to establish a set of eleven committees of economic experts (over 150 members in all) to construct the draft for the New Economic Model.[37]

In Czechoslovakia, the process occurred rather more slowly. However, reformers acquired some sympathetic friends in high places as early as 1962, when economic reformer Ota Sik (recently promoted to head the Institute of Economics of the Academy of Sciences) became a full member of the Central Committee and an active participant in that body's subcommittee for economic affairs as well as in the State Commission for Organization and Management. Two new additions to the Politburo, Drahomir Kolder and Josef Lenart, seem to have been sympathetic to moderate reform suggestions, in sharp contrast to the Stalinist holdovers they had replaced as the result of Khrushchev's second destalinization campaign. Although the May 1962 Plenum of the Central Committee had announced its decision to replace the disgraced Chairman of the Planning Commission, it was only after sixteen more months and a major cabinet shake-up that the badly divided leadership was able to agree on a replacement, who turned out to be Oldrich Cernik (later Premier during the short-lived Prague Spring of 1968 and an important supporter of the economic reform package). The Central Committee did not accept Sik's plea for official appointment of a committee of economic experts until January of 1964, but by early 1963, Sik had already created such a group informally (under the auspices of the Academy of Sciences), and they were actively working on what later became the draft of the economic reform package approved by the Central Committee late in 1964.[38]

The genesis of the Bulgarian economic reform program is more than usually shrouded in mystery, and it is not at all clear who were the main authors of the recommendations. The Eighth Party Congress in November of 1962 led to very substantial changes in the composition of many Party and state bodies, but it is hard to tell the degree to which this opened up the economic policy-making process to reformers. The changes were closely connected with First Secretary Todor Zhivkov's efforts to consolidate his power by purging his major politburo rivals (Yugov and Chervenkov) and their supporters. The purges were carried out with Khrushchev's evident approval, and the dismissals were in many cases explicitly linked with Khrushchev's own renewed efforts at 'destalinization." The Congress passed resolutions calling (rather vaguely) for reforms in the system of planning and management. Petko Kunin, an economist and former Minister of Industry only recently released from a fifteen-year prison term he had received as a "Kostovite" in the purge trials of 1948, was elected to the Central Committee and began advocating reformist ideas in print shortly thereafter. The new Deputy Chairman of the Planning Commission (Evgeny Mateev) had positive things to say about the Liberman discussions in May of 1963,[39] at about the same time that Todor Zhivkov made his initial favorable report on the subject to the Politburo. Although Zhivkov's May proposals were said to have been "accepted in principle" by the Politburo, they were never actually published, and their relationship to the "Theses" finally promulgated as the basis for reform experiments at the end of 1965 is still not known with any certainty. It is known that several different versions of the reform were tried out on an experimental basis at over fifty different enterprises, and it is quite clear that the whole issue was a highly conflictual one within the Politburo. It may be that the schemes were largely devised by the various ministries themselves (in consultation with the Ministry of Finance) rather than by any single commission or panel of experts specifically anointed for the purpose by the Party's Politburo.[40]

In Romania, advocates of economic reform seem to have made no visible headway in achieving access to policy-makers in the first half of the 1960's, and, indeed, there was no genuine Romanian participation in the Liberman discussions at all. The Albanians, like their Chinese allies, discussed the Liberman-style reforms only to denounce them in the most vitriolic manner possible, citing them as additional evidence of the covert restoration of capitalism in the U.S.S.R. If there were Albanian believers in similar measures, they maintained a prudent silence.

In Poland, economists of a reformist persuasion had gained considerable prominence in 1956-1957 and, through the institutionalization of the "Economic Council" and the cooptation of academics into relevant Party and state committees and commissions, they seemed assured of considerable access to policymakers. By 1959, however, the changing political climate had led to the effective scuttling of the implementation of the Economic Councils 1957-58 reform "Theses." The Polish leadership's loss of enthusiasm for economic reform was evidenced by the return of a number of previously disgraced Stalinist economic policy-makers of the early 1950's to positions of power (E. Szyr and J. Tokarski became deputy premiers with primary responsibility for economic affairs, and T. Gede became First Assistant to the Chairman of the Planning Commission) and the demotion of several prominent reform supporters who had been coopted into top leadership posts in 1956 (most notably Jerzy Morawski, who lost his Politburo membership and his position as a Central Committee Secretary). Contrary to the trend in other East European countries, the early 1960's in Poland was a period in which the cause of reform continued to lose ground. Tokarski and Gede added other responsibilities to their spheres of authority in the planning apparatus. The reformist Central Committee Secretary Jerzy Albrecht was demoted to the Finance Ministry and lost his seat on the Politburo. During 1963, Oskar Lange's Economic Council was formally abolished, and reform-minded Central Committee Secretary W. Matwin lost his Party post. In 1964, the same Party Congress that grudgingly approved certain much watered-down economic reform

theses also simultaneously elevated the hard-liner Eugeniusz Szyr to
Politburo membership and entrusted him with their implementation.

While Polish reformist economists retained a meaningful residual of their
former access to policy-making (especially via the Ministry of Finance),
it was clear that Gomulka's regime was progressively withdrawing into
itself. By then, Gomulka himself seems to have concluded that the
intellectuals needed to be kept more firmly "in their place."[41] No
broadening of access seemed in prospect, but the Party policy-makers were
already relatively familiar with much of what the reformers had to say as
a result of the earlier discussions. (Indeed, few, if any, proposals were
put forward anywhere in the other East European countries during the
debates of the 1960's that had not already been discussed or at least
suggested by someone in the Polish debates of 1956-1957.42) The problem
was simply that Gomulka and his close advisors neither solicited the advice
of the reformist economists nor saw fit to heed it when it was offered.
The relative success in maintaining and even slightly accelerating overall
growth rates (albeit at increasingly worrisome costs to the standard of
living) using the existing system probably discouraged the leaders from
reaching out to a broader selection of economic advisors and from
considering structural reform a matter of urgency.

Official Commitments to Reform the Economy

In a sense, the initial decision to allow and even encourage extensive
public debate on the suitability of the existing system of economic planning
and management demonstrated that the dominant leaders within the
particular Communist Party had already determined that some degree of
modification was probably necessary or desirable. But as subsequent
events made clear, the decisions were by no means unanimous or internally
consistent. Clearly not all members of the political elite shared common
perceptions as to the causes of the difficulties in economic performance
that were being encountered to one degree or another throughout most of
the region, they did not agree on the likely efficacy of the proposed
remedies, and in any case many powerful leaders had strong personal or
group interests that were being threatened by some of the reform proposals.
Analysis of the elite and group conflicts that emerged in the course of
adoption and implementation of the reforms needs be undertaken on a
country by country basis, and this task constitutes the subject matter of
following chapters. Here we wish only to record the basic outlines of the
reform proposals that were in fact formally endorsed by the various
Communist parties of East Europe as a result of the debates of the early
and mid-1960's, to point out some patterns which become apparent when

we compare the various reform "blueprints," and, finally, to suggest a simple model to account parsimoniously for the variations in these initial outcomes.

The basic outline of the process by which the various economic reform packages came to be adopted was relatively similar throughout the region. Following Khrushchev's example, leading figures in the Party called for the economics profession to take a more active role in suggesting practical means by which to improve the functioning of the economy, thereby opening the way to the public debates and discussions we have reviewed. Meanwhile, behind the scenes, one or two leading Party officials with supervisory but not operational responsibilities in the area of economic policy (typically a Central Committee Secretary) would be designated (either by the First Secretary at his own initiative or by a collective decision of the Politburo) to organize a team for drafting preliminary proposals. Drawn into the working group would be not only the planning commission technicians, Party economic specialists, and administrators who normally helped to define the basic policy options for the leadership but also recognized academic experts from the universities and the research institutes. The "outsiders" normally were men with some past administrative or Party experience (to insure that they would be both loyal and "practical" men), and their role was both to suggest ideas of their own and to act as transmitters and interpreters of the more worthwhile ideas of their colleagues being turned out as a result of the broader public discussions. The working group would eventually produce a report for discussion at a meeting or meetings of the Politburo, leading to modifications and reformulations. Typically at least two formal documents emerged, several months (or longer) apart: a statement of the basic concepts and principles to be followed, and then a more detailed "blueprint" in which specific measures and timetables for transition would be worked out. These documents were normally formalized as resolutions of the Central Committee (or, if the timing was convenient, of the Party Congress). Following Party approval of reform measures, appropriate parliamentary legislation, ministerial decrees, and administrative directives had to be worked out and the actual transition process undertaken, typically with a great deal of bureaucratic pulling and hauling that led to revisions of the original timetables and even to reversals of earlier decisions of the Party leadership. In some countries, a deliberate process of "experimentation" was followed, in which a few enterprises would be shifted over to some version of the new system, with modifications to the basic plan being anticipated as a result of the initial experience before the system would be made universally applicable. Both because of technical difficulties and because of political resistance, the duration of the innovation process from initial public discussions to actual implementation of the new system throughout the entire economy (when that actually occurred) averaged about five to seven years. Table 2.4 displays the basic chronology of the reform processes in Eastern Europe.

TABLE 2.4
Chronology of the East European Economic Reforms

Country	Began Debates	First Experiments	Blueprint's Acceptance	To be Complete
Abania	none	none	none	none
Bulgaria	Nov 1962	Jan 1964	Jan 1964 (principles)	Dec 1966, later postponed to Dec 1967, later postponed to Dec 1968
Czecho.	Feb1963	Apr1964	Oct 1964 (principles) Jan 1965 (detailed)	967
G.D.R.	Oct 1962	Jan 1963	Jul 1963 (principles) Dec 1965 (changed principles & detailed)	Jan 1968
Hungary	1954-55,57 Nov 1962	none	Nov 1965 (principles) May 1966 (detailed)	Jan 1968
Poland	1954-1955 1956-1958 Oct 1962	Sporadic since 1956	Nov 1957 (principles) Mar 1964 (principles) Jul 1965 (detailed) Dec 1968 (principles) Dec 1969 (detailed) Dec 1971 (principles) Jun 1972 (detailed)	Not specified Not specified Dec 1970 (abandoned Jan 1971) Not specified
Romania	Sep 1966	Jul 1967	Oct 1967	Not specified

The degree to which the reform blueprints approved by the Party incorporated the more important proposals of the advocates of decentralization varied quite sharply. By comparing the blueprints and guidelines with a check-list of these proposals, it is possible to rank-order the countries' reforms on a continuum ranging between basic retention of the established Stalinist economic model and basic acceptance of a model more closely approximating market socialism. Some of the important questions for differentiating the extent of the reforms would be the following (answers for each country are tabulated in Table 2.5):

TABLE 2.5
Provisions of East European Reform "Blueprints" Compared
(Status as of 1964-1967)

Country	(1)	(2)	(3)	(8)	(5)	(6)	(12)	(9)	(10)	(11)	(4)	(7)
Yugo.	+	+	+	+	+	+	+	+	+	+	+	+
Hungary	+	+	+	+	+	+	+	+	+	+	+	+/-
Czecho.	+	+	+	+	+	+	+	+	+	+	+	+/-
Bulgaria	+	+	+	+	+/-	+/-	+/-	+/-	+	-	-	-
G.D.R.	+	+	+	+	+/-	+/-	+/-	+/-	-	-	-	-
U.S.S.R.	+	+	+	+	+/-	+/-	-	-	-	-	-	-
Poland	+	+	+	+	-	+/-	+/-	+/-	-	-	-	-
Romania	+	-	-	+	-	-	-	-	-	-	-	-
Albania	-	-	-	-	-	-	-	-	-	-	-	-

Key: + = Yes   +/- = qualified yes   - = no

(1) Are significant rates of interest to be charged against the revenues of the enterprise for the extension of credit by banks or other state agencies?

(2) Are substantial charges to be levied against enterprise revenues as payment for the acquisition or continued use of state-owned capital, as opposed to the previous practice of cost-free provision by the central authorities?

(3) Is enterprise profitability to be regarded as one of the three most important criteria for judging enterprise performance?

(4) Is enterprise profitability to be the single most important criterion for evaluating enterprise performance?

(5) Is the remuneration of the enterprise director to be determined to a substantial degree by enterprise profitability?

(6) Is enterprise profitability to be the principal determinant of above-wage bonus funds for non-managerial employees?

(7) Is the size of the total wage-fund of the enterprise to be substantially determined at the enterprise level, as opposed to being assigned from above as a compulsory plan target?

(8) Is the size and composition of the work force to be substantially at the discretion of enterprise management?

(9) Is the assortment and quantity of output to be substantially at the discretion of enterprise management?

(10) Are enterprises to have substantial discretion in negotiating the prices to be paid for their output on delivery?

(11) Is enterprise membership in industrial trusts or combines to be non-compulsory, reducing the ability of sectoral administrators to prevent competition between enterprises producing similar products?

(12) Are enterprises to be allowed substantial discretion to undertake investment projects using their own or borrowed funds?

The least controversial measures appear to have been those improving the possibilities for rational cost accounting. That is, there seemed to have developed a general sense that planning in a complex economy requires increased attention to the calculation of costs in value terms and that lower level managers should be given incentives to cut costs wherever it would be possible to do so without violating explicit plan directives. The accounting system, moreover, needs to take into account the fact that non-labor factors of production are scarce and that their rational utilization can be made more likely if managers are required by the cost accounting system to recognize that requisitioning of unneeded or only marginally productive machinery decreases overall social productivity: hence the widespread acceptance of interest-like charges for loans, more-than-token payment for new machinery or construction, differentiated land-rents for extractive industries, and the like. The acceptance of some variant of profit or profitability as an important measure of enterprise efficiency (or at least as a measure of *changes* in enterprise efficiency over time) also reflects this rather elementary but nonetheless hard-won insight.

More controversial, less often adopted, and most bitterly resisted in the implementation stage were measures that eroded the detailed administrative control of the central authorities over investment, product assortment, wages, and (especially) prices. Better accounting methods were most often seen as a means of encouraging more efficient fulfillment of the plan, not as a means for enabling decentralized decision-makers to improve on the plan. Plan fulfillment rather than profit maximization was most often retained as the most important criterion for evaluating enterprise performance with profitability becoming only one of many planned targets to be achieved. Except in Hungary and Czechoslovakia, the reform blueprints basically could be summarized as follows: improved accounting, better planning, and only marginal decentralization of decision-making to the level of the factory or enterprise.

Determinants of Economic Reform Radicalism: Some Hypotheses

Examination of Table 2.5 reveals rather clearly that there were substantial differences in the degree of "radicalism" of the economic reform programs to the implementation of which the various Communist parties of Eastern Europe committed themselves in the mid 1960's. How might we explain these variations? An adequate answer requires, of course, as detailed as possible an explanation of the decision process in each country. However, it is also instructive to view these decisions first at a more macro level as adaptive responses of self-steering, self-maintaining systems confronted by changes in their environment of varying magnitude.

The first hypothesis suggested by this chapter's preliminary examination of the period of the reforms is that

> The more serious the "performance gap" displayed by the economy in the period just prior to and during the reform discussions, the more likely the Party leadership was to adopt one of the more "radical" or innovative economic reform blueprints.

The rationale for this hypothesis is relatively straightforward. Since the political-economic system contains mechanisms that tend to maintain existing structures, a substantial external stimulus is required to overcome these homeostatic forces sufficiently to produce major rearrangements. The adequacy of the hypothesis can be subjected to statistical test if we stipulate operational measures of "degree of seriousness of the performance gap" and "radicalism of the economic reform program adopted." Table 2.5 displays a pattern in the adoption of various proposals sufficiently regular to justify the construction of a Guttman-type scale (coefficient of reproducibility well above .90) that gives us at least an ordinal measure of the dependent variable, the reform's radicalism. (Actually, if we merely count the number of different major changes adopted by each country, then arguably the measure meets the stricter standards of a ratio-scale.)

There are a variety of plausible methods of operationalizing the seriousness of the performance gap. Since previous experimentation with a number of such alternative methods yields essentially the same results, it seems most expedient for purposes of exposition to use the simplest. We may simply refer back to Table 2.3 (which identified periods of serious performance gaps according to three criteria: growth performance relative to the country's own recent past and relative to the contemporary performances of other capitalist and communist countries) and count the number of criteria according to which each economy was "underperforming" during the relevant periods of the early 1960's. Table 2.6 displays the resulting coded data. Computation of the simple linear correlation between the two measures yields an R of .87 (R^2 = .75), which is statistically significant at the .01 level. The countries experiencing the most serious underperformance in economic growth did indeed tend to adopt the most innovative reforms, as hypothesized.

TABLE 2.6
Economic Performance and Radicalism of Reform

Country	Ranking on Degree of Reform	Number of Kinds of Performance Gaps
Albania	8	0
Bulgaria	3	2
Czechoslovakia	1.5	3
G.D.R.	4	2
Hungary	1.5	2
Poland	6	0
Romania	7	0
U.S.S.R.	5	1

Yet although the statistical correlation supporting the first hypothesis is rather high, it still leaves a good proportion of the variance unaccounted for. This is to be expected, since common sense would generally suggest that a simple stimulus-response model is hardly adequate to describe fully so complex a phenomenon as the policy-making process of a modern state. It is hard to believe, for example, that characteristics of the political elite would not play some sort of mediating role in shaping the policy-makers' response to the stimulus of threatened economic decline. Individuals and groups vary considerably in their degree of openness to change, even under similar pressures. Under institutional arrangements where political elites are able to exercise control over the generation (or at least the diffusion) of innovative ideas for policy changes (through censorship, for example, or through restriction of access to relevant information and to relevant decision-makers), it is entirely possible that decisions on issues of economic reform might be restricted to an artificially narrow range of alternatives, quite apart from the intensity of the stimulus provided by the existence of an economic performance gap. Indeed, we have already seen that the East European Party elites displayed considerable differences in their willingness to encourage wide-ranging debates on economic questions in the wake of the Soviet Liberman discussions. They displayed even greater differences in the degree to which a broader range of expert economic viewpoints was solicited in the process of drafting the various "blueprints" and "guidelines" that were the basis of Politburo and Central Committee discussions. We may reasonably hypothesize that, *ceteris paribus*,

> The greater the extent to which official policies acted to discourage or suppress the independent articulation of ideas and policy proposals, the less likely the Party leadership was to adopt one of the more "radical" or innovative economic reform blueprints.

To test this hypothesis, we need a measure of the degree to which the policy process was closed to inputs that did not come from certifiably like-minded men. One possibility would be to attempt some sort of rank-ordering based on the account of the consultation processes given in the earlier section "Reformers' Access to Policy Makers." This approach encounters weighty objections. In the first place, in several countries (notably Albania, Romania, and Bulgaria), little information has come to light as to what sort of consultations may or may not have been taking place in private during the relevant period: the fact that no one has talked about them does not *necessarily* ensure that they did not occur (though one is entitled to one's doubts). Deletion of the doubtful cases leaves too few remaining for statistical analysis. Moreover, since the author gathered the data in that section with the present hypothesis already in mind, it is possible that the data would incorporate an unconscious bias in the coding process. It seems preferable for these reasons to concentrate on more public kinds of articulation (or non-articulation) of policy alternatives.

Luckily, help is at hand. Raymond B. Nixon and his associates have generated useful data for testing this hypothesis as part of a cross-national comparative study of the determinates of press censorship in the years 1960 and 1964.[43] Their coding approach involved using panels of experts familiar with the press laws and practices of the various countries to categorize their stringency, basing their judgements not only on a close reading of the printed media but also on background materials compiled by Western press agencies for the use of foreign correspondents. Nixon's nine-point scale proved sufficiently sensitive to discriminate between the degrees of censorship exercised in East European countries during the years 1960 and 1964.[44] East European countries' scores for the year 1964 are excerpted in Table 2.7 (a coding of "9" represents the greatest degree of press censorship in Nixon's world-wide comparison, while "1" represents the highest degree of press freedom).

TABLE 2.7
R.B. Nixon's Codings of Degree of
Press Censorship

Country	Degree of Censorship Stringency, 1964
Albania	9
Bulgaria	8
Czechoslovakia	8
G.D.R.	8
Hungary	7
Poland	7
Romania	8
U.S.S.R.	8

Source:R.B. Nixon, "Freedom in the World's Press," *Journalism Quarterly* XLII (1965) pp. 6, 13.

Relating the degree of censorship exercised during 1964 (the period when the reform blueprints were being drafted) to the rankings of the various country on the degree of economic reform endorsed (from Table 2.6) by means of correlation analysis again gives us an appropriate test of our hypothesis. One would expect that the countries with the most rigid censorship would also be those that adopted the least radical economic reforms. The strength of the correlation is somewhat less this time: $R = -.47$ ($R^2 = .22$). While it is of the expected sign and of a respectable magnitude, the small number of cases renders the correlation coefficient statistically significant at only about the .14 level, which is outside conventionally accepted thresholds of significance.

It would seem that a somewhat freer flow of ideas is not in itself sufficient to bring about economic reform. But what about the effect of looser censorship *in conjunction with* the stimulus of a serious economic performance gap? It might still be that the availability of independent proposals from outside the policy establishment would amplify the effects of a performance crisis, while having little or no impact in times when the economy was already performing satisfactorily.   It appears that this is indeed the case. If one includes *both* the seriousness of the performance gap *and* the press censorship variable in a regression equation to predict the degree of economic reform undertaken, the total variance accounted for increases quite dramatically. Despite the small number of cases, the multiple correlation coefficient of .99 is statistically significant at better than the .001 level. Whereas the performance gap variable alone accounts for 75 percent of the variance and the censorship variable alone accounts for only 22 percent, together they *jointly* account for 98 percent. Moreover, when one examines the coefficients of partial correlation (that is, measurements of the relationships between each of the independent variables and the dependent variable, *controlling for the effects of the other independent variable*), one finds that both are considerably higher than the corresponding simple correlations and that each is significant at better than the .01 level.[45]

TABLE 2.8
Relationship of Radicalism of Economic Reform
to Degree of Censorship and Economic Performance Gaps

	Economic Reform with Performance Gaps	Economic Reform with Censorship	Economic Reform with Performance Gaps and Censorship
Bivariate correction coefficient.	.87*	-.47	
Partial correlation coefficient, controlling for other independent variable	.99**	-.97**	
Multiple correlation coefficient			.99**

* significant at .01 level (single-tailed test)
** significant at .001 level

The degree of radicalism in undertaking the economic reforms of the 1960's seems to be accounted for in remarkably parsimonious fashion by the magnitude of the economic performance gaps confronting the various East European leadership groups in conjunction with the degree of the regime's willingness to entertain proposals emanating from outside the closed administrative hierarchy. In this simplified model of the process, domestic factors appear to have played the determining role in the decisions whether to undertake such major alterations of fundamental economic institutions. Yet one must also bear in mind that another variable likely to have a major impact on the prospects for economic reform is glossed over in such an explanation: the influence exerted by the leaders of the Soviet Union.

The highly penetrated character of postwar East European politics has been apparent in economic policy matters almost from the very beginning. It was Stalin's insistence on the restructuring of their economies in rigid imitation of Soviet economic institutions that resulted in East European Communists' repudiation of their own once-heralded diversity and creativity in economic planning and management during the 1944 to 1947 period. By 1948, enthusiasm in emulation of even the smallest details of Soviet economic practices and institutions came to be seen as a touchstone of "socialist internationalism," while even minor deviation from Stalinist economic prescriptions was perceived as an indication of disloyalty to the alliance. Both the Eastern European regimes' synchronized adoption (and, later, repudiation) of Malenkov's "New Course" economic policies of 1953-1954 and their simultaneous execution of massive investment and agricultural collectivization drives in 1958-1961 testify to the fact that Soviet pressures for economic emulation by her junior allies continued well after the departure of Stalin from the scene. This suggests the possibility that, at least for those East European countries still closely aligned with the USSR, the adoption of economic reforms might be yet one more manifestation of a generalized propensity to imitate Soviet policy initiatives. In that case, we might hypothesize that

The more closely aligned the country is with the Soviet Union, the more its economic reform package resembles that of the Soviet Union in its degree of radicalism, while the less closely aligned the country, the greater the likely disparity between its economic reform package and that of the Soviets.

In order to evaluate the hypothesis, it is necessary to have a measure of the degree of similarity between the various East European countries' economic reform programs and that of the Soviet Union as well as a measure of the relative closeness of each country's alignment with the Soviet Union.

The raw materials for assessing the degree of similarity between Soviet and East European economic reform programs are to be found in Table 2.5 above. But the summary scores of the reforms' "radicalism" used to test previous hypotheses will not serve for the present hypothesis, since it does not deal with radicalism per se (departures from the old Stalinist model) but rather with the degree of deviation from the revised Soviet model as represented in the Soviet reform program of 1965. A more suitable measure for the purpose at hand can be derived by assigning numerical values to the coding categories in Table 2.5 ("measure adopted" = 1; "measure not adopted" = 0; "measure partially or ambiguously adopted" = 0.5) and then calculating any of a number of conventional statistical indicators of strength of association between Soviet positions across the twelve reform components and those of each of the various East European regimes. Table 2.9 displays Pearson correlation coefficients, but any other conventional measure of association would produce the same rank ordering.

The problem of how most reliably and productively to assess the relative extent of Soviet influence on the various East European countries is a knotty one. The author's own previous efforts to deal systematically with this measurement problem employed and compared a variety of approaches, including expert judgmental assessments as well as more objective indicators of military cooperation, cultural penetration, and trade dependency.[46] Results of this earlier analysis suggest that, for the period under consideration at least, a reasonably validated measure for testing the hypothesis is provided by the work of Henry Teune and Sig Synnestvedt.[47] In the course of their efforts to assess the validity of various objective measures of 119 countries' "degree of alignment" with the US and with the USSR as of the year 1963, Teune and Synnestvedt administered a questionnaire featuring an eleven-point judgmental scale of 89 North American scholar-experts, consisting of both international relations generalists and area specialists. (Agreement among respondents was high.) The rank ordering of the European Communist countries according to their average scores on Teune and Synnestvedt's "alignment with the USSR" scale is also displayed in Table 2.9 (in descending order of alignment).

TABLE 2.9

Alignment with the USSR and
Similarity of Economic Reforms to the Soviet Reforms

Country	Alignment Ranking*	Similarity of Economic Reform**
G.D.R.	1	.91
Bulgaria	2	.74
Czechoslovakia	3	.27
Hungary	4	.27
Poland	5	.73
Romania	6	.58
Albania	7	0.00
Yugoslavia	8	0.00

* From Henry Teune and Sig Synnestvedt, "Measuring International
Alignment," *Orbis* IX (1965), p. 180.
** Pearson correlation coefficients, calculated from data in Table 2.5
supra.

The hypothesis is supported moderately strongly by these data. Visual
inspection of Table 2.9 reveals that the two countries generally regarded
as Moscow's most reliable allies (the G.D.R. and Bulgaria) adopted the
reform programs most closely resembling that of the U.S.S.R., while the
two European Communist countries generally understood as being completely independent of Soviet control (Albania and Yugoslavia) diverged
the most widely from the Soviets in their approach to economic reform
(albeit in diametrically opposite directions). However, among the remaining countries whose degree of alignment with the Soviet Union fell
somewhere in between these extremes of servility and independence, a
considerable variation is exhibited in the character of the economic reforms
that cannot be readily accounted for by the hypothesis. Indeed, Romania
and Poland, widely regarded as mavericks within the Soviet bloc, exhibited
greater similarity to the Soviets in their economic reform packages than
did Czechoslovakia and Hungary, which were at the time perceived as
much more acquiescent to Soviet demands. Computing the Spearman
rank-order correlation coefficient between these measures of alignment
with the Soviet Union and similarity in economic reform programs yields
a moderately strong R of .80 ($R^2 = .63$), which is statistically significant
at the .01 level.

The highly penetrated character of most of the East European Communist countries was clearly manifest in the economic reform process. A necessary precondition for the East European leaders' efforts to adapt their institutions to the special demands of their respective domestic situations was the prior acceptance by the regional hegemonic power, the Soviet Union, of the basic legitimacy of modifying what many had come to think of as quintessentially "socialist" organizational modes. It was a matter of great good fortune for the East European advocates of economic reform that their own countries' economic problems coincided with a serious performance gap in the U.S.S.R. itself and that the principal Soviet leader at the time had concluded that taking a more innovative and less reverential attitude to Soviet economic institutions of the past was a matter of considerable urgency. Khrushchev's green light to the development of economic science and his encouraging public discussion of economic reforms for the Soviet Union during the early 1960's was simultaneously an invitation and a suggestion for his East European comrades to do likewise. The Soviet stamp of respectability made it much more difficult for East European opponents of economic reforms to declare East European reformers completely beyond the pale or to prevent the discussion of their ideas within the economic profession. The precise boundary lines of orthodoxy on economic matters had been rendered exceedingly fuzzy by the Soviet leadership (who appear themselves to have been internally divided on the issues of economic reform[48]), and it would have been dangerously premature and presumptuous for East European leaders closely aligned with the U.S.S.R. to proscribe altogether views that were still being actively considered in Moscow.

Yet, at least in the period 1961-1967, the Soviet role in promoting economic reform in Eastern Europe seems to have been primarily permissive rather than prescriptive. It is relatively clear that the detailed provisions of the various economic reform packages were worked out by the various East European regimes themselves and not simply copied from Soviet models as "pilot projects" for the convenience of Soviet leaders. The East European economic debates were much more sophisticated and far-reaching than those in the Soviet Union, and the reform blueprints adopted in East Europe diverged rather considerably from the most favorably discussed proposals in the Soviet media, especially with respect to the issues of price formation and the decentralization of pricing decisions. The patterns of elite conflict which developed over the adoption and implementation of the economic reforms also suggest that the Soviets had not actively insisted upon the East European comrades' participation in the development of new models, since in many cases it was precisely those leaders who had hitherto demonstrated the most unflinching loyalty to Moscow's demands who became the most obdurate opponents of economic innovations. The Soviet press during 1964 and 1965 printed a number of sympathetic accounts of the economic reforms being devised in East European countries,[49] but there were no public criticisms of other socialist countries for failing to launch economic reform schemes (this was never an issue in the contemporary Soviet polemics against China and Albania, nor was it any part of the Soviet criticism of Romania's resistance to Comecon integration). Favorable Soviet attitudes toward economic experimentation no doubt helped disarm potential opposition within the East European Party leadership, but there is little to indicate that top Soviet leaders played any active promotional role.

The Soviet Union's permissive attitude toward economic experimentation in other socialist countries tended to erode somewhat as the Soviet economic reform package took on a more determinate character. Yet even after the public presentation of the Brezhnev-Kosygin reform blueprint at the Central Committee plenum in September of 1965, one finds little evidence to indicate that the Soviets determinedly applied pressure for other European socialist countries to abandon any of the more "advanced" features of their respective blueprints. In fact, the basic principles of the much more radical Hungarian reform were first made public a full two months *after* the Soviets' official pronouncements. While individual Soviet economists (including some very prominent ones) not infrequently expressed doubts or reservations about particular features of other countries' economic reforms on grounds of practicality or workability, it was not until some months after the 1968 intervention in Czechoslovakia that harsh ideological criticisms of "market socialist" provisions already approved by fraternal Communist parties began to emanate from authoritative Soviet sources, and even then they were directed specifically against "revisionist" elements in the Czechoslovak Party. During the period of maximum hostile criticism of Ota Sik and the Czechoslovak economic reform (1969), the Soviet media continued to present balanced (and even, sometimes, favorable) accounts of the rather similar Hungarian reforms in economic planning and management.[50]

By virtue of the Soviet Union's dominant position in Eastern Europe, Soviet tolerance was absolutely necessary to the initial adoption of the economic reforms. Soviet experimentation and reform of their own economy legitimated and facilitated economic reform in the other East European countries by removing the threat of a Soviet veto and by weakening the position of domestic conservative forces who otherwise might have defended the existing system of economic planning and management by insisting upon the necessity of emulating the Soviet Union in so important a matter. Yet the Soviets did not attempt to make East European participation in economic reformism of any particular type absolutely obligatory. Under such favorable international conditions, even in the more heavily penetrated countries of Eastern Europe, the character of the economic blueprints adopted and the actual outcomes of the struggles to implement them were left to be determined mainly by the balance of domestic political and economic forces in each country, and this has continued to be reflected in the diversity of economic planning and management arrangements in the region. While hardening Soviet attitudes on economic questions after 1968 clearly reinforced the positions of the already strong domestic anti-reform forces that continued to exist in every East European country and thereby contributed to the pronounced diminution of reforming zeal throughout most of the bloc, it is equally clear that Soviet conceptions of the acceptable institutional arrangements for planning and management did not narrow so far as absolutely to preclude reforms considerably more radical than their own, so long as basic political stability could be assured. Soviet power imposed certain background constraints at all times, but to understand the East European politics of economic reform in the 1960s, we need to look primarily at domestic economic and political forces.

CHAPTER III

ECONOMIC REFORM, ELITE CONFLICT, AND THE LEADERSHIP FACTOR

> "Those who govern, having much business on their
> hands, do not generally like to take the trouble
> of considering and carrying into execution new
> projects. The best public measures are therefore
> seldom adopted from previous wisdom, but forced
> by the occasion."
>
> Benjamin Franklin
> *The Autobiography*
> The Modern Library edition
> (Random House)
> New York 1950

Interpreting Eastern Europe's economic reforms of the mid-1960's as the rational adaptive responses of political systems to varying challenges of declining economic performance enhances our understanding of the differentiated forms increasingly being taken on by East European economic institutions. Yet the organismic model implicit in such an interpretation can provide us with little guidance in seeking to understand the concrete processes by which such adaptive institutional changes were historically produced. Even in the most monolithic political systems, a major structural change is not simply the product of rational decision by a single global intelligence but rather an outcome of complex interactions between individuals and groupings pursuing diverse ends and entertaining differing conceptions as to the likely outcomes of alternative courses of action. The homeostatic and adaptive mechanisms that are at work to preserve and transform the basic structure of the macro system do not represent disembodied forces but rather consist of the activities of discrete human beings in varying degrees of conflict and cooperation.

Enacting and implementing major changes in economic planning and administration entailed major political conflicts in every East European country where such proposals were seriously entertained. By virtue of the highly centralized structure of authority prevailing in Communist systems, effective participation in determining the nature of the reforms (if any) was at least initially restricted to a relative handful of people at or near the top of a given country's fused political-economic hierarchy. The practical power of ultimate decision on issues of such fundamental importance naturally rested with the Communist Party's Politburo (or Presidium), whose members acted in close consultation with an inner core of economic advisors and top administrators. In addition to the Politburo members themselves, the principal actors included the Central Committee secretary or secretaries for economic affairs, the chiefs of the Central Committee's relevant economic committees and commissions, those members of the Council of Ministers with the broadest responsibilities in the economic sphere (in addition to the premier, typically two or three vice-premiers, the ministers of Finance and Foreign Trade, and the chairman of the State Planning Commission), and the heads of major state economic commissions (for prices, labor and wages policy, material-technical supply, statistics, and so on). At a slightly further remove from the central locus of economic decision-making represented by the twenty-odd people just mentioned, great influence on somewhat more specialized aspects of economic policy was exercised by the heads of the various economic ministries and their chief subordinates, as well as by a number of upper-middle-ranked officials serving in the staff agencies attached to the Council of Ministers and to the Central Committee. Provincial Party secretaries (especially from the more developed regions) often involved themselves quite substantially in both the planning and the execution of national economic policies with important implications for the regions of their responsibility (particularly salient were decisions concerning the regional distribution of investment, materials, and production targets). When it was deemed useful by more important decision-makers, special commissions or part-time consultants could also be called upon, drawing on the expertise available in the universities and research institutes or in the offices of some of the mass organizations (such as the trade union apparatus, for example). In the initial stages of the active struggle for adoption of major economic reforms, the people whose views really "counted" in any given country's decision whether or not to proceed probably numbered little more than one hundred (if that many).

Most of those who wielded substantial influence in the formation of economic policies were persons who owed their measure of power and status precisely to their incumbency in functional roles inextricably bound up with the established highly-centralized system of economic planning and management, so it is hardly surprising that the main proposals for radically altering the organizational structure in the direction of greater decentralization did not come up to the top "through channels." As we have already seen, such proposals were initiated primarily by advocates based outside the economic establishment. They came from "ivory tower" theoretical economists in the universities and research institutes, or from "in-and-outer" types whose careers had alternated periods of admini- strative or staff work with academic positions.[1] In addition to the "committees of experts" formed at the behest of top political leaders, an important means by which reformist ideas entered the policy process seems to have been the maintenance of strong professional ties by at least some economists working in staff positions inside the planning apparatus.

For economic reformism to be translated into a concrete program acceptable to the leaders of the Politburo, it was first necessary that at least some of these top leaders should take the initiative to break through the bureaucratic conservatism that tended to dominate economic thinking at the levels just below, to bring forth new initiatives. Several factors combined in the early and mid-1960's to make this more likely to happen. First, of course, there was the example of the Soviet Union's Liberman debates and Khrushchev's clear mandate for greater economic experimen- tation expressed at the Twenty-Second Congress of the C.P.S.U.:

> Our task in the course of building communism is to make ever greater use of and to improve the finance and credit levers, ruble control, prices and profit. We must enhance the importance of profits, of profitability. It is in the interest of better plan fulfillment that enterprises be given greater opportunity to determine the use of their profits, to make broader use of them for encouraging their collectives to do good work and for expanding production.[2]

Given the ingrained habit of many top East European Communist leaders automatically to feel obligated to emulate Soviet domestic policy initiatives, some sort of action along these lines must have seemed in order even to some of the more conservative who had heretofore given absolute loyalty to the established Soviet institutions of an earlier vintage. Those who were already of a somewhat reformist bent were even more positively encouraged to press for action. Khrushchev's sudden ouster did not deter East European economic experimentation, since the new Brezhnev-Kosygin team moved rather quickly to develop and implement a reform package of their own in September of 1965, less than a year after assuming power.[3]

Sudden changes of heart by incumbents newly impressed by reformist logic and Soviet endorsement were not a negligible factor in the new acceptability of economic reformism, but perhaps a more important element was the rather substantially increased turnover in the policy-making elites, especially among those with responsibilities in the economic sphere. In part, the rash of demotions, transfers, retirements and outright sackings was simply the predictable consequence of the abysmal performances being turned in by several of the national economies. Those who had presided over economic policy were being held to account for their failures to manage successfully. Czechoslovakia, the G.D.R., Hungary, and Bulgaria all acquired new premiers, new Planning Commission chairmen, and new Central Committee secretaries for economic affairs during 1962-1964, and there were substantial numbers of other replacements in the economic establishments at the cabinet and immediate sub-cabinet levels. For the most part, the new replacements were younger, better educated than their predecessors, and charged with a mandate by their Politburo superiors to "shake things up" and to bring forward positive programs calculated to produce better results.[4]

However, there was much more involved in the extensive personnel changes in the Party leadership of the early 1960's than simply the punishment of economic maladroitness. Khrushchev's drive to consolidate his political position in the Soviet Union through his second destalinization campaign kicked off around the meeting of the Twenty-Second Congress had its ripple effects in a number of East European countries, where attacks on the "subjective" economic policies of the past were coupled with a more political attack exposing "abuses of socialist legality during the period of the personality cult." As in the Soviet Union, East European destalinization and the struggle against "dogmatism" involved efforts by one or more factions of the local Communist Party leadership to discredit and to unseat powerful rivals. Allocating the blame for unsuccessful economic performance could easily become a tactical weapon in the factional infighting.

While it is difficult to untangle the relative proportions of substantive economic policy disagreements and personal rivalries in the motivations for replacing a number of key economic policy-makers in the early 1960's, it nevertheless seems clear that this process often facilitated the adoption of economic reform blueprints. Where prominent leaders of the Stalinist old guard were demoted or forced to retire (Dogei, Kiss, and Marosan in

Hungary [1962]; Chervenkov, Tsankov, and Yugov in Bulgaria [1962]; Bacilek, David, and Siroky in Czechoslovakia [1962-1963]), the likelihood of Politburo approval for economic reforms was enhanced for several reasons. First, destalinization's changes in the composition of the leadership altered the ideological climate and led to a somewhat more tolerant or pragmatic attitude in evaluating innovative proposals to solve pressing economic problems. Second, from the point of view of the remaining leaders, administrative reorganization might offer further opportunities to weed out the supporters of their fallen rivals from positions of influence at the secondary and tertiary levels of the state and Party hierarchies and to use the vacancies to reward their own friends and advance their own policy preferences.

The issue of economic reform was not the only substantive issue involved in the factional struggles that took place in East Europe during the early 1960's. Indeed, the linkages between policy positions and factional affiliations seem often to have been quite tenuous. Therefore, the dramatic changes that took place in the composition of the Hungarian, Czechoslovakian, and Bulgarian Politburos in the wake of the Twenty-Second Congress of the C.P.S.U. by no means settled the question of what to do about the economy. Many of the most rigid opponents of any kind of "revisionistic" economic changes had, it is true, been removed, but there was everywhere still quite substantial room for disagreement among the surviving oligarchs on these matters. The most that can be said is that the combination of economic difficulties and the personal changes in the Politburos opened up opportunities for ambitious "entrepreneurs" within the leadership to sponsor innovative proposals and still to entertain realistic hopes of winning over a working majority of their colleagues *if* they were particularly skillful in the application of persuasion, bargaining, and compromise.

An extremely important factor in determining the prospects for achieving relatively radical economic reform in each country was the attitude toward the issue taken by the Communist Party's First Secretary. When the First Secretary clearly favored the reform and was willing to expend his formidable political resources to mobilize support for it despite opposition, adoption of the reform blueprint and its subsequent practical implementation were considerably facilitated. Where the First Secretary was either hostile toward much of the reform or unwilling to risk a major battle against strong opposition to secure its passage, the most probable outcome was either no reform or one so watered down and inconsistent as to be largely ineffective in achieving its stated goals. (If the economy's performance therefore continued to be unsatisfactory, pressures could be expected to build up within the Politburo either to find an alterative policy that would be mutually acceptable or to make changes in the composition of the leadership that would make effective action possible.) Even if a reform package could somehow be pushed through without the strong personal commitment of the First Secretary, the consequences for the cohesiveness and effectiveness of the top leadership would be severe, and without determined prodding and pushing from a unified Politburo and Secretariat, implementation was apt to be incomplete and slow because of the predictable opposition of lower-ranking power-holders personally and corporatively threatened by the changes.

According to Leninist norms of "democratic centralism," the adoption by the highest Party bodies of a major programmatic document, such as an economic reform blueprint, ought to be followed by the most vigorous and cooperative efforts of all subordinate Party and state organizations and members to carry out the full letter and spirit of the decision at the level of everyday practice. Nevertheless, when policy decisions have important and adverse personal consequences for those charged with carrying them out, severe strains are apt to be placed on Party discipline. The economic reforms created many such conflicts of interest for the incumbents of positions of political-economic power at the levels just below the top policy makers of the Politburo and the inner circle of the Government: the officials connected with the central planning apparatus, with the various state committees, with the economic ministries and their branch administrations, and with the specialized Party apparatus assigned the day-to-day task of supervising and guiding their activities.

The number of people occupying leading positions in these economic bureaucracies varied from country to country but could be roughly estimated as falling between four or five hundred in the smaller and less developed countries to about a thousand in the larger and more developed countries. Under the highly centralized command economy inherited from the Stalinist past, theirs were the vital functions of translating the decisions and priorities of the top leadership into concrete directives to the enterprises and of coordinating and supervising their implementation through the direct allocation of material resources and the discretionary dispensing of rewards and penalties. For most of these people, implementation of decentralizing and market-oriented economic reforms would imply a definite decline in personal power and prestige (and probably in the material perquisites that went along with them). If financial-economic policy instruments superceded multitudinous administrative directives and detailed super-vision, many bureaucratic functions would be taken over by the impersonally determined arrangements of more autonomous enterprises contracting with each other directly (and with commercial banks) in order to obtain their resources and dispose of their products. No longer the wielder of near-absolute power as the sole authorized interpreter of the will of the leadership, the bureaucrat would become a more limited functionary whose directives could be challenged by enterprise managers as incompatible with the social priorities "objectively" embodied in the price system and in the statutory obligation to maximize enterprise profitability.

Under more radical versions of economic reform, large numbers of formerly indispensable and well-rewarded officials would become redundant and would presumably have to find other employment. Others would presumably keep their positions but would have to reconcile themselves to the curtailment of their powers and prestige and to presiding over a much smaller staff.[5] Since the functions of the ministerial authorities would be changing, incumbent officials would often find themselves having to learn new skills and to devise new operating procedures — with the attendant risk of being found incapable. Even the less radical reforms (as in the G.D.R. or, later, Romania and Poland) that chose more limited decentralization by devolving many of the former ministerial powers to the level of gigantic new *khozraschet*-based branch administrations (rather than to the enterprises) still involved transferring a lot of bureaucrats from the ministerial headquarters in the capital city to the branch association offices, which typically were located on the premises of the largest member enterprise, often in a less desirable provincial city or town.

In addition to the vertical redistribution of power and status downward through the processes of decentralization, the economic reforms of the 1960's tended to effect a horizontal redistribution as well among the most important central economic bureaucracies. For example, the enlarged role of fiscal and monetary policy instruments relative to administrative directives and the "system of material balances," the new importance of a commercialized banking system in evaluating small-to-medium-scale investment projects, and the emphasis on developing more sophisticated techniques of financial accounting and financial control of the enterprises all tended to enhance the importance of the Ministry of Finance in the making of economic policies, at the expense of the ministries set up to administer particular industries or sectors of the national economy. (Not coincidentally, many of the earliest and most committed supporters of the economic reform movement within official circles were present or former Ministers of Finance: Rezso Nyers and Maytas Timar in Hungary, Jerzy Albrecht in Poland, Petko Kunin and Dimitur Popov in Bulgaria, Bohumil Sucharda in Czechoslovakia.) The emphasis on rationalizing prices to cover costs, the elimination of subsidies, and the stress on elaborating more "objective" methods for calculating the effectiveness of investment outlays were threatening to the interests of traditionally politically favored sectors (such as heavy industry and mining), while ministries that had formerly been discriminated against (especially those for consumer goods, food processing, textiles) stood to gain a larger share of investment funds and manpower allocations.

Given the loss of power and status and the possible personal dislocations entailed in the economic reform proposals, the enthusiasm for reform among the members of the more privileged and politically well-connected stratum of central economic officials was about what one would expect, and, indeed, they were often the source of the most determined covert opposition during the phase of reform implementation. Because the massive job of elaborating specific procedures and directives and timetables for the transition of particular economic branches and enterprises to the new system was necessarily entrusted to the existing administrative organs, they were in an excellent strategic position to engage in delaying tactics, improper reassertion of supposedly-abolished controls through legalistic technicalities and other forms of bureaucratic foot-dragging and silent sabotage. Without the most vigilant insistence and constant active intervention by the top Party leadership, without mobilization of external control agencies to ensure timely and good-faith efforts by the responsible officials to carry out the spirit and the letter of the reform, the "new system of economic planning and management" could all too easily "die the Death of a Thousand Cuts" and never become a functioning reality.

Adoption of the East German Economic Reform

The G.D.R. was the first of the East European countries to respond to the implications of the Soviet Liberman debates. Liberman's article on "Plan, Profits, Bonuses," originally published in *Pravda* on September 7, 1962, was reprinted in the G.D.R. before the month was out and was quickly followed by translations of most of the subsequent Soviet discussion it had inspired. Party chief Walter Ulbricht, who had just returned from a month-long vacation in the U.S.S.R., immediately registered his own positive evaluation of these developments in Soviet economic thought in a speech to his Party's October 3-5, 1962, Central Committee Plenum. Summarizing Liberman's principal proposals, Ulbricht declared:

> Our economists and planners should carefully follow and evaluate this discussion. At the same time, they should develop their own conceptions so there can be a fruitful exchange at the economists' conference that will shortly be

coming up.   The wide public discussion in the Soviet Union of important economic questions underlines the growing role of economists and planners.[6]

From this point, events moved extremely rapidly, clearly with Ulbricht's blessing and encouragement. A veritable flood of mostly-favorable articles appeared in the technical economic press, the Party's official daily, and in the Party's theoretical journal. Included among the public supporters of "Libermanism" were not only the formerly-censored heretic Fritz Behrens but also the Deputy Minister of Finance Walter Halbritter (who soon became Deputy Chairman of the State Planning Commission and later a candidate member of the Politburo).[7] The "Draft Program" of the S.E.D. (published in November for purposes of "discussion" prior to the January 1963 Party Congress) already contained many of the features that later would become the "New Economic System" (N.E.S.). By the time of the "economists' conference" in early December, the basic concepts of the N.E.S. had been largely codified by an informal Party working group organized in the Central Committee apparatus and supervised by Party Secretaries Erich Apel and Gunter Mittag. At the Sixth Congress in January, Ulbricht again closely identified himself with the proposals for economic reform and proposed that the Congress authorize a special committee to work out the detailed proposals to implement the general principles he had just enunciated.[8] Of the ten principal participants in the new working group, only three were not employees of the Central Committee apparatus,[9] although other "outsiders" were consulted in one capacity or another during the drafting process. The fathers of the N.E.S., Mittag and Apel, were elected candidate members of the S.E.D.'s politburo, the Executive Committee, in recognition of their new importance. By June of 1963, the Council of Ministers had already approved the lengthy set of directives prepared by Apel and Mittag's working group, officially inaugurating the "New Economic System" — just eight months after the opening of the German version of the Liberman debate.[10]

Walter Ulbricht himself made the first public announcement of the new decisions.[11] It was now revealed that since January the basic elements of the new system had already been in "experimental" application in ten factories and, in Ulbricht's view, could already be pronounced a success. Full-scale implementation of the various features of the N.E.S. would take place in a programmed fashion over 1964-1967, beginning with a comprehensive restructuring of the existing system of pricing raw materials and other producers' goods (the prices then in effect were still based on relative valuations prevalent in 1944). As the price system became more rational, fuller development and implementation of "economic levers" would progressively displace administrative directives, making possible greater autonomy for the enterprises and especially for the V.V.B.s (Vereinigung Volkseigener Betriebe — Unions of State Enterprises) in operational decisions. In addition to greater reliance on such financial categories as sales, interest, rents, and profits in measuring enterprise performance, the N.E.S. envisioned a reduction in the number of physical targets specified for the enterprise in the plan and an increased reliance on material incentives based on the financial results of the enterprise for both management and the general work force. The V.V.B.s, which were formerly branch administrations within the ministries supervising a number of similar enterprises, became themselves economic rather than administrative bodies, operating on a *khozraschet* basis and a financial incentive system quite similar to that created for the managers of individual enterprises. It was to the V.V.B.s rather than to the enterprises that most of the directive authority given up by the central organs were transferred. Price-setting and the administration of the system of material balances remained relatively centralized, although substantial new discretion in these matters was delegated to the level of the V.V.B.s (but not to the enterprises).[12]

As this brief account would suggest, the initial adoption and implementation of the N.E.S. in East Germany does not seem to have been hampered by any major degree of conflict between factions within the Politburo. Although there was evidently quite a lot of transferring, demoting, purging, and replacing going on at lower levels as a direct result of the decision to implement the N.E.S., the resulting tensions seem not to have led to any serious disunity at the very highest levels of the Party. The Politburo and Secretariat showed extreme stability and continuity in membership for the remainder of the decade, despite several fairly disruptive policy changes (not only in the N.E.S., but also in the organizational structure of the Party itself).[13] Ulbricht was able to count on solid backing from his Politburo comrades when he led the way into undertaking the N.E.S., and when substantial retrenchments in the N.E.S. were made in the later 1960's, essentially the same group fell once again into ranks behind him.

The high degree of unity manifested by the East German Politburo may be explained by several factors. To begin with, the N.E.S. did not involve very radical decentralization, and the role of spontaneous market forces would be slight because prices would still be carefully controlled. Administrative directives were not abandoned in principle and would continue to operate. Ulbricht's past successes in purging his principal opponents in 1953 (Zaisser and Herrnstadt) and in 1958 (Schirdewan,

Wollweber, and Oelssner) was also no doubt an important factor in minimizing friction, since there seems to have been no major rival for the leadership remaining in a position to challenge Ulbricht's policy. Ulbricht's unusually close personal relations with the Soviet leadership no doubt also played a substantial role in his ability to avoid challenges to his initiatives in the N.E.S.: what he was proposing had surely been thoroughly discussed with the Soviet comrades in advance.[14] The one instance of serious dissent within the Politburo in this period (and the manifestation was indeed extreme) was N.E.S. architect Erich Apel's strong objections to the terms of the Soviet-G.D.R. Trade Treaty of 1965. Apel is thought to have believed that a substantial reorientation of East German foreign trade would be necessary for the technological upgrading of the economy and the return to higher rates of growth. When Ulbricht refused to buck the Soviets on so delicate a matter, Apel committed suicide a few hours before the scheduled signing of the treaty.[15] Apel's departure from the scene was followed rather promptly by a certain back-tracking in the specific details of the N.E.S., which were modified at the December 1965 Central Committee Plenum by the decision to subordinate the V.V.B.s more closely to the new branch ministries, which were to be interposed between the V.V.B.s and the Planning Commission and would acquire the power to modify the former's plan proposals before presenting them to the latter. This decision seems to have been the result of a German desire to emulate the Soviet Union, which had just re-established industrial ministries and repudiated Khrushchev's scheme of organizing production on the basis of regional *sovnarkhozy*, but it did have a somewhat more "recentralizing" significance in Germany than in the U.S.S.R., because the German V.V.B.s (unlike the Soviet branch administrations) were operating on a *khozraschet* basis. The re-establishment of industrial ministries implied somewhat diminished independence of the V.V.B.s from "administrative" control, but the V.V.B.s still remained the central institutions of the N.E.S., as before.

Whatever may have been the private reservations of the East German Politburo members about the wisdom or orthodoxy of the N.E.S., the group stuck together quite firmly, in full accordance with the norms of democratic centralism. Ulbricht's firm leadership and the manifest unity and determination of the Politburo and Secretariat, along with the careful marshalling of regional Party bureaus to supervise the transition, seem largely to have prevented serious bureaucratic foot-dragging and insured the orderly implementation of the N.E.S. "Guidelines." While East Germany's was not one of the more radical economic reforms, it was one of the most fully implemented, and subsequent modifications that took place during the late 1960's were carried out in an equally methodical fashion, without apparent splits in the Party leadership. The process of modifying the German mechanism for economic planning and administration has at all times been orderly and politically well-controlled.

Adoption of the Bulgarian Economic Reform

The adoption of the economic reform in Bulgaria presented quite a contrast to the rather well-orchestrated process in the G.D.R. The Bulgarian Party leadership had been riven by factions and intrigues for years, as First Secretary Todor Zhivkov contended for power with his deposed predecessor as First Secretary, Vulko Chervenkov (still retained on the Politburo),and his own Premier, Anton Yugov, both of whom had factional support deeply entrenched in the Party and state apparatus. The Twenty-Second Congress of the C.P.S.U.'s call for a second great campaign against the remnants of the "personality cult" touched off a drive by Zhivkov to consolidate his own power and eliminate his chief rivals, a decision which evidently enjoyed Khrushchev's encouragement and open personal support.[16] Chervenkov was purged in November of 1961, and, after intense politicking that forced the delay of the scheduled Party Congress by three months, Yugov also lost his positions. The November 1962 Party Congress was dominated by denunciations of Chervenkov and Yugov (as well as their closest supporters), and the new Central Committee and Politburo elected at that time were markedly different in composition from the old ones. Almost a third of the former Central Committee members were dropped and the total size of that body was enlarged by another 12 percent, permitting Zhivkov substantially to increase his base of support at that level. On the Politburo, Zhivkov for the first time enjoyed a majority of supporters, albeit only by a five-to-four margin. In addition to his position of First Secretary, Zhivkov now assumed the premiership and transferred the secret police from the Ministry of the Interior to his own personal control. Fifteen new ministers were appointed to the newly-enlarged twenty-eight man Council of Ministers. While Zhivkov had unquestionably greatly consolidated his position, nevertheless he still faced substantial opposition and dissatisfaction in the middle and lower ranks of the Party apparat.[17]

The Eighth Party Congress of November 1962, which formalized Zhivkov's political ascendancy, also passed a resolution employing some of the rhetoric then current in the Soviet economic debates and recognizing the need for some degree of reform of the existing system of economic planning and management. The resolution was relatively non-specific, but referred to the need for greater participation from below in the drawing up of enterprise plan targets and the utility of enhancing the role of material incentives to ensure better plan fulfillment.

That official interest in relatively serious reforms was genuine, was demonstrated symbolically by the election of Professor Petko Kunin to the new Central Committee. A highly respected Communist economist of the 1940's, he had been a Politburo member before World War II and had served as Minister of Industry and Minister of Finance during the period 1947-1949. Kunin was caught up in the 1949 purge of "Titoists" and sentenced to fifteen years at the same trial that brought his associate, Politburo member and CC Secretary for Economic Affairs, Traicho Kostov, the death penalty. Kunin's principal offense seems to have been resistance to the wholesale copying of Soviet-style ultracentralized economic planning and management.[18]

The May 1963 Plenum was devoted almost entirely to economic matters. At that meeting, Zhikov himself put forth a program for radical restructuring of the economic model. Evidently his proposals were not received with anything like the unanimous acclaim his successes at the Congress might have led him to expect. The debate was reported to have been "frank," and the published resolution of the Plenum confined itself to reaffirming the basic economic decisions of the congress and to approving certain relatively minor reorganizations of the economic administration in the twenty-seven regional councils. Zhivkov's own report was never published.[19]

The public version of the Liberman debates did not get underway in Bulgaria until rather late — in fact, not really until after Zhivkov had already presented his "Theses" at the May 1963 Plenum and been rebuffed. The discussion was kicked off by a relatively mild summary of the Soviet Liberman debates written for the Party's ideological monthly *Novo Vreme* by the deputy chief of the Planning Commission, Evgeny Mateev. It was followed up in November by a more sensational article by Professor Angel Miloshevsky of the Karl Marx Economic Institute, who endorsed Libermanism and went beyond it to advocate broader rank-and-file workers' participation in managerial decisions, in a way that left little doubt that he had something like the Yugoslav Workers' Council system in mind. (This suggestion was quickly and roundly condemned.) More "moderate" and "realistic" suggestions by Bulgarian economists were the norm. The contribution by Professor Kunin in December probably had more impact, by virtue of his new status as a full member of the Central Committee, and Kunin himself went quite far in the radical direction, advocating a broad range of managerial discretion for self-supporting enterprises, improved and rationalized pricing and cost-accounting, profit as the main determinant of managerial incomes, competition between alternative manufacturers of similar products, and some form of profit-sharing as an important supplement to the wages of manual workers.[20]

Zhivkov's rejected "Theses," perhaps in somewhat modified form, were again brought forward for discussion in January 1964 at an unusual joint meeting of the Politburo and the Council of Ministers. At this time, they were "adopted in principle," but only as a basis for elaborating plans for limited experiments in selected enterprises.[21] The first such experiment was at the "Liliana Dimitrova" textile plant in Sofia, and the system tested evidently closely followed that recommended by Professor Kunin. By mid-1964, more than fifty pilot experiments were underway, and the public debate by economists became more and more detailed and specific in the advocacy of reform proposals. There had still been no public endorsement of any of these specific proposals by the Politburo, but as early as February 1964, Finance Minister Dimitur Popov had announced to a national meeting of accountants in Sofia that a "completely new system of planning and management" was in the process of being prepared, that the experiments should have been sufficiently long by the end of 1965, and that the new system ought to be applied throughout the country by the end of 1966.[22] It appears that Zhivkov and his closest supporters on economic issues may have been trying to stampede the Politburo with a *fait accompli*. If so, the ploy was only partially successful.

Early in 1965, the Politburo evidently balked again at agreeing to publication of an official draft blueprint for public discussion. A larger-scale extension of the program of "experimentation" was apparently all that could be agreed upon. By the end of 1965, enterprises employing over a third of the industrial work force and producing over 40 percent of industrial output had become part of the experiments.[23]

Endless "experimentation" seems to have been part of a more general delaying strategy by opponents of the reform within the Politburo. Certainly it was contrary to Zhivkov's preferences, as indicated by the Party's embarrassing failure to make good on his public promise (in a midsummer interview with a group of Austrian journalists) that the official Politburo Theses on the economic reform would be made public before the end of August 1965.[24] Zhivkov was able to get an official "Draft" for discussion through the proper collective decision process only in December of 1965.[25] Even then, his revised "Theses" were to be subjected to appropriate public debate and amendment before being finally approved. The Central Committee Plenum that was to have finally endorsed the reform "Theses" at the end of January 1966 was twice postponed and did not meet until the end of April, testifying to the degree of disagreement that still raged in the Party's upper echelons. When formal Central Committee approval finally was secured, it was still not unambiguous, since the resolution approved only the "basic principles" of the draft and instructed the Politburo to make appropriate additions and deletions "taking into account the report of comrade T. Zhivkov *and* the statements of the participants in the Plenum."[26]

The "Theses" that were finally approved at the cost of so much conflict still seemed to represent a rather radical departure from the past system, despite a number of internal inconsistencies.[27] While the principle of central planning was not fundamentally questioned, enterprises were to take the initiative in drafting their own plans for approval by the central authorities, and it was implied that vetoes by the center were intended to be exceptional. The number of compulsory targets written into the final version of the enterprise plan was supposed to be limited to only four (rather than the several dozen of the old system): (1) volume of physical production of principal products; (2) upper limits on the extent of capital investment undertaken from the enterprise's own funds; (3) upper limits on purchases of enumerated basic materials in short supply; and (4) limits on foreign exchange to be made available for the purchase of materials and machinery. Enterprises were to use their discretion in such a way as to maximize the ratio of profits to total enterprise capital ("profitability") while remaining within the constraints imposed by plan indicators and laws governing the payment of wages and bonuses, the transfer of capital, and so forth. Additional investment for modernization of the enterprise and the expansion of its production was to be undertaken from self-financed sources — either retained profits and depreciation funds or interest-bearing bank credits — although the state would continue to finance major new investments in "priority sectors." An important part of the wage fund would be determined in proportion to the profitability of the enterprise, subject only to the requirements of minimum-wage legislation.

Perhaps the most innovative and original aspect of the Bulgarian new economic model was the price system. Affirming that prices should continually be brought closer to "socially necessary labor costs," the blueprint spelled out a scheme providing for three different types of price determination for different classes of products. Some prices would continue as before to be set by the central authorities (although purportedly on a more "scientific" and flexible basis) — mainly prices for capital goods and certain basic consumer "necessities." For many other (perhaps most) goods, the state would fix only maximum and minimum prices, with market forces being allowed to determine the exact level at any given time (mainly goods traded between individual enterprises not deemed of "fundamental" importance to the economy, on the basis of negotiated contracts). Finally, prices of some goods would be left entirely free to fluctuate in the marketplace (mainly for seasonal agricultural products and consumer items subject to rapid shifts in demand due to changing fashions).

As the extreme difficulties in obtaining Party endorsement of the reform blueprint presaged, the process of the reform's implementation was marked by disorganization and delay. Many of the old compulsory indicators formerly imposed by the ministries on the enterprises and supposedly abolished by the reform were reintroduced by the newly strengthened branch associations (counterparts to the G.D.R.'s V.V.B.s) "on their own initiative" as a means of controlling their constituent enterprises. Enterprises were supposed to become "self-financing" and to have their incentive funds regulated by profitability, yet as late as 1968, industrial ministries were still assigning plans to certain enterprises involving "planned losses" and paying large subsidies to less efficient enterprises by seizing the profits of more efficient enterprises, without apparent penalties.[28] The principle of "self-financing of investment" was blatantly disregarded in the traditionally favored sector of heavy industry, where virtually all investment continued to be provided on a cost-free basis from the state budget, with the result that, as late as 1967, only 10 percent of total investment was being financed through interest bearing bank loans.[29] Moreover, the interest rates the banks charged to different enterprises were inversely related to enterprise profitability to provide back-door subsidies and thus seriously distorted the financial calculations for making investment decisions.[30]

Most damaging of all was the delay by the central authorities in implementing the price reforms, which made most of the measures designed to employ financial levers in guiding enterprises' decision-making counter-productive. If prices remained essentially arbitrary and reflected neither planners' real priorities nor those of consumers, then there was little reason to expect that efforts by the enterprises to maximize their profits would result in socially optimal decisions. Zhivkov's speech to the April 1966 Central Committee plenum projected that the new pricing system would be fully in operation by the middle of 1967.[31] It was not, and it was belatedly announced in November that, even by the middle of 1968, only the prices to govern inter-enterprise transactions would be ready, and not the new consumer prices.[32] And when the July 1968 Central Committee plenum met, even this revised deadline had not been met.

The July 1968 plenum, which was supposed to have marked the successful completion of the transition to the new economic model, instead turned out to be the occasion for a rather extensive revision of the 1966 blueprint. The changes constituted a substantial retreat in the direction of recentralization, as was made abundantly clear in the final resolution of the plenum:

> The Party and public supervision of activities of state agencies has not been well-organized and is insufficient. . . . It is necessary to increase the responsibilities of the government, of the ministers and of other leaders within our state and economic apparatus.[33]

Among the specific measures approved by the plenum were an increase in the number of obligatory targets assigned to the enterprises from the original four to ten, the creation of a new cabinet-level Ministry of Supplies and State Reserves to handle the physical rationing of machinery and materials (marking a substantial diminution in the role of independent enterprise contracting in favor of centralized allocation), and the substantial augmentation of the powers of the branch associations over the enterprises (very much along the lines of East German V.V.B.s). Subsequent measures further confirmed the recentralizing trend over the next few years. While never formally disavowed, all references to the three-category price system were dropped from public statements.[34]

By the end of 1968, official Bulgarian conceptions of their "new" economic system had been systematically revised to include an expanded role for centralized planning, a permanent role for a larger number of compulsory targets than had previously been envisioned, and a *de facto* rejection of the earlier plan to let some prices in the industrial sphere be determined by market forces. What was left of the original blueprint was the stress on a greater degree of enterprise self-financing, a more important role for profitability in determining material incentives, and the desirability of improving the scientific basis of centralized price-setting. To this they had added a much-expanded role for the large conglomerate branch associations in economic planning, the administration of production, and (especially) in the subordinating of scientific-technological research to the needs of production. This was essentially the same position toward which Soviet and East German theorists were converging at this time.

There seem to have been two major reasons for Bulgaria's ultimate failure to institutionalize the relatively radical model of economic planning and management elaborated by the reformers in the early and mid-1960's. The first reason was Todor Zhivkov's inability to engineer a sufficiently solid commitment to the basic concepts of the reform among the top leaders of the Bulgarian Communist Party. Despite his apparent triumph at the

Eighth Party Congress in 1962, the Party continued to be plagued by serious problems of factionalism (including even an abortive and amateurish attempt at a military coup in April of 1965). The ouster of Nikita Khrushchev from the Soviet leadership late in 1964 removed one of Zhivkov's most powerful sources of support and seems seriously to have undermined his ability to ensure the acceptance of his policy initiatives.[35] Zhivkov's evident lack of elite support necessitated an inordinate number of compromises in the drafting of the economic reform blueprint (thereby introducing serious internal inconsistencies that threatened the workability of the new system from the outset) and made it impossible for him to take appropriately punitive action against bureaucratic resistance to the businesslike implementation of many of the reform's more controversial but important features. To overcome the log-jam, it would probably have been necessary to mobilize additional support from outside the usual policy-making establishment and carry out a purge of the leadership, but this Zhivkov was either unable to do or unwilling to risk.[36]

By late 1967 Zhivkov seems largely to have reconciled himself to abandoning the effort to achieve full implementation and to have begun concentrating on more modest measures aimed at improving the efficiency of centralized administration through greater reliance on the branch associations and improved centralized price-fixing. At the July 1968 plenum, he admitted somewhat sorrowfully that

> even today we lack the mechanism to implement some of the basic principles of the new system . . . and wherever the mechanism has been worked out, it has not yet been applied.[37]

He went on to repudiate the practicability of "planning from below" and suggested that the emphasis in efforts to improve economic performance should shift from organizational innovations aimed at improving efficiency to a more systematic, planned exploitation of the benefits of the "scientific-technological revolution," which, he claimed,

> makes it possible under socialist conditions to administer the economy without any break in the chain, to avoid duplication, and to reach full coordination of functions and activities among the individual units.[38]

Unable to achieve implementation of his reform, Zhivkov himself pronounced its obituary.

Apart from the domestic difficulties with the reform and contributing to them, a second important factor in Bulgaria's turn away from the reform's more decentralizing and market-oriented features was a major change in the international ideological and political climate. By 1967, it had become relatively clear that the Soviet leaders were proceeding much more cautiously in their own economic reforms than some had expected on the basis of the September 1965 blueprints.[39] As the shape of the new Soviet model gradually emerged, the "emulative impulse" in Bulgaria no longer worked in favor of open-minded experimentation as it had a few years earlier. By the middle of 1968, criticisms of Czechoslovakia's liberalizing political reforms had become widespread throughout most of the Soviet bloc, and at least some authoritative East German and Polish Party spokesmen (but not yet the Soviets) had already broadened their anti-Czechoslovak polemics to include the charge of "economic revisionism." Following the decisions of the July plenum and the Bulgarian participation in the August intervention in Czechoslovakia, even G. Filipov, the newly appointed chairman of the "Permanent Commission on the New System," occupied his time penning the most scornful possible polemics against the Yugoslav and Czechoslovak idealization of "market socialism" as evidence of a lingering petty bourgeois mentality with ultimately counter-revolutionary implications.[40] Under the circumstances, domestic opponents of the reform were able to add to their usual repertory of arguments the one that perhaps finally tipped the balance: excessive reliance on decentralization and market forces in the economic sphere endangers the leading political role of the Party and is incompatible over the long run with maintaining comradely relations with the rest of the Soviet bloc, as had already been tragically demonstrated in Czechoslovakia.

Trying to assess the relative weights of international and domestic factors in bringing about the Bulgarian decision to abandon a substantial portion of their original economic reform program is a thankless task because the factors were in constant interaction with each other. The precariousness of the balance of power within the Bulgarian Party leadership was one important reason that the policy-making process was sensitive to influences from the Soviet Union and other Communist countries: very little was required to tip the balance one way or the other. The economic reform got under way in a situation where the performance gap in the economy was acute and the international climate was congenial to economic experimentation and innovation. Even so, vested interests hostile to the reform remained powerful enough to delay the institutionalization of the new system long enough for reformist pressures to slacken because of cyclical economic recovery and because of disillusionment born of continual frustration. Zhivkov's skills as a leader proved insufficient to the task of bargaining for enough elite support and he was unwilling to risk Dubcek's strategy of mobilizing additional support from outside the relatively narrow political-economic establishment. The near stalemate was finally broken when the international situation changed in such a way as to strengthen the opposition to the reform by effectively denying socialist legitimacy to the most controversial measures in the eyes of at least some of their former elite supporters. At this point, the only prudent course was to beat a hasty retreat and to seek "moderate" approaches to solving the country's economic difficulties that would involve little or no deviation from the methods being worked out in other more stable Communist countries and which held out greater promise of domestic political tranquility.

Adoption of the Czechoslovak Economic Reform

The adoption and implementation of economic reform in Czechoslovakia coincided with, and contributed to, the most intense and far-reaching intra-Party conflicts. In addition to the manifest bankruptcy of established economic policies (Czechoslovak national income actually declined by about 2 percent in 1963), at least two other major issues severely strained the unity of the Communist Party of Czechoslovakia: (1) the question of how to respond to Soviet pressures (and increasingly vocal popular demands) to undertake the exposure of "violations of socialist legality" that had taken place during the exceedingly bloody purges of the late 1940's and early 1950's; and (2) the question of how best to order the political relationship between the two major nationalities that made up the bulk of the country's population, and, in particular, how best to respond to the growing dissatisfaction of the Slovak regional political elite with the extreme centralization of political and economic power in Prague.

The top political leadership in the Politburo and Secretariat of the Czechoslovak Communist Party were singularly disadvantaged by their own past records in their efforts to adapt their regime to the economic and political challenges they faced in the decade of the 1960's. Czechoslovakia had avoided almost entirely the consequences of the first great destalinization campaign launched by Khrushchev at the Twentieth Congress of the C.P.S.U. in 1956 by the simple expedient of delaying action until the Polish and Hungarian disorders of that year retroactively vindicated their cautious policy. Consequently, in the early 1960's, the Politburo and Secretariat still comprised nearly the same group who had risen to power by perpetrating the bloodiest and most far-reaching of all the East European purges of the Stalinist period.[41] Acknowledging the bogus character of the charges, as destalinization pressures demanded, would necessarily have resulted in the discrediting of most of the Party's top leadership. Moreover, two of the principal categories of victims in the purge trials were Party members accused of Slovak "bourgeois nationalism" and economic officials whose dissent from the policy of overcentralization of the economy in 1949 was taken as proof of their intent to sabotage the economy.

Party First Secretary and President of the Republic Antonin Novotny was deeply implicated in the fabrication of charges in the purges and had been closely identified with the policies of extreme centralization in both the economic and political spheres throughout his entire political career. By conviction and by past commitments, he was in no position to act as champion of reform in any major issue area, including the economic. Nevertheless, the conjunction of the extreme economic crisis of 1962-1965 with the intensification of Soviet demands for destalinization after the Twenty-Second Congress of the C.P.S.U. in October 1961, made some sort of response unavoidable.

The Twelfth Congress of the Communist Party of Czechoslovakia, held in December of 1962 (after an unexplained postponement of several months duration), had been expected to produce important changes. By and large, these expectations were disappointed. The new party statute did not importantly modify the monolithic and authoritarian character of power, no incumbent members of the Politburo were demoted, and uprooting the "cult of personality" turned out to consist largely of the symbolic demolition of the Stalin monument and the removal of the embalmed corpse of former Party First Secretary Klement Gottwald from public display. However, the release from prison of some thirty unjustly convicted purge victims was announced, and there was a vague promise of further review of the political trials held between 1949 and 1954.

The principal subject for discussion at the Twelfth Congress was the deepening economic crisis. The line taken by Novotny in his report was that "subjectivist tendencies" on the part of the planners, the weakening of labor discipline, and the pernicious results of the mild decentralization that had been accomplished in the mini-reform of 1958 were the chief causes of the difficulties. The resolution of the Congress was rather vague on the subject, calling for measures to increase the efficiency of the enterprises, but without specifying any means to the end.

Several practical effects of the Congress were to have an impact on the subsequent course of economic policy, however. Several new members were added to the Politburo, men who were not seriously implicated in the purges and who were selected at least in part for their economic expertise: Drahomir Kolder and Jozef Lenart became full members and Alexander Dubcek became a candidate member. All three were later to display a much more open-minded attitude toward the idea of economic reform than their senior colleagues on the Politburo. Moreover, Professor Ota Sik, who had been closely involved in designing the proposals for economic reform in 1956-1957, had recently become head of the Institute of Economics of the Academy of Sciences and was elected a full member of the Central Committee, where he soon became quietly active in promoting his reformist views in both Party and academic circles.

The major changes, however, came in the months after the Congress. The Czechoslovak version of the Liberman debates somewhat belatedly got under way in February of 1963, with the publication of Professor Radoslav Selucky's attack on "The Cult of the Plan."[42] Although directed specifically against the economic model inherited from the past, Selucky's article was quite self-consciously a part of a much broader attack on the legacies of the Stalinist past and coincided with other thinly veiled public attacks on the Party's slowness in rehabilitating the victims of the purges, including especially the Slovak "bourgeois nationalists" and the surviving victims of the "economists' trial" of 1954. Novotny, on the defensive, soon thereafter attacked Selucky by name and warned against "internal enemies" who, "under the guise of combatting the cult of personality," called for "abandonment of the gains of socialism." Novotny went on to call for the *strengthening* of the authority of the economic plan.[43] Nevertheless, critical articles by economists continued to appear sporadically throughout 1963.

The year 1963 finally saw some rather drastic changes in the composition of the Party's top leadership. Although Novotny managed to hold on to his position, he did so by gradually disassociating himself from his closest long-time associates and throwing them to the wolves one by one as their roles in engineering the purge trials were publicly exposed. In April of 1963, the Central Committee removed Karol Bacilek and Bruno Kohler from the Politburo and Secretariat. (Bacilek had also been the Party's regional secretary for Slovakia: he was replaced by Alexander Dubcek in both jobs.) In June, Pavol David was expelled from the Politburo. In August, Viliam Siroky, the Prime Minister, was removed both from the government and the Politburo. By the end of 1963, only four persons in leading Party posts had occupied high office between 1949 and 1954.[44] Moreover, Premier Siroky's fall in September led to a major reshuffling of the cabinet and the replacement of a number of key economic administrators and decision-makers. The new Premier, Jozef Lenart, and the new Planning Commission chief, Oldrych Cernik, were both men considered to be open to proposals for changes in the system of planning and management, although by no means were they fanatical reformers. Drahomir Kolder, the new Central Committee Secretary for Economic Affairs, a pragmatist, had concluded that drastic measures were necessary, however painful. Ota Sik, in his various capacities and with his new authority as a member of the Central Committee, had already established an informal working group of academic economists to develop a comprehensive set of proposals for economic reform, without official Party sanction.[45] Sik's article, published in September,[46] was the first semi-official acknowledgement by an important (if secondary) Party official that most of the harsh criticisms by such radical economists as Selucky and Evzen Lobl were essentially valid. This opened the way for an extremely frank exchange of views at a November conference of academic and government economists sponsored by the economic weekly *Hospodarske Noviny*. Publication "without comment" of selections from the discussions at the conference constituted the first public indication that concrete suggestions for rather radical economic reforms were being seriously entertained by at least some important policy makers, despite continued outspoken condemnations of economic "revisionism" by First Secretary Novotny.[47]

At the December 1963 Plenum of the Central Committee, something of a showdown on the issue of economic reform seems to have occurred. Ota Sik spoke out sharply against the economic policies and the economic organizational forms of the past and went so far as to state in so many words that, since Czechoslovakia had already depleted its manpower reserves and did not enjoy the relative self-sufficiency of the larger and better-endowed Soviet Union, Czechoslovakia could no longer afford to model its economic institutions on those of the U.S.S.R. Sik openly advocated a new economic model more suited to Czechoslovakian conditions, which would involve a creative blending of both plan and market elements.[48] That he made a positive impression on a substantial number of those present was indicated by the fact that a special Central Committee meeting in January of 1964 finally appointed an official Party committee under Sik's chairmanship to study and report on approaches for improving the system of planning and management, with the report to be submitted to the Politburo for its consideration. While the existence of the special committee was not made public at the time, Central Committee Secretary Kolder's public statements immediately afterwards gave the first official confirmation that important reforms were being considered. Kolder called for less "administrative" and more "economic" management, endorsed the need for strengthening the role and effectiveness of material incentives, and solicited the development of innovative proposals for encouraging and rewarding efficiency so that they might be tested on an experimental basis in selected enterprises.[49]

Novotny and his allies were evidently still actively resisting the very idea of economic reform, however. Novotny's speech in mid-March attacked critics of the established economic model, accusing them of "olympian arrogance," of "one-sided," "incorrect," and "subjectivist" opinions, and of attempting to "denigrate the overall development" of Czechoslovak socialism.[50] The Politburo disapproved the report of Sik's special committee at its April meeting, publicly lamenting that some of its contents represented out-and-out "economic revisionism."[51] Nevertheless, by this time the economic crisis had made it obvious that some sort of measures would have to be taken. (National income had grown only 1 percent in 1962 and had actually declined by 2 percent in 1963, with no recovery in sight.) A compromise agreement for at least limited reforms was evidently extracted from Novotny soon after the April meeting, since at the end of May, Novotny himself acknowledged in a speech to an unprecedented nationwide conference of chairmen of Party organizations in enterprises that "a new system of management" was being elaborated.[52] Nevertheless, Novotny went on to insist that, while "dogmatism and sectarianism" might be the most serious threat to the workers' movement at the international level as Khrushchev had recently reiterated, in Czechoslovakia, "revisionist and liberalistic tendencies represent the main danger . . . in our present situation."[53]

On October 17, 1964, the Party daily finally published the "Draft Principles of a System for Improving the Economy's Planned Management," which evidently represented a somewhat revised version of the Sik committee's April draft.[54] These "Draft Principles" were supposed to be discussed and passed on at the December 1964 Central Committee meeting, but the sharp polarization of views among the Party leadership and the extended debates resulted in their being held over for additional debate at the January 1965 meeting. Novotny's New Year's speech to the nation clearly indicated his continued leadership of the opposition to the more radical aspects of the reform, assuring the public that the economy would "continue to be directed and planned." Referring to the mini-reform of 1958-1959, Novotny charged that the troubles plaguing the economy had arisen largely because "most of the measures degenerated into so-called decentralization."[55] Novotny and his fellow skeptics were successful in getting the "Draft" recommitted to the Central Committee's standing Economic Commission for "further study," but at the end of January, the Central Committee finally endorsed the "Draft Principles" and instructed appropriate state agencies to prepare more detailed guidelines for putting the basic principles into practice. In March, the Council of Ministers passed a resolution setting up a timetable for the transition to the new system, providing for full implementation in conjunction with the beginning of the new Five-Year Plan on January 1, 1966. Initial "experiments" in selected enterprises had already begun in late January, and more were begun in April, involving 440 enterprises (which together produced about one-fifth of the country's industrial output [56]). It appeared that the reformers had won out.

The adoption of the "Draft Principles" (which outlined the most radically market-oriented and decentralized economic model yet seen outside Yugoslavia) by the Central Committee over the strong opposition of the First Secretary constituted little less than a formal repudiation of the economic policies of the past fifteen years, policies which had in large part been imposed by the leader who was now supposed to force the needed changes on a reluctant bureaucracy. The fact that Novotny still retained his position at all testified to the ambivalence of the Party leadership and to the closeness of the divisions on the issue of economic reform. (In point of fact, Novotny continued to speak openly against the spirit and many of the specific features of the reform long after its adoption by the Central Committee and even after its formal endorsement by the Thirteenth Party Congress in June of 1966.[57]) The strategy of the reformers was to mobilize the economics profession and the pressure of the mass media to assure prompt implementation while the movement for economic reform still maintained its momentum and while the more conservative elements of the leadership were still off-balance as a result of the continuing revelations about the purges of the Stalinist period and the manifest stagnation of the economy under their stewardship. The strategy of the reform's opponents was, naturally, to delay long enough that order could be restored in the mass media and Party discipline once again reasserted over the Party intelligentsia.

The advocates of radical economic reform had generally opposed proposals for widespread experimentation before finalizing and implementing the new system throughout the economy. Nevertheless, by September of 1965, the government announced a modification in the schedule. Instead of full implementation by the beginning of 1966, there would be at least another full year of experimentation, with no final deadline established for the total transition to the new system.[58] What followed was a long process of delay, faulty implementation, the imposition of "temporary" exceptions to the basic principles of the reform, the flatly illegal retention of certain compulsory directives by branch administrations unwilling to give up their former prerogatives, inconsistency in application of supposedly general rules and other forms of bureaucratic resistance, which was only partially checked by the efforts of the new, more reform-oriented cabinet installed in November of 1965. Despite this, as the Thirteenth Party Congress approached, the implementation of the reform was in fact making measurable progress. The most radical economic reform in East Europe (outside of Yugoslavia) was slowly being transformed from an abstract blueprint to a working model approximating market socialism — or so it still seemed.

The Thirteenth Party Congress in June of 1966 turned out to be a limited victory for the forces within the Party which were struggling for change in the areas of economic reform, cultural policy, and Czech-Slovak relations. After enlarging the Central Committee and replacing some of the former members, the turnover in membership amounted to about 40 percent, and the new Central Committee even now included a sprinkling of rehabilitated victims of the purges. Thereafter, Central Committee meetings became much more open and included a great deal of criticism of Novotny's shortcomings in administering the affairs of the Party. A frequent subject of such criticism was the slow progress being made in implementing the economic reforms.[59] While the Congress produced no substantial changes in the composition of the Politburo and Secretariat, it did pass a resolution calling for accelerating implementation of the economic reform, which was to be in effect from January 1, 1967, the soonest that the new price system could be worked out.

In the course of 1967, the economic reform ran into serious difficulties, principally because of the inadequacies of the centrally-fixed prices that had just gone into effect at the wholesale level. The effect of the wholesale price reform was to raise prices more than was economically justified, resulting in levels of enterprise profitability about double those that had been allowed for in the plan. When these enormous profit increases were translated into employee bonuses and larger-than-planned enterprise investment funds, the result was extremely serious shortages of both consumer goods and investment goods and inflationary pressures, which in turn greatly strengthened the arguments of the anti-reformers in favor of recentralization, physical rationing, additional controls on the allocation of enterprise funds (especially wage and bonus funds), and a return to management by *ad hoc* directives. The result was that the first year of the "full adoption" of the new system in many ways marked a retreat from the relative autonomy that had been grudgingly conceded during the last year of widespread experiments. For example, the share of "free" (category three) priced goods in total retail sales dropped from 25 percent in 1966 to only 13 percent in 1967.[60]

The new economic crisis coincided with (and probably helped to stimulate) the growth of serious political unrest, not only among the intellectuals, but also among students and workers. The clumsy (and largely ineffective) attempts by Novotny to repress growing criticism by police methods (the suppression of the Writers' Union weekly, the expulsion of several outspokenly critical writers from the party and their jobs, and, especially, the brutal tactics employed against peaceful student demonstrators in September) contributed to Novotny's growing isolation within the Party leadership. At the October 1967 Central Committee Plenum, Novotny came under concentrated attack for his shortcomings in three areas: his lack of leadership in implementing the economic reform, the clear loss of the regime's moral authority among a very large fraction of the general population that was repelled by the intensification of repressive measures against even moderate dissent, and the unsatisfied demands of the Slovak party leadership for a more satisfactory degree of regional autonomy and a more equitable share of investment funds for regional development.

By the autumn of 1967, Novotny had not only alienated the advocates of economic reform and of a more permissive cultural policy but also much of the Slovak leadership and even some of the more hard-line elements within the Politburo (such as Jiri Hendrychs) who were appalled by the sheer ineffectiveness of Novotny's leadership and who considered him a liability for the Party. By the end of the year, Novotny's fate was sealed, when Soviet First Secretary Leonid Brezhnev, after conferring with the Party leadership on the current crisis, refused to lend his personal support for Novotny's retention. After a three-month long debate over who should succeed him, the January 1968 meeting of the Central Committee transferred the Party leadership to Alexander Dubcek, who was acceptable to both the Slovaks and the (predominantly Czech) backers of the economic reform.[61]

The struggle over the implementation of the economic reform was by no means ended with the ouster of Antonin Novotny, nor even was its success assured as the "Prague Spring" got well under way and additional changes in the leadership occurred. The coalition that overthrew Novotny was based on the convergence of a number of dissatisfactions and was not united on the proper approach to take toward the problem of economic reorganization. While Dubcek and his closest associates were on record as favoring the more rapid implementation of the reform, other more "political" reforms occupied center stage during most of 1968, and the policy-making structure for the economy remained divided and poorly coordinated. (A relative conservative, Lubomir Strougal, was named to head the Economic Council while Ota Sik became a Vice-Premier.) The new statute to implement the economic reform (called for in the Party's April 1968 "Action Program") seemed to be going through an interminable drafting process and full implementation was now scheduled to occur only in January of 1969. In the meanwhile, economic policy was largely improvisational in character. Moreover, the expansion of citizen participation in public policy-making fundamentally altered the parameters of economic decision, as will be explored in more detail in the next chapter. In particular, the reformers now had to garner support for the New Economic System from an increasingly restive and self-assertive working class, and their success was by no means assured, even in the absence of Soviet intervention.

The patterns of elite conflict which were involved in the Czechoslovak economic reform from its inception to its abrupt termination following the Warsaw Pact intervention and the imposition of policies of "normalization" were unique in their intensity and in their ultimate political consequences. The stubborn opposition of a powerful and seemingly well-entrenched Party First Secretary had to be overcome if the radical reforms adopted under the pressure of the most severe economic crisis in East Europe since the post-war reconstruction were to be implemented in practice. The reform had to be brought into harmony with the core political values of both the Communist Party and Czechoslovakia's diverse population. That the economic reformers succeeded as well as they did may perhaps be attributed to the fact that the positions of the established political leadership had been undermined not only by their manifest failures in maintaining acceptable economic performance but also by the revelations of their sheer moral bankruptcy stemming from Soviet-initiated public reexamination of the purges of the Stalinist era. The discrediting and consequent removal of many of the established leaders and the return to political life of many of their surviving victims created the opportunity for a nucleus of reform-oriented men to enter the upper ranks of the economic policy-making establishment through a process of co-optation. In turn, they were able to secure the adoption and partial implementation of a radical economic reform partly by appealing to the obvious necessity of improving economic performance in their discussions with the existing leaders and partly by mobilizing additional support from the margins of the existing policy-making establishment — most notably by reactivating the Central Committee as a meaningful forum for the discussion and debate of alternative policies and by appealing to public opinion through a part of the mass media that for a variety of reasons was acquiring a meaningful, if limited, degree of autonomy from the formerly extremely rigorous censorship.

Even so, the ultimate success of the reformers in getting the economic reforms fully implemented and institutionalized against the determined opposition of the Party First Secretary was very much in doubt (witness the extensive rollbacks of the reform's most radical aspects during 1967). Overcoming bureaucratic opposition to the reform's implementation required the mobilization of external control agencies which, by the very nature of the existing political system, were largely under the control of the Party apparat. It was the partly fortuitous coalescence of several rather different sources of opposition to the personal rule of Antonin Novotny (along with the securing of tacit Soviet consent) that made it possible finally to break his hold on the apparat and to begin the process of converting the Party into an instrument for insuring social control over the implementation of policy by the state bureaucracy. Unfortunately, however, the extreme intensity of elite conflict that had by this time been engendered made it nearly impossible to reconcile important segments of the Party to the impending political and economic changes. Embattled conservative forces then sought and received the support of the Soviet Union in order to prevent their complete elimination from the political arena. Having finally gained the upper hand after years of frustration, the reformers were not inclined to follow a policy of reconciliation, even if newly mobilized public opinion would have permitted this, and the implications of such a thoroughgoing attack on the existing political establishment seemed to the Soviet leadership inevitably destructive of both the Party's dominant role in Czechoslovak political life and the country's reliability as a Soviet ally.

Adoption of the Hungarian Economic Reform

The Hungarian economic reform package, like that elaborated in Czechoslovakia, was one of the most radical blueprints for change in the system of economic planning and management to be adopted by an East European Communist Party. Like the Czechoslovak economic reform, the Hungarian "New Economic Mechanism" (N.E.M.) envisioned expanding enterprise autonomy to the point of virtually abolishing compulsory plan directives, with enterprises to be guided primarily indirectly (or "parametrically," as the theorists of the reform preferred to term it) through a flexible price mechanism incorporating centrally fixed prices, fixed maximum-minimum "range" prices, and completely "free" prices and through conventional macroeconomic policy instruments. Enterprises would be expected to maximize their profits (after charges for the use of raw materials and socially-owned land and capital), and the material remuneration of management and (to a lesser degree) of the workers would be substantially dependent upon the successful attainment of profits in the marketplace. Like Czechoslovakia (and unlike Bulgaria and the G.D.R.), Hungary would assign the principal economic role to the autonomous enterprise and would retain "branch associations" only as convenient organizations to provide desired services (mainly marketing research and the provision of technological assistance) to the enterprises and not as decision-making bodies with power to give administrative directives with binding force.

Although the Hungarian N.E.M. rather closely resembled the Czechoslovak NES in its general conceptual outlines, the political process by which the Hungarian political leadership came to adopt and implement their reform differed rather strikingly from the exceptionally bitter and conflict ridden zigzag course followed in Czechoslovakia. The reform proposals did indeed generate significant conflict and disagreements within the top leadership of the Party, but extreme care was taken by First Secretary Janos Kadar to manage the intensity and disruptiveness of these conflicts so as to maintain at all costs at least the minimum degree of unity necessary for the Party to preserve its effectiveness as a mechanism for ensuring the controlled implementation of agreed-upon national policies. Kadar, unlike Novotny, lent his personal support to the cause of economic reform almost from the beginning, which was a crucial factor in securing a relatively smooth transition.

The top leadership of the Hungarian Socialist Workers' Party was by the 1960's already somewhat better prepared to undertake institutional reforms than their Czech and Slovak counterparts. Although the Hungarian uprising of 1956 had been bloodily repressed by the intervention of the Soviet military and the reformist-revolutionary government of Imre Nagy had been physically liquidated, the political elite that was installed by the Soviets to carry out the "normalization" of political affairs did not represent a simple restoration of the Stalinist cadres who had been disgraced in the aftermath of the Soviet Twentieth Party Congress earlier that year. Kadar himself had been tortured in prison as a victim of Rakosi's purges, and his elevation to the first secretaryship had been part of the same liberalizing trend that returned Imre Nagy to the premiership. Kadar's disengagement from Nagy's government at the height of the crisis and the loyalty he demonstrated to the Soviet Union by collaborating in the Soviet invasion and the subsequent repressions made it possible for him to survive politically. Since the Party had literally disintegrated in the course of the uprising, it had to be reconstituted once again from the ground up. While the political realities of "normalization" dictated that the Party would utilize a great many experienced cadres from Rakosi's Stalinist regime, the rebuilding process did make it possible for Kadar to exclude many of the worst offenders. Kadar's own orientation was generally considered "centrist" and he made it his primary task to ensure that there would be no repetition of the rigid sectarianism *or* the blind factionalism that had characterized the period 1953-1956 and culminated in the disaster of a mass popular uprising.

The renewal of the Soviet destalinization campaign in late 1961 made it possible for Kadar to consolidate his position and politically profitable for him to lessen his dependence upon the more conservative wing of the Party. In September of 1961, Kadar personally assumed the premiership. The year 1962 saw the quiet removal of three of the more "dogmatic" members of the Party leadership (Imre Dogei, Karoly Kiss, and Gyorgy Marosan) and the promotion to the Politburo of economic reformers Rezso Nyers and Miklos Ajtai, who now assumed primary responsibilities in the economic policy area. Although Kadar's speech at the Eighth Party Congress in November 1962 reiterated his familiar formula that the Party must wage a "two-front struggle" against "dogmatism" and "revisionism," he added parenthetically that at the current juncture greater efforts would be necessary against the former than against the latter. In the interests of Party unity, even those ousted from the Politburo for having "failed to see in the proper light" the purge trials of the Stalinist period (and their own roles in them) were allowed to remain members of the Central Committee. Other Politburo members who had had rather prominent positions during the Stalinist period, such as Antal Apro and Gyula Kallai, were allowed to retain their Politburo membership.

There is considerable evidence that a number of aspects of Kadar's policies that had been the subject of intra-Party controversy for several years continued to engender opposition in certain circles within the Central Committee and among the regional Party *apparatchiki*. Kadar's guiding principle (reaffirmed more vigorously following the Soviet Twenty-Second Congress) was what he referred to as the "Alliance Policy": that is, a policy of reconciliation and careful bridge-building between the Party and the masses of the population who had become alienated from the regime as a result of the excesses of "dogmatism" in the pre-1956 period. In response to Rakosi's famous slogan of the early 1950's ("whoever is not with us, is against us"), Kadar counterposed the motto that "whoever is not against us, is with us." The principal operational manifestations of the Alliance Policy were: a greater solicitude for the development of the standard of living as a policy goal, de-emphasis on class origins as a criterion for determining the career opportunities of individual citizens, increased opportunities for non-Party members to hold positions of leadership in economic and cultural organizations, an emphasis on persuasion in preference to coercive methods for securing the cooperation of the public with Party policies, and a considerable diminution in anti-religious propaganda. Opposition to the Alliance Policy by "dogmatists" was evidently a problem of considerable magnitude during 1961-1965, judging by the constant stream of articles exposing particular instances of abuses by local officials, exhorting them to reform, threatening sanctions against the perpetrators of such offenses, and publicizing the Party discipline meted out to the unrepentant. The necessity of such prolonged polemics against "dogmatism" was persuasive evidence that the problem continued to be a widespread one, and, indeed, Kadar acknowledged that such had been the case at the Ninth Congress in November of 1966.[62]

Decentralizing economic reforms, such as those proposed in 1957 by the "Varga Commission," seem initially to have been favorably looked upon by Kadar, who had appointed this earliest committee of economic experts in December of 1956. Implementation of a few of their recommendations was in fact accomplished (most notably the initiation of a system of profit-sharing bonuses for workers in 1958 and a relatively sophisticated reform in the technique of central price-setting in 1959). Because of Soviet objections and because of the necessity of maintaining the still-fragile unity of conservative and centrist Party cadres in the delicate post-1956 political situation, most of the more radical and market oriented recommendations of the Varga Commission were rejected as unsuitable during the general "tightening up" that got under way in 1958.[63] However, with the return to a more relaxed political atmosphere in the aftermath of the Twenty-Second Congress, there was also a revival of economic reformism. In his report to the 8th Congress of the Hungarian Socialist Workers' Party in November of 1962, Janos Kadar himself signalled the new direction in economic policy. With the completion of agricultural collectivization that year, Hungary had entered the era of full construction of socialism. Now, he said, the new tasks were largely economic. "The boosting of productivity, the raising of profitability, the expansion of production are today the principal battlefronts."[64]

The Soviet Liberman discussions did not themselves create much of a stir in Hungary, except as an indication that a reopening of the issues raised by Hungarian economists in 1954-1955 and 1956-1958 was once again feasible. In addition to somewhat freer discussions of economic problems and policies in the economic journals and the general circulation press,

1963-1964 saw the publication of several iconoclastic treatments of the practical results of Stalinist economic practices by prominent economic historians, most notably Gyorgy Ranki and Ivan Berend, which set the stage for radical analysis of the organizational and structural sources of contemporary shortcomings. In general, the level of sophistication of the Hungarian economic literature was considerably higher than that displayed in either the Soviet Union's Liberman debates or the growing Czechoslovak literature.[65] Hungarian economists at this time were more widely aware of both "bourgeois" micro-economic price theory and of the finer points of the theory of "market socialism."

Despite the Hungarians' apparent lack of concern for the Liberman debates as such, Hungarian economists and political leaders were extreme-ly concerned with the lagging performance of the economy and were already carrying on theoretical work of some sophistication in devising possible solutions. At the May 1963 Central Committee Plenum, the Central Committee's new Secretary for Economic Affairs, Rezso Nyers, presented a detailed report identifying the principal problems facing the economy and proposing that he be authorized to undertake a major study to discover suitable reforms which would be able to alleviate the slowdown in economic growth, the persisting balance of payments problem with the West, the insufficiently rapid rise in the standard of living, and the poor quality of enterprise management. Nyers' general recommendations were for increasing the sphere of enterprise autonomy, greater application of "commercial methods" in handling the intractable problem of material-technical supply, and greater use of material incentives to stimulate enterprise efficiency. (Hungary had already introduced limited "profit-sharing" bonuses in 1958 and had carried out a relatively sophisticated price revision in 1959.) Although the Central Committee took his report "under advisement," they did not authorize any major study to develop a comprehensive reform and the text of his speech was not published.[66] Nevertheless, certain long-advocated partial reforms were approved. On January 1, 1964, Hungary instituted a 5 percent annual interest charge on the assets of the enterprises, in order to discourage hoarding of unnecessary capital and to facilitate more rational economic calculation at the level of the enterprise. This was the first such interest charge instituted in East Europe (except for Yugoslavia).

It was not until the December 1964 Central Committee Plenum that Nyers received the requested authorization to undertake the drafting of a comprehensive, market-oriented reform of the entire system of economic planning and management. That this was a matter of rather heated discussion seems relatively clear, and the actual text of the official resolution was never published. Word of the decision came out only indirectly, in the public speeches and writing of some of the participants.[67] Despite the relative secrecy of the undertaking, participation in the process of drafting the reform was in fact remarkably widespread. Nyers quickly appointed a collection of eleven special committees, consisting of a total of about 150 Party officials, economists, managers and engineers. Both Party and non-Party experts were included.[68] These committees of experts submitted preliminary reports by November of 1965, and, based on these reports and the recommendation of Rezso Nyers, the November 1965 Plenum decided "in principle" to undertake the kinds of reforms being put forward. Nyers and his committees were instructed to work out the more detailed and specific "main directives" that would be necessary. These were approved by a narrow margin at the May 1966 Plenum.

Although general theoretical discussions of individual reform proposals had gone on for several years in the press, the actual period of public debate of the officially proposed reform measures was relatively short. Nyers' report to the November 1965 Plenum was published immediately following the end of the meeting, along with the resolution approving this report as the "guidelines" for discussion, pending final consideration of the issues raised at another Central Committee meeting to be held "in the first quarter of 1966."[69] (In point of fact, the degree of opposition within the Central Committee must have forced a postponement of the final vote by several months, since May is in the middle of the second quarter.) The public discussions in the economic media were largely favorable, but not uncritical. In general, potentially divisive *ideological* criticisms of the scheme were not published, while the technical-economic criticisms were welcomed and sometimes incorporated in the final draft.

The debate on the final draft accepted at the May 1966 Plenum was evidently extremely heated within the privacy of the Party headquarters. According to Nyers' later remarks,[70] Janos Kadar took an active role in the debates and, in effect, laid his own prestige on the line in backing the N.E.M. against its opponents, some of whom were said to have argued that Hungary had been "economically stronger" under the stalinist policies of Matyas Rakosi in the early 1950's. While Nyers gives no figures on the vote, he makes it plain that the N.E.M. was accepted only by a relatively narrow margin. Another Politburo member, Valeria Benke, writing in the Party's theoretical monthly very shortly thereafter, also emphasized Kadar's personal identification with the reform:

> The Party documents pertaining to the reform of the economic mechanism are the results of almost one and one-half year of collective work, joint efforts, thorough investigation, research and analysis and extensive, creative debates. . . . The "Guidelines" were discussed by leading Party and social bodies, by various associations, ministries, high authorities, scientific institutions and universities. Simultaneously with this, the draft of the reform was worked out by Communist and non-Party experts, economists, technicians, Party workers and practical economic workers. . . . This complicated work had been inspired and encouraged by the leading Party bodies and by Janos Kadar in person.[71]

Kadar seems to have played an increasingly important role in mapping out strategy to secure the N.E.M.'s acceptance once the principles of reform had been ratified by the Central Committee. At his insistence, the eleven special committees of experts had included not only academic economists, but also a healthy sprinkling of Party and state officials who would eventually be involved in carrying out its implementation and whose active support would therefore be essential. After the May 1966 Plenum, these committees were very substantially expanded for the final working out of legal texts for the enacting decrees and regulations. (This is in sharp contrast with the procedure followed in Czechoslovakia, where the economic reformers' status as a quasi-insurgent group in an adversary relationship with much of the Party and state apparatus resulted in a situation where the theory of the reforms was worked out by economists under Ota Sik's direction and then basically turned over to the state bureaucracy for implementation once its formal acceptance had been secured. The Czechoslovak procedure provided only minimal opportunities for the reform's authors to interact with and co-opt the reform's opponents and gave the latter the maximum potential for sabotage.)

Kadar's concern for unity led him to expand still further on the need for coopting those who might feel threatened by the reform in his address to the members of the preparatory committees just before their numbers were to be expanded for the final work of implementation. Evidently he wanted to insure that this group of the highly committed fully understood the strategy to be pursued:

> Above all it is necessary for all those people who are in key economic positions . . . to be well acquainted with the essence and basic principle of the reform. . . . Even the preparatory work should be done in this spirit, and afterward it should be implemented in this same way. This is necessary so that a larger group of people should have confidence in the reform, because, when this group

of leaders understands it, a larger group has to be told what has to be done, and in this, the cooperation of the economic leaders is vital.[72]

Benke then went on to report that Kadar specifically charged the members of the preparatory committees (both Party and non-Party) with the duty of contributing in the greatest possible way to the mobilization of support for the reform. No longer should these architects of the reform give "individual interpretations" or raise "debatable issues," but rather they should put their past differences aside and carry out propaganda efforts in full support of the Central Committee Resolution — as it had been passed, not as they wished it had been passed.[73]

That such elaborate efforts were necessary and effective was indicated by Kadar himself on the eve of the N.E.M.'s implementation. Speaking to the Central Committee late in November of 1967, Kadar recalled the atmosphere of the Central Committee debates of 1965:

> When we spoke about the reform more than two years ago there were essentially different opinions — not only among economists but also among those now present and even on basic questions. We pursued a correct road . . . because we took the basic issues one after the other, discussed them, clarified them and settled them . . . and thus achieved unity.[74]

The Ninth Party Congress, which met November 28 to December 3, 1966, seems to have marked a turning point in the struggle over economic reform in Hungary. While repeated references to foot dragging by older "dogmatists" continued to be made over the next few years in discussing difficulties in the implementation of the N.E.M., the substantial expansion of the size of the Central Committee that took place at the Congress evidently diluted their strength sufficiently that Kadar could now be more confident in his support from that quarter: of the 101 members, twenty-six were newly elected and only fifty-eight had been full voting members of the previous Central Committee. Missing from the line-up were several former Politburo members who had been hardline critics not only of N.E.M. but also of Kadar's stands on a variety of other issues as well, including former Premier Ferenc Munnich and long time Trade Unions Council President Miklos Somogyi.[75] A major reorganization of the Council of Ministers in mid-1967 placed long-time supporters of the N.E.M. in nearly all of the key administrative positions, thus assuring as smooth as possible a transition, at least from the perspective of controlling bureaucratic obstructionism.

The principal factor that threatened to block the implementation of the reform was the international one. The N.E.M. went into full effect on January 1, 1968, at a time when, as we have noted, the international climate within the Soviet bloc had begun to chill distinctly with regard to the question of "market socialism." By this time, however, the groundwork for the N.E.M. had been so thoroughly laid that the top Hungarian leadership regarded themselves as unalterably committed to the basic outlines of their new system. Specific references to Hungary's N.E.M. were few, but the harsh foreign polemics against "the revisionist conceptions of Ota Sik" were pitched at a sufficiently theoretical level to cause some concern, since criticism of N.E.M. seemed logically implied by many of the attacks on the Czechoslovak reform. The armed intervention in Czechoslovakia by Warsaw Pact forces in August led to considerable fear among the Hungarian population that this event also portended the reversal of Hungary's political and economic gains of the recent past. The Hungarian leadership immediately took the position that nothing of the sort was implied, that the troubles in Czechoslovakia were essentially the result of the weakness of the Communist Party's leadership and not an inevitable result of new economic institutions. Politburo member Istvan Szirmai assured a mass rally in Budapest on August 27, 1968, that "the policy of the Party will remain unchanged both in substance and in methods."[76] Politburo member Karoly Nemeth reiterated on August 30, 1968, to another mass rally, "It is the unalterable decision of the Central Committee to pursue its previous policy, both in its internal life and in its foreign affairs. . . ."[77] The mass media throughout the country were intensively mobilized to convey the same message over and over — nothing would change.

The basic unity of the top Party leadership in support of N.E.M. seems to have stood them in good stead. The Hungarian leaders did not intend to back away from their policies unless it became absolutely necessary. There is no evidence that anyone in an important leadership position tried to take advantage of the international situation to scuttle the N.E.M. As time passed, much of the worry about Soviet disapproval tended to fade away, as favorable articles about the N.E.M. began to appear in the Soviet press.[78] It seems to have been enough for the Soviets to have the assurance that the Party in Hungary had the political situation well in hand, that the leading role of the Party was in no apparent danger, and that the Hungarian leadership had not the slightest intention of abandoning their close international political and economic links with the rest of the Soviet bloc. The Hungarian economic reform continued its orderly development throughout the remainder of the decade. When pressures arose that led to its modification, they were largely of economic and domestic political origin, as will be discussed in the following chapter.

The decisive factor in carrying through the Hungarian N.E.M. to a successful conclusion seems to have been the political skills demonstrated by Janos Kadar and his highly self-conscious efforts to prevent the inevitable disputes over the question of economic reform from causing a bitter and lasting division within the Party's top leadership. Kadar's consistently cautionary and moderate line on the necessity for persuasion rather than coercion in the relationship between the Party and the general public also found its counterpart in intra-Party relationships. Where possible, Kadar's strategy was to go to considerable lengths to reassure those who had doubts about his policy initiatives. Where necessary to preserve the basic integrity of his policies, however, Kadar was willing to mobilize his political powers to put a stop to overt manifestations of obstructionist activity. At the Ninth Congress, Kadar acknowledged that the newly-reaffirmed centrist-reformist line of the Party had not been attained without serious opposition:

> A section of our Party members have shown lack of understanding as to the novel solution of certain questions with regard to progress and our present-day conditions. Differences of opinion have arisen about . . . the equal rights of citizens, . . . the assessment of the economic position, and the development of the standard of living. The varying opinions on certain details spring fundamentally from the complex nature of our era. . . . With those who fail to understand certain details of the Party's policy, patient persuasion is the correct and expedient method. There are, however, those who knowingly opposed the Party's policy and entered the road of factionalism. We have firmly dealt with such Party members in accordance with the Party statutes.[79]

Characteristically, Kadar's punitive measures went no further than necessary to assure practical results: the great majority of the N.E.M. opponents who had to be removed from key positions were not publicly denounced or disgraced, and many of them were simply transferred to honorific posts where they would be unable to interfere. This policy considerably lowered the stakes for those who perceived themselves as unable to function successfully under the new system by offering the hope of a dignified retirement or a transfer to some other field of endeavor. (This was in sharp contrast to the factional struggles in Czechoslovakia, where, as conflict developed, reformists and their entrenched opponents made clear to each other that no quarter would be given: as a result, surrender was nearly impossible and continued resistance by all available means was virtually assured.)

The Economic Reform Deadlock in Poland

Proposals for reforming the system of economic planning and management have been put forward in greater numbers, over a longer period of time, and with greater theoretical sophistication in Poland than in any other Communist country. The writings and the more informal intellectual exchanges of such distinguished Polish economists as Oskar Lange, Michael Kalecki, and Wlodzimierz Brus had an enormous and widely acknowledged impact on socialist economic thought throughout the bloc and provided many of the theoretical underpinnings of the more radical economic reform programs introduced in Hungary and in Czechoslovakia. Yet ironically enough, despite Poland's status as a pioneer in the theory of market-oriented and decentralizing economic reform, Poland has lagged considerably behind most other European Communist countries in the translation of reformist theories into actual practice.   Despite major campaigns by reformers resulting in the Party's nominal affirmation of commitments to economic reforms in 1956-1957, 1961-1965, 1969-1970, 1971-1973, and 1981-88, the measures adopted have been modest (and poorly coordinated with each other), and the practical steps necessary for their implementation have been repeatedly blocked by bureaucratic resistance or fear of mass opposition.

In most respects, the high-water mark of the Polish economic reform movement was in 1957. The unique political climate prevailing in Poland following the dramatic events that brought Wladyslaw Gomulka to power in October of 1956 was particularly favorable for the proponents of far-reaching economic reforms. Indeed, one of Gomulka's first acts after assuming power was the appointment of an "Economic Council" as a new organ of the government. Chaired by Oskar Lange and including such prominent advocates of economic reform as Brus, Lipinski, Bobrowski, Popkiewicz, and Kalecki, the Economic Council was to be a permanent governmental body charged with the sole responsibility of developing the institutional reforms that would periodically prove necessary to insure the continuous progressive development of the national economy.   During 1957, the Economic Council's deliberations led to the elaboration and publication of two basic documents setting forth both the theoretical basis of a distinctive "Polish economic model" and prescribing concrete reforms of economic planning and administration to translate the theory into a functioning reality.[80]

The proposals of the "Theses" of the Economic Council called for a radical decentralization of the economy along essentially "market socialism" lines. Enterprises would be autonomous and self-governing, with the basic managerial authority vested in an elected worker's council and exercised under their supervision by the enterprise director, who would serve at the council's pleasure. (The workers' councils had already sprung into being spontaneously during the ferment of 1956 and were by no means the invention of the economic experts, who were merely ratifying what they took to be the established basic institution of the post-October order.) Enterprises would be substantially free to formulate their own production plans, to determine their own staffing procedures, and generally to make the basic micro-economic decisions on current production and on investment for expansion or modernization on the basis of available prices for the human and non-human factors of production. Enterprise revenues would be expected to cover not only the costs of materials and wages but also interest payments on borrowed funds, land rents, and the costs of purchasing and replacing the fixed capital of the enterprise. Profits of the enterprise (after payment of levies to the state for the use of socially-owned land and capital) would be available to the enterprise for additional investment or for distribution (in cash or as fringe benefits) to the employees.

The model differed from Lange's earlier conceptions in several important respects. The assumption that the Central Planning Board could flexibly set all prices and still achieve an approximation of optimal pricing was largely abandoned. The planners would attempt to set the prices of "key commodities" only (mainly widely used raw and semi-finished materials) while leaving most price determination to market forces (that is, allowing enterprises and purchasers to negotiate their own prices by means of contract, relying upon the competitive pressures of multiple suppliers and consumers to prevent monopolistic distortions).

Whereas Lange's pre-war model had envisioned managers as salaried civil servants obeying "Rule 1" and "Rule 2" simply out of respect for the law, in the new Polish model, managerial decision-making was to be guided directly by the injunction to maximize enterprise profitability (formally equivalent to the two rules in Walrasian equilibrium) and by direct financial incentives in the form of "profit-sharing" for both the director and the entire enterprise work force. (In effect, the enterprise would be renting the productive plant and machinery as well as the working capital from the state, with the work force retaining that portion of profits attributable to "good management" after turning over to the state the proportion representing simple returns to capital.)

The role of the central planners would be to anticipate the main lines of development, to shape investment policy where this involved establishing new enterprises or the provision of "public goods," to determine the basic proportions at the macro-economic level (investment rate, division of consumption between individual and collective forms, control of wage policies to prevent inflation, and so on), to insure smooth adjustments in the pricing mechanism, and a variety of other "visible hand" activities. In the transition period, the central authorities would continue to exercise a great many "administrative" prerogatives (especially wage and price limitations), but it was projected that the planning authorities would rely increasingly upon fiscal and monetary policy instruments and selective subsidies in the future, as the new system stabilized itself.

Although the proposals of the Economic Council were at first politely received by Polish political leaders, it soon became apparent that neither First Secretary Wladyslaw Gomulka nor most of the other top leadership were prepared to undertake such sweeping reforms. While the first set of "Theses" (pertaining mainly to organizational regroupings within the industrial sector) were officially "accepted in principle by the Polish government,"[81] the theses on the reform of the system of wages and prices were for the most part not accorded the same reception. Very few of the proposed reforms were actually implemented on an economy-wide basis, and, instead, a very large number of small-scale "experiments" employing different variants of the simplified administrative, cost-accounting, and incentive systems were undertaken in 1958.

The strategy of "experimentation" bought valuable time while Gomulka and his more conservative associates reconsolidated the Party's economic and political controls, most notably through the effective emasculation of the workers' councils by shifting most of their prerogatives to "Conferences of Workers' Self-Management" made up of one-third elected delegates and two-thirds appointed delegates of the management, the trade unions, and the Party committee. In addition to the neutralization of the workers' councils, the years 1958 and 1959 saw the return to prominence of a number of economic policy-makers of the early 1950's (most notably Eugeniusz Szyr and Julian Tokarski, who became vice-premiers, and Tadeusz Gede, who became First Deputy Chairman of the Planning Commission) and the demotion of some of the reform's more active advocates within the administration (Jerzy Morawski and Jerzy Albrecht, formerly secretaries of the Central Committee of the Party). While the Economic Council was not formally abolished until 1962, it became essentially inactive after 1959 because it was clear by then that its reformist recommendations were no longer taken seriously by the political leadership. In January of 1960, the new state of affairs was formalized by the repeal of most of the organizational changes introduced at the recommendation of the Economic Council back in 1957 and the reassertion of the discretionary authority of the Planning Commission to carry out detailed supervision of the construction of enterprise plans and their implementation.[82]

The main reasons for the retreat from the commitment to economic reform beginning in 1958 were both economic and political. From an economic point of view, a "go-slow" policy was justified principally by reference to the serious inflationary pressures that had built up because of the large wage increases won by the workers during 1956-1957 (average wages in industry rose by 11 percent and 19 percent in those two years).[83] The unwillingness of the Party leadership to loosen central authority with respect to prices and wages made it practically impossible to carry out any extensive restructuring of prices to bring them into closer correspondence with actual costs of production, and this in turn cast very serious doubt on the propriety of relying solely (or even mainly) on profit or other financial indicators for the guidance of micro-economic decision-making. Moreover, the decision by the Party to accelerate the rate of investment in 1959 led to a situation of excess "tautness" in the plan, with very serious disparities between the supply of and demand for producers' goods: under these circumstances, central rationing of materials was almost inescapable if planners' priorities were to be given effect in production.

From a political point of view, the retreat from economic reform was in part a byproduct of Gomulka's efforts to unify the Party by allowing a partial restoration to power of representatives of the Party's more "conservative" wing, who had tended to be shoved aside in policy-making during the "revolutionary" period of 1956-1957 but who were still powerfully represented among the local and regional cadres. The general reassertion of Party controls over Polish life was reflected in the economic sphere as a reassertion of Party controls within the enterprise (the undercutting of the workers' councils) and the greater subordination of the enterprise to the central planning apparatus (which was assumed to be closely supervised by the Party). The return of old-line economic administrators to positions within the economic policy-making establishment naturally led to a stronger tendency toward preserving the older economic model. Moreover, Poland's embrace of radical economic reform was not approved of by the Soviet leadership nor, indeed, by the leaders of any other Soviet bloc state, and, while the new etiquette of intra-bloc relations discouraged open interference in internal matters, it was clear that such deviation created tension in Polish-Soviet relations. The anti-revisionist campaign was in full swing throughout the bloc in the late 1950's, and the Polish leadership could scarcely avoid drawing the necessary conclusions. The salience of foreign pressures was made very clear in the debates at the Central Committee Plenum of February 1958, where the principal argument advanced by the extreme hard-liners (such as W. Klosiewicz and S. Lapot) against the new economic model was that it would create "a basic disproportion" between the Polish economy and that of other Communist countries and would hinder close cooperation with them.[84] Writing some years later, Wlodzimierz Brus (a former vice-chairman of the Economic Council) cited the pressure against the reforms from other socialist countries as the decisive factor in their ultimate defeat.[85]

Despite the government's increasingly anti-reformist complexion, the proponents of economic reform retained important footholds in the universities and research institutes and were still able to promote their views to some degree. The pages of the economic weekly *Zycie Gospodarczy* regularly provided a forum for genuine, if somewhat con-strained, criticism of the existing system of planning and management. Moreover, Gomulka's efforts at cementing Party unity involved a certain tolerance for limited diversity of views on policy questions, which enabled such reformist sympathizers as Jerzy Albrecht to continue to hold positions in the government's economic policy-making apparatus. Since Gomulka himself never built a large personal faction of his own within the Party, his approach to maintaining the unity of the Party concentrated on a careful balancing off of other factions in such a way that he and his closest associates on the Politburo maintained the balance of power. The condition of remaining in the leadership, however, was acceptance of the necessity for the Party to maintain a basically "centrist" line, avoiding splits by avoiding radical departures either to the right or to the left.[86]

The Soviet Twenty-Second Party Congress and the Liberman debates which followed gave a certain encouragement to Polish reformers, and Oskar Lange used the discussion of Gomulka's report from Moscow in November of 1961 to launch a new wave of critical analysis of the economic performance of the existing highly-centralized economic model.[87] Reformist proposals received another fillip in July of the following year, when a five-day congress of East European economists met in Warsaw (under Lange's chairmanship) to discuss methods of improving economic performance through more effective use of foreign trade and improved planning and administration. Increasing difficulties with fulfilling the demands of the highly ambitious five-year plan for 1961-1965 seemed to presage a more receptive political climate for reformist proposals.[88]

Yet the expectations of the reformers were largely disappointed. Gomulka's announcement of the scrapping of most of the highly ambitious targets of the current five-year plan at the end of November 1962 made no mention whatever of changes in either the structure of production or the model of planning and management as a possible solution to the difficulties, but rather concentrated on the need for greater discipline on the part of planners to avoid over-ambitious targets without adequate reserves to meet contingencies. Gomulka himself was clearly not going to take the initiative in formulating or mobilizing support for an economic reform program.[89]

Nevertheless, support for measures of economic rationalization tended to grow as the first half of 1963 brought but little improvement in the economic situation. The report of the Politburo on the plan for 1964 took a somewhat more open-minded attitude toward proposals for changes in the system of incentives as a means of improving plan fulfillment.[90] The "theses" prepared for discussion at the Fourth Party Congress (June 1964) showed clear reformist influences,[91] and the Congress itself approved in its resolution a statement that "profitability of production and strict cost accounting should be the basic criteria of all economic activity."[92] Yet the same Congress which gave verbal endorsement to those relatively vague proposals for economic reform also elevated several of the economic planners most critical of radical economic reform proposals to membership in the Politburo (Eugeniusz Szyr and Franciszek Waniolka).

The Polish economic reform program[93] that emerged in 1964-1965 was constructed principally by incumbent economic policy-makers, especially long-time Chairman of the Planning Commission Stefan Jedrychowski, with only a minimal involvement of outside experts. (The Economic Council had been formally abolished at the end of 1963.) It bore the marks of its creation at the hands of reluctant reformers. The process of bureaucratic bargaining and compromise produced a reform characterized by a piecemeal and uncoordinated approach. The new "system" was not the result of a single master conception but rather a laundry list of miscellaneous measures aimed at correcting particular immediate shortcomings, and this led to very difficult problems of inconsistency between the various provisions as well as to a lack of attention to the careful sequencing of institutional changes necessary for a smooth transition.[94] Polish commentators not only acknowledged the *ad hoc* character of the reform but also attempted to portray this as a mark of pragmatic realism and a positive virtue:

> Poland bases her reforms' implementation on the principle of *evolutionary* changes consisting of experiments, of introducing new solutions of limited scope. . . . The reforms' implementation is considered as a *constant* process. . . . The reforms being carried out in Poland are not based upon any new theoretical or ideological orientation but mainly on *practical observations*. . . . The solution of all these complex problems is not possible on the basis of a single theoretical approach.[95]

In order to limit the demand of enterprises for excess allocations of machinery and materials allocated free of charge under the old system, the Polish reform provided for charges on the value of enterprise capital, the financing of enterprise investment from revenues or from interest-bearing bank loans, and even for a rudimentary differentiated rent on land. However, the interest rates charged were very low for the most part (an average of 3 percent on investment credits and an average annual rate of about 5 percent on the gross value of fixed assets — which was very much less than the marginal rate of productivity of investment). Moreover, the rates of interest charged were varied systematically from industry to industry, with favored but relatively unprofitable industries (heavy industry and mining, especially) enjoying concessionary rates. Free budgetary grants of investment funds continued to be provided for a very substantial fraction of Polish industry, accounting still for more than one-quarter of all investment in 1968.[96] Such systematic favoritism rendered ineffective any attempt to compare the relative social profitabilities of various industries and tended to freeze existing patterns of investment allocations.

Another aspect of the reform was supposed to be the improvement of the system of material incentives. Instead of the old gross output target, the chief indicator of enterprise success (and the chief determinant of managerial bonus payments) was to be a version of "profitability" (to be precise, the ratio of profits to prime costs). Bonuses were to be paid for achieving the planned level of the profit/cost ratio, with penalties for underachievement but no additional bonus for overfulfillment. This system provided some incentive for holding down costs, but the fact that the expected level of the profit/cost ratio would be redetermined every year for every enterprise in the plan according to the "ratchet principle" meant that managers still had strong incentives to engage in many of the unlovely practices of the old system: concealment of reserves, foregoing of opportunities for "once-only" profits, prolonged bargaining with the central authorities as to where the planned targets should be set, and so on. By basing the bonus on planned profit rather than on absolute profit attained, the "objective meaning" of profitability as a synthetic indicator of efficiency was effectively vitiated, and managerial bonuses became once again primarily a function of skill in bargaining for an easy plan rather than of economic performance. Moreover, the new bonus system did not *replace* the old bonus system (which provided for more than a dozen different specialized bonuses for the fulfillment of various aspects of the plan) but was added to it, accounting for only about half of the available bonus funds. While the maximum size of the profitability bonus was to be based on attainment of planned profitability, the degree to which the bonuses could actually be paid out was dependent upon simultaneous fulfillment of a number of additional conditions, most of them having to do with the proper observance of the assigned assortment and quantities of output. The overall result was an incentive system so complex as to be quite literally incomprehensible to the managerial personnel whose behavior was supposed to be regulated. (A survey of white collar workers in industry in 1967 revealed that 62 percent of the population sampled did not understand how their bonuses were computed. Not very surprisingly, 71 percent offered the opinion that their bonuses had no incentive effect whatever on their work.[97])

Tight central regulation of prices and wages remained a major concern of the Polish authorities under the new system, and Stefan Jedrychowski, the chief of the Planning Commission and a major architect of the reform, maintained that this principle constituted "the essence of socialist planning."[98] In Poland there was no appreciable experimentation with ceiling prices, free range prices, or free prices for industrial products, in sharp contrast to the more innovative approaches taken in Czechoslovakia, Hungary, and Bulgaria. On the contrary, economists advocating a much larger role for market forces in price formation were criticized by the reform's principal architect as "anti-socialist" and "utopian."[99] Moreover, beyond adherence to the principle of centralism in price-fixing, the blueprint's account of *how* prices should be fixed was wildly contradictory. Prices were to be "stable" but also "flexible," should "reflect demand" but also "direct demand," should "promote efficiency" but also insure profitability to all enterprises "conforming their production to the prescriptions of the plan.[100] Comprehensive reform of the price structure was put off indefinitely, but new "factory prices" covering about 40 percent of industrial output were introduced in January of 1967, principally in those industries importantly involved in international trade. Official concern with controlling inflationary pressures and the continued priority given to increasing the overall rate of investment as the chief means of promoting growth led the designers to retain detailed central control over both the total work force of individual enterprises and their absolute wage funds. (In this last respect, the Polish reform did not go even as far as the Soviet blueprint of 1965.)

The failure to carry out a thoroughgoing price reform meant that profitability was less useful as a synthetic indicator of enterprise performance than it otherwise might have been, and therefore planners felt justified in prescribing additional compulsory targets as a counterweight to the "pathological" consequences that might result from price imperfections. This logic, however, easily lent itself to the justification of retaining old habits of "petty tutelage" endemic to the ministerial bureaucracies. The proliferation of supplementary indicators threatened to erode the very autonomy of managerial decision-making that was supposed to liberate local initiative in the cause of improving efficiency. As each piecemeal reform was introduced, pathological tendencies derived in good part from the absence of complementary reform often appeared and were responded to by *ad hoc* administrative methods.

As was also the case in the U.S.S.R., East Germany and Bulgaria, many of the directive powers nominally taken away from the ministries devolved, not upon the enterprises, but upon the *zjednoczenia* or industrial associations. Membership was compulsory for the enterprises, and the association director's rights to requisition and redistribute enterprise profits, promulgate binding directives, and overrule enterprise decisions were formidable. Thus, compulsory targets theoretically abolished at the level of the ministry could be (and often were) reintroduced by the industrial associations at the "suggestion" of the ministerial authorities.

Bureaucratic tactics of delay, misinterpretation of general policy guidelines, and even outright refusal to cease and desist from the issuance of unauthorized directives were quite common during the period 1965 to 1967. This resistance to the genuine implementation of what was already a rather watered-down economic reform was evidently quite effective and was repeatedly complained about by the advocates of further rationalization. *Zycie Gospodarcze* interviewed a prominent industrial director in April of 1966, inquiring as to the effect of greater enterprise autonomy on his own day-to-day work. The response elicited was:

> To be quite frank, I must say that in my position I have noticed no difference. The scope of decisions I can make has remained identical, as it was before. . . . Over the years, methods of operating have taken hold and we cannot get

away from them. No one has the power and — in a certain sense — the courage.[101]

Council of Ministers decrees following the June 1965 Plenum had ordered reductions in the compulsory plan indicators directed to the enterprises that should have cut their numbers by some 30 percent. Yet M. Malicki's survey of enterprises in Warsaw in the summer of 1966 (more than one year after the decrees) revealed that the number of binding targets being handed down was exactly the same as before the "reform."[102] Similarly, the much ballyhooed goal of increasing the investment funds available to the enterprise managers for their own discretionary use in upgrading productivity went almost entirely unfulfilled. While about 10 percent of total investment funds had remained at the enterprise level during 1965, the new system theoretically allowed for up to 22 percent to remain there: but in actual practice, the industrial associations took advantage of their powers to increase the required levels of enterprise contributions to the association reserve funds and effectively soaked up all of the new enterprise resources.[103] By mid-1967, *Zycie Gospodarcze*'s editor-in-chief was publicly charging that, although two full years had passed since the Party's Central Committee had given its final approval to the "new methods of planning and management," nevertheless "the actual implementation of the reforms at all levels still leaves much to be desired." The reason for this was not merely "the old habits and conditioned reflexes which are the heritage of the old system," but also the deliberate strategy of bureaucratic opponents of the reform who "stand by the old methods and the familiar routine in the hope that the old ways will return."[104]

The relative ineffectiveness of the attempts to implement the economic reforms of 1964-1965 was directly traceable to the failure of the Party to speak with one voice on the issue and to mobilize its formidable organizational resources for the systematic overcoming of bureaucratic passive resistance. The Party's declarations of policy in favor of economic reform were sufficiently vague (and internally inconsistent) to allow those with vested interests opposed to any genuine decentralization or marketization of the economy to sabotage implementation with impunity, so long as Gomulka and his closest associates in charge of the Party apparatus did not see fit to make such violations grounds for the summary imposition of Party or administrative punishment. This Gomulka was not prepared to do for several reasons.

In the first place, neither Gomulka nor his most intimate and trusted advisors (Zenon Kliszko, Ignacy Loga-Sowinski, and Marian Spychalski) were trained in economics, and only Loga-Sowinski (a long-time trade union activist and, since 1956, the head of the trade union federation) had administrative experience even tangentially related to the planning and management of the industrial sector of the economy. Apart from his very deep convictions about the political necessity of extreme gradualism in the socialization of agriculture, Gomulka's attitudes toward complex questions of economic administration and growth strategy were essentially orthodox, and his attitude toward the "intellectuals" who were the foremost advocates of economic reform was one of intense suspicion.[105] In general, Gomulka held himself aloof from the whole issue of economic reform, regarding the maintenance of a very high rate of accumulation and investment and the insistence upon stricter labor discipline as the chief factors to assure Poland's economic growth.[106] Gomulka was enough of a pragmatist to go along with limited rearrangements of economic practices and institutions when the economy was experiencing difficulties, but he was by no means an initiator or even a very convincing advocate of any particular approach to economic reform.

A second reason for the relative passivity of the Party's inner circle when it came to mobilizing support for the rapid and businesslike implementation of the economic reforms was a more explicitly political one. Gomulka's "centrist" policies corresponded to Gomulka's position as final arbiter presiding over a Party leadership that remained unusually factionalized, despite the rather extensive purges of the Party rank and file in 1957-1959. In the early 1960's, the Party's Central Committee, Secretariat, and Politburo still contained adherents to several rival cliques: former adherents of the "Natolin" group, which had opposed Gomulka's return to power in 1956 and which espoused a return to the hard-line policies and close rapport with the Soviet Union that characterized the early 1950's; former adherents of the "Pulawy" group, which had supported Gomulka's ascendancy but which increasingly became disappointed at Gomulka's failure to institute sweeping political liberalization and economic reforms; Gomulka's small band of close supporters who had been purged and imprisoned along with him in the late 1940's and who were returned to power by him after 1956; and several smaller groupings based principally upon personal loyalties arising out of long association and common background and experiences (ex-Social Democrats who had come over with Premier Jozef Cyrankiewicz at the time of the merger of the two working class parties in 1948, Edward Gierek's "technocrats" with long experience in common fields of economic planning and administration, and so on).[107]

A major factor in the intensification of the intra-Party factional struggle during the 1960's was the rise to prominence of a new grouping, composed principally of veterans of the wartime Communist underground and known as the "Partisans." While their political activities were characterized by a very considerable degree of opportunism, their political program was describable as a blend of militant Communism with xenophobic and ethnically exclusionary nationalism. Calling for a revival of the ideological fervor and the spirit of self-sacrifice of the wartime partisan struggle as the prerequisite for restoring dynamism to Polish society, the Partisans set out to purge from the ranks of the Party leadership, by any means necessary, those elements which they held responsible for the "degeneration" of the Polish revolution into cynicism and *petite bourgeois* egoism — the Jews, liberals, and "revisionist" intellectuals. Their anti-intellectualism and their personal antagonisms toward the reformist "Pulawians" led the Partisans to adopt a hostile attitude toward proposals for economic reform emanating from these quarters. While economic issues were not uppermost in the Partisans' minds, their inclination was basically toward a kind of unsophisticated economic "fundamentalism."

While Gomulka seems to have had little sympathy for the Partisans' anti-Semitism, their general policy orientation was essentially that espoused by the domestic wing of the Polish Workers' Party under Gomulka's leadership during World War II and the immediate postwar years, and a number of the Partisans who had been Gomulka's comrades-in-arms during that period had shared his fate during the purges of the late 1940's. Partisan leaders such as Mieczyslaw Moczar, Ryszard Dobieszak, Franciszek Szlachcic, and Grzegorz Korczynski were raised to high positions in the police and intelligence services after Gomulka's return to power, and others, like Zygmunt Duszinski, and Alexander Kokoszyn, were placed in key positions in the military establishment. (Adam Bromke, writing in the early 1960's, identified General Wojciech Jaruzelski as having close contacts with the Partisan faction as well.)[108] From this power base, the partisans set out to expand their political influence during the early 1960's, achieving their first major success with the virtually complete takeover of the mass organization for World War II veterans, the "Z.Bo.Wi.D." In July and November of 1963, their intrigues led to the expulsion from the Politburo and Secretariat of the Party of two prominent (Jewish) leaders of the reformist "Pulawy" group, Roman Zambrowski and Wladyslaw Matwin.

The Fourth Party Congress of June 1964 (originally scheduled for March 1963) climaxed a period of serious Party infighting. Gomulka himself had been attacked by some of the diehards of the "Natolin" faction within the

Central Committee, who had gone so far as to circulate a clandestine pamphlet accusing him of a "rightist-nationalist deviation" and even of adhering to a "bourgeois ideology."[109]   The "Pulawy" group attempted to recoup some of their declining political fortunes by taking advantage of the economic difficulties of 1963 to push for a more comprehensive economic reform, culminating in an angry indictment of Gomulka's economic policies by Zambrowski at the March 1964 Central Committee meeting.   There were even rumors that the "centrist" secretary of the Silesian Party organization and Politburo member, Edward Gierek, was working to bring about Gomulka's honorable retirement.[110]

Gomulka's political survival in 1963-1964 was the result of an intricate set of maneuvers whereby he played off the various factions against each other and made strategic policy compromises calculated to isolate his most fervent critics and to regain support for his "centrist" line among their more cautious sympathizers.   With the aid of the Partisans in the security apparatus, the ringleaders of a Natolinist conspiracy were exposed, and several were removed from their posts (including Central Committee members Klosiewicz, Mijal, and Nieszporek).   Yet at the Fourth Congress, the former Natolinists Szyr and Waniolka, who had remained loyal to Gomulka, were promoted to the Politburo.   The Partisans acquired candidate-membership in the Politburo for their ally Ryszard Strzelecki (who became a full member later that same year at the death of Aleksander Zawadzki), and the Partisans' chief leader, General Mieczyslaw Moczar, became Minister of the Interior shortly afterwards.   The most "radical" of the reformists in the Pulawy group (Zambrowski, Morawski, and Matwin) lost their seats on the Central Committee, yet others, such as Finance Minister Jerzy Albrecht, retained important policy-making positions and even were rewarded by the Congress's vague endorsement of a new economic reform.   The position of Premier Cyrankiewicz and his small group of ex-Social Democratic associates was reaffirmed (despite the fact that the Partisans had been seeking his ouster), and a number of younger second and third echelon leaders in the Party *apparat* and the state administration who were not identified with any particular faction or strongly-held ideological position were promoted to the Central Committee and even the Secretariat.   Edward Gierek came to some sort of understanding with Gomulka and emerged as his informally designated heir-apparent.

The result of all these Byzantine maneuverings was to leave Wladyslaw Gomulka still in his overall dominant position within the Party.   Yet this was achieved only at the price of preserving the factional divisions within the Party's top leadership, with resulting gross inconsistencies and incon-

gruities in the realm of policy-making and policy implementation. A
tightening up of police controls over the intelligentsia and the launching
of a major ideological campaign to combat the menace of revisionism were
pursued simultaneously with the drafting of the economic reform. The
result was that the program of economic reform unveiled during 1965 was
designed principally by relatively uncommitted technocrats and
administrators rather than by the most ardent proponents of far-reaching
change. And practical implementation of the already much-compromised
reforms was entrusted to the very bureaucracy whose perquisites they
threatened.

The political precondition for any kind of reform at all was that it should
not completely alienate any of the politically potent factions remaining in
Gomulka's shaky grand coalition. A determined effort to push through a
consistent set of economic reforms and to ensure their thorough implementation would very likely have precipitated a major and public split in the
Party's ranks of a kind that could easily have led to serious political
instability, yet a complete failure to act would also have been dangerous
because of the long-run threat posed by the increasingly high costs of an
"extensive" growth strategy to the masses' standard of living. Under the
circumstances, Gomulka chose to temporize rather than to take the risks
which would have been associated with a second mobilization of popular
forces against the Party and state "establishment" on the pattern of
1956-1957. Such a course would once again have imperiled the leading
role of the Communist Party in Polish political life and would likely have
triggered responses from the Soviet leaders that would have been dangerous
to the *modus vivendi* so laboriously worked out by Gomulka over the
previous decade.

The movement for more radical economic reform, which was already
faltering scarcely two years after the Party's formal endorsement of partial
reform, received a near mortal blow during 1968. The Arab-Israeli "Six
Day War" of June 1967, in which the Polish government followed the
Soviet line of support for the Arabs, provided the Partisans with a pretext
for advancing their own political fortunes by launching a witch-hunt against
covert "Zionist" sympathizers within the Party. The first targets of the
purge were journalists whose reporting of the war had been insufficiently
anti-Israel, but in December, the Partisans achieved major successes with
the replacement of the (Jewish) editors of *Trybuna Ludu* (the Party daily)
and *Zycie Warszawy* (the principal daily newspaper in the capital) by
opportunists willing to cooperate more enthusiastically with the Partisan-
dominated security services in the exposure of Zionist plots and their
intimate connection with the promotion of revisionist policies in the youth

organizations, the Writers' Union, the universities, and even within the Party itself. After the student demonstrations of March 8, 1968, protesting the government's increasingly repressive cultural policies and expressing support for Polish emulation of the emerging reformist policies of the Czechoslovak government, the purge intensified, spurred on by a propaganda campaign carefully orchestrated by the Partisans and carried out by their supporters at the editorial desks of the country's principal newspapers.[111] Party cells were advised by the media to take a principled stand against "cosmopolitans" in their midst and expel them "without waiting for directives 'from the top',"[112] thereby bypassing the normal Party channels (which the partisans did not yet control) and confronting the Party leadership with *faits accomplis*. At somewhat higher levels of the Party, the participation of the sons and daughters of several prominent Party leaders of the Pulawy faction (mostly, but not entirely, of Jewish extraction) in the university demonstrations was made the pretext for the condemnation and demotion or expulsion of their parents, greatly weakening the more reformist wing of the Party. The most prominent victims of the post-March purges were Finance Minister Jerzy Albrecht (who lost not only his state positions but also his seat on the Central Committee) and Edward Ochab (the former First Secretary of the Party who had opened the way for Gomulka's return to power in 1956).

The purges of "Jews, liberals and revisionists" not only drastically diminished the influence of the more principled advocates of economic reform within policy-making circles but also threatened to eradicate them on their own home grounds, the universities and research institutes. More than one hundred faculty members were dismissed at Warsaw University alone, and hundreds more were fired at other institutions, including the Academy of Sciences. Economic reformers were among the most prominent targets of the purges, denounced not only as "Zionist agents" but also as "the principal carriers of the deadly bacilli of economic revisionism."[113] They were accused of plotting to bring about a new economic system in which "real power will pass into the hands of a narrow group of economic experts" and in which "the leading role of the Party would be reduced to a minimum" — a system that would "deify the market mechanism" and promote "enrichment as the central value of life."[114] While some of the most internationally respected figures (such as Michael Kalecki and Edward Lipinski — Oskar Lange had died in 1965) were simply pushed into retirement, others (such as Wlodzimierz Brus) were not only dismissed and subjected to public vilification but also forcibly deported to Israel. Many of their younger and less prominent followers suffered demotions and transfers or were even hounded out of their professions entirely. Others, protected by the professional solidarity of their colleagues, managed to hold on to their positions by performing self-criticism and keeping a low profile until the campaign against them died away in October of 1968.

By the time of the Fifth P.U.W.P. Congress in November of 1968, Gomulka had managed to bring the factional fighting under control and had turned aside the partisans' bid for complete dominance of the Party. While the new Central Committee dropped thirty-one of the eighty-three members elected at the previous Congress (including all of the Jewish members except Szyr and Starewicz, most of the non-Jewish Pulawians, and all but three of the former members of the pre-merger Socialist Party), the vacancies were not for the most part filled by any influx of readily identifiable Partisans. On the contrary, most of the new members were in their late thirties or early forties (too young to have played much part in the wartime activities of the Party), well-educated, and noteworthy principally for their experience in economic administration. The Partisans' principle leader, General Moczar, had been advanced to a position as a Central Committee Secretary and candidate member of the Politburo in July, but the Congress did not promote him to full membership in the Politburo (which had been widely expected) nor did it add any of his followers to that body as even candidate members. Moczar's old enemies, the ex-Natolinians Szyr and Waniolka, were ousted from the Politburo and from their positions in the economic planning apparatus, but they were replaced by men with reputations as essentially pragmatic economic administrators (one of whom, Boleslaw Jaszczuk, had been a member of Oskar Lange's Economic Council — albeit one of the less radical ones).

Gomulka's advancement of a younger, better-educated, and less dogmatic generation of "pragmatists" and "technocrats" as a counterweight to the ambitions of the Partisans brought about a rather rapid and surprising turnaround in the field of economic policies. While endorsing no wholesale revamping of the economic system, the Fifth Congress took note of and condemned the lackadaisical manner in which the rather mild reforms approved by the Party in 1965 had been implemented by the economic bureaucracy, and this was followed by a major shake-up of the economic leadership. The long-time chairman of the Planning Commission (and Politburo member) Stefan Jedrychowski was replaced by Boleslaw Jaszczuk as the Party's chief spokesman on economic matters. Also replaced at the same time were the two deputy chairmen of the Planning Commission and the chairmen of the Committee on Labor and Wages and the Committee on Science and Technology. There followed shortly thereafter a series of changes at the ministerial level, including the ministers of Finance, Light Industry, Food Industry, and Internal Trade, as well as the chairmen of the Price Commission and the National Bank.

The April 1969 Plenum of the new Central Committee was devoted almost entirely to discussion of the economy and particularly of the serious shortfalls in the 1968-1969 plans. (Planned growth rates were being attained only because of above-plan increases in industrial employment, which were driving labor productivity down and causing severe inflationary pressures because of the resulting over-expansion of the wage fund.) Reaffirming the Fifth Congress's pledge to have the long-delayed reforms in full operation by January 1971, the Plenum called for strengthening the role of the industrial associations in elaborating the economic plan, for a more rigorous insistence on curbing the practice of granting "free" investment funds to favored branches instead of interest-bearing bank loans, for an improvement in the structure of wholesale and retail prices so that they would more closely correspond to actual social costs, and for a closer linkage between enterprises' financial performance and the availability of funds for increasing wages and bonuses. Specific measures to these ends were elaborated and approved by subsequent meetings of the Central Committee in 1969 and 1970, spurred on by the deteriorating economic situation.

The new determination to implement the economic measures that had long been a part of the Party's official program was manifest in the more energetic performance of the Party and state organs responsible for overall guidance of the economic bureaucracy.   Unfortunately, however, implementation was being carried out under extremely unfavorable economic circumstances, and the preoccupation with the current economic crises led the architects of the plans for transition to take certain decisions which were to have the most serious political consequences. Specifically, Gomulka's new economic policy-makers were extremely concerned at the very serious inflationary pressures that had built up as a result of the overly rapid growth of employment in the socialist sector, which had expanded the wage-funds paid out above the planned levels at the same time that bottle-necks and shortfalls were preventing the consumer goods branches of the economy from achieving even their modest planned levels of output. Implementation of the new systems of price determination and of material incentives would therefore coincide with rigorous "austerity" in incomes policy. In effect, the measures to implement the new incentives program as of January 1, 1971, provided also for freezing the total wage fund at the 1970 level until at least the middle of 1972.[115] Since the new scheme also envisioned a tightening of labor norms and a greater differentiation of workers' incomes according to individual and group productivity, this implied that many of those adjudged to be relatively less productive would suffer cuts in their money incomes (or even involuntary discharge[116]). The announcement of very large increases in the prices of foodstuffs in mid-December of 1970 (which was also part of the economic reform package, designed to insure that prices covered costs of production and to redirect demand away from foodstuffs toward durable consumers' goods) multiplied the adverse impact of wages policy on working class living standards. Increases of 15 to 30 percent in food costs (with the greatest increases decreed for the price of meat) meant that the freeze in nominal money incomes was transformed into an actual reduction of average real wages for manual workers.[117]

The announcements of the price increases triggered the massive strikes, demonstrations, and violence that led to Gomulka's ouster by the Party's Politburo and his replacement as First Secretary by Edward Gierek. The price for restoring order in the factories was the prompt repeal of both the price increases and the new system for determining remuneration, the sacking of Boleslaw Jaszczuk and the other policy-makers closely associated with the austerity policies, and the promise of very substantial improvements in the standard of living over the next few years. Although the changes in the leadership brought about by Gierek's consolidation of his personal position (the removal of Gomulka's "inner circle" from the Politburo and Secretariat, followed by the demotion of Moczar and his partisan followers[118]) replaced many of the policy-makers formerly most antagonistic towards major reforms in the system of economic planning and management with younger, better-educated, and more "pragmatic" elements, the political realities dictated that price reform and changes in the system of material incentives could scarcely be attempted without the grave risk of renewed mass unrest.[119] Since major modifications in the structure of prices and material incentives were essential preconditions of any "radical" market-oriented and decentralizing reforms along the lines of Hungary's or pre-invasion Czechoslovakia's, the "comprehensive program of economic reforms" called for by Gierek at the February 1971 Plenum of the Central Committee[120] (and investigated by a new "commission of experts" appointed immediately thereafter) eventuated only in a series of "partial solutions" introduced in 1971-1973, with other more comprehensive measures to be postponed until the 1976-1980 five-year plan.[121] The "fourth wave" of the movement for economic reform in Poland, like the first three, never surmounted the political barriers to advance beyond the stage of administrative rearrangements within an essentially centralized and non-market oriented system.

CHAPTER IV

POLITICAL IMPACT OF THE ECONOMIC REFORMS

> "There is nothing more difficult to take in hand,
> more perilous to conduct, or more uncertain in
> its success, than to take the lead in the introduction
> of a new order of things. Because the innovator
> has for enemies all those who have done well
> under the old conditions, and lukewarm defenders
> who may do well under the new."
>
> Machiavelli
> *The Prince*
> Everyman Editions
> London 1958(p.29)

The economic reform proposals elaborated during the 1960's represented an effort to secure better performance from the socialist economy by rationalizing economic organization to conform to a higher stage of social and economic development in which it was assumed that "intensive" approaches to growth would have to replace "extensive" approaches. But an economic system is never merely the realization of pure reason, nor is it the simple result of rational assignment of economic roles to individuals according to the principle of comparative advantage. Concrete economic systems are also historically developed power structures that function in accordance with particularized divisions of power and authority among individuals and among the various institutions and departments. Proposed reforms normally encounter opposition not merely due to the inertia of established habits but also due to the self interest of incumbent power-holders who foresee the loss or erosion of their own privileged positions as a likely by-product.

In the countries ruled by Communist parties, the deliberate fusion of the economic elite with the political and social elites makes it particularly likely that instrumentally-conceived changes in economic institutions will rather quickly become political conflicts precisely because of the lack of any clearly delineated economic sphere of life "outside of politics." The proposed economic reforms of the 1960's were of such scope and magnitude that literally millions of people would be affected by the resulting redistributions of power, status, and material well-being. When people became aware of the personal consequences they might expect, many of them were mobilized into more or less explicitly political activity seeking some measure of control over the outcomes.

As should be evident from the account thus far, the highly concentrated distribution of political and economic decision-making power in East European countries, along with the elite's near-monopoly of access to relevant information, virtually assured that the early stages of the economic reform process would involve only a relatively small number of people who were strategically placed to exert influence on economic policy-making: the upper ranks of the Party leadership and their staffs, the important officials of the central economic planning and administrative apparatus, and (largely at the discretion of the former) co-opted economic experts from the universities and research institutes. To the extent permitted by the authorities, advocates of economic reform tried to widen their base of supporters through publicity, primarily employing popular essays of a critical and deliberately provocative character in the mass media. Public discussion of the previously undiscussible alerted the more politically sophisticated attentive public that changes in the established system were being seriously entertained by at least part of the top Party leadership and that consequently there might opportunities to exert influence on the outcome by making appropriate representations through whatever particularized channels of access might be available to them. Public discussions intended by the leadership to prepare the public for institutional or policy changes tended to call forth expressions of opinion not only by the reformist intelligentsia but also by members of other elite groups with a more skeptical or hostile attitude toward reform, and the net effect was to crystallize larger opinion groups within the ranks of the informed public. (Where this process of public discussion was most inhibited, the advocates of economic reform tended to be disadvantaged, since the inability to mobilize a somewhat broader public in support of reform proposals meant that most of the input into the elite decision process would come from the existing political and economic administration, most of whose members had vested interests that predisposed them to oppose important aspects of the reform.)

While the relatively sophisticated participants at earlier stages of the reform process were acting in anticipation of the results that the economic reform might be expected to have, most people in Eastern Europe were neither trained in economics nor accustomed by virtue of their daily pattern of activities to think about the economy in systematic terms. The common man was rather unlikely to form any very strongly-held convictions about the consequences of esoteric modifications in the economic mechanism so long as the reform remained in the stage of preliminary theoretical discussions. But once the stage of practical implementation or large-scale experimentation arrived, ordinary people suddenly found themselves having to adjust their daily routines and plans to a number of rather unsettling changes that affected them both as consumers and as participants in the process of production. While some of these changes were of a positive nature, many others were not, especially in the initial stages of the transition.   The result was a substantial heightening of social and economic tensions during the first years of trying out of the new economic models, and the regulation and canalization of these tensions therefore became a major preoccupation of political leadership at all levels, imposing significant constraints on the policies that the Party was able or willing to pursue. These effects were most marked where the reforms were most radical — in Czechoslovakia and Hungary — but were by no means absent elsewhere.

Managers, Apparatchiki, and Bureaucrats

Reforms of economic planning and management during the 1960's mainly had to do with adjusting the relationship of the socialist enterprise (the basic unit of organization responsible for the actual carrying out of productive activity) to the supervisory agencies in the capital responsible for assuring that enterprise activities conformed to the political, economic, and social preferences of the country's top political leadership. The general thrust of the reforms was toward enlarging the sphere of discretionary decision-making at the enterprise level to take better advantage of the (necessarily dispersed) knowledge of particular circumstances of time and place that crucially affect the efficiency of production. Simultaneously, the enhancement of enterprise autonomy would free the central planners from their constant preoccupation with details of current production and distribution so that they might better devote their limited manpower to elucidating the longer-term macro-economic choices which would determine the basic directions of future economic development. The increase of enterprise autonomy was to be accomplished by reducing the degree of detail specified in the centrally imposed plan as legally binding targets for enterprise management. "Vertical" relations of domination and subordination between the enterprise and the superior agencies would be de-emphasized, while "horizontal" relationships of bargaining and exchange among enterprises would assume a larger role in the day to day affairs of economic management.

Recognizing that increased discretion at the level of production was a necessary but not a sufficient condition for the improvement of economic performance, reformers identified two further problems to be solved. Enterprise decision-makers would require not only *autonomy* to make meaningful decisions but also *information* which would enable them to determine the socially optimal course of action and *incentives* actually to pursue that course once it was identified. The reformers believed that the primary method of transmitting the necessary information about social preferences (understood as some combination of consumers' preferences and the preferences of the national political leadership) ought to be a system of prices reflecting both costs of production and relative scarcities (supplemented to varying degrees by legal restrictions and administrative interventions). With a properly designed price system in place, profitability would become an adequate, if imperfect, gauge of net social benefits. The element of motivation would be provided by linking the material interests of the management and work force to the financial results of enterprise activities, normally by means of forming wage and bonus funds of the enterprise in determinate proportion to enterprise profitability.

Under the established system of planning and management, the functions of determining the socially optimal choice in micro-economic decision-making and motivating the relevant actors to behave accordingly were performed in quite different fashion and by incumbents of different social roles. The state plan approved by the top Party leadership was defined as the only scientifically based representation of the social interest. In effect, those members of the state bureaucracy who disaggregated plan targets from the level of the ministry to the level of the branch and on down to the level of the individual enterprise in the form of administrative directives based their claim to legitimate authority (and hence status and material privilege) on their mediating role between the truth of Marxist-Leninist science as apprehended by the Party and the concrete implementation of Party policy through the regulation of production and distribution. For the enterprise to serve the social interest, it was only necessary that the director obey the commands of his superiors in the bureaucracy and in turn secure obedience by his own subordinates. Obedience to the directives of the plan was ultimately sanctioned by coercion[1] (since plan directives had the binding force of law), but the more proximate sources of motivation to secure fulfillment of the plan were material incentives[2] (distributed principally according to rank and relative success of the enterprises in achieving or over-achieving administratively assigned gross production targets derived from the plan) and moral incentives[3] (whose manipulation in support of planned objectives was a principal task of the primary Communist Party organizations and the Party's most important "transmission belt" within the factory, the trade union committee). The desire for promotion and the attainment of greater prestige, power, and authority was also a powerful motivating factor for ambitious individuals, and these rewards too were dispensed primarily by the Communist Party *apparat* (through the *nomenklatura* system[4]) based on the aspirant's proven record of active and enthusiastic participation in the implementation of Party policies (one of the most important of which was always the fulfillment and over-fulfillment of the economic plan).

The logic of decentralization, objectivization of social priorities in a flexible price system, enterprise guidance by means of "financial levers" in preference to direct administrative directives, and greater emphasis on a rationalized system of material incentives rather than threats or moral exhortations, implied drastic changes in the functional importance and practical influence of various roles in the economic organization as well as in the requisite skills for successful performance of these roles.

To the degree that the enterprise director acquired discretionary control over such key decisions as the assortment and quantity of planned output; the technological variants and mix of materials used in production; the size, composition, and remuneration of the work force; the level and character of investment for the expansion or the technological modernization of the enterprise's productive plant; and the conditions under which the products of the enterprise are to be sold — to that degree the bureaucratic strata in the branch administrations and industrial ministries would be rendered superfluous.

In the more extreme versions of the reformist program, the industrial ministries would be abolished altogether and the branch administrations would be reduced to the status of (smaller) service organizations for the autonomous enterprises, supplying marketing research, disseminating useful technological developments and the like. For example, Ota Sik, the principal architect of the Czechoslovak economic reform, writes that

It was necessary, first and foremost, to reduce the size of the giant bureaucratic apparatus that had been built up during the period of command planning. Czechoslovakia had . . . eighteen economic ministries, each with three, four or five main departments — a bureaucratic apparatus that made any kind of economic reform quite impossible. . . . We intended to do away with the large number of industrial ministries and go back to a single small industrial ministry alongside a few general economic ministries, such as are also known and necessary in Western countries . . . a ministry of finance, a ministry of foreign trade, and a small . . . planning commission. The struggle . . . was not easy.[5]

In Hungary, where a deliberate decision was made rather early on to avoid massive disruptions of established managerial careers,[6] in order to minimize opposition to the N.E.M. from that quarter, it was nevertheless found necessary to reduce the number of employees of the industrial ministries' headquarters from about 7000 to about 5000 over the first few years of the reform.[7] Most of this reduction was in clerical and secretarial staff, evidently, but Granick reports that his interviewees estimated that the cuts in professional staff of the five main branch ministries ranged from as high as 60 percent to as low as 30 percent between 1968 and 1971, suggesting that perhaps as many as several hundred people with high-status jobs had to accept transfers, mostly to the staffs of larger enterprises or of branch associations.[8] Even the very mild Romanian decentralization of 1969 displaced about 35 percent of the ministerial headquarters staff.[9]

The resistance of the bureaucrats in the state administration to devolution of decision-making to the enterprise, not very surprisingly, was quite determined and, in most countries, rather successful. Most of the reform programs stopped well short of granting the enterprises the degree of autonomy envisaged in a market socialism model, and consequently the sectoral ministries and branch organizations continued to play a very large role in micro-economic decision-making, even though that role was somewhat more limited than in the pre-reform period. In part, this outcome can be attributed to sheer political muscle: people occupying high-level ministerial positions had had to be politically well-connected in the first place to achieve such eminence, and where their collective interests were at stake, the aggregated influence of their friends and patrons within the Central Committee and Politburo constituted a formidable protective force. Moreover, the workability of pure reliance upon "economic" levers was open to serious question for many reasons, not the least of which was the difficulty encountered in devising a price system that genuinely guaranteed the dominance of planners' preferences over consumers' preferences. Whenever serious deviations from established preconceptions about optimal economic outcomes became manifest, there were strong immediate incentives favoring (and few internalized inhibitions restraining) *ad hoc* administrative interventions to "correct" the situation. (And often a vicious circle would develop whereby a single intervention designed to combat a particular problem would lead to disequilibria in other areas, which in turn would call forth additional administrative measures.) Where the bureaucratic establishments retained overall responsibility for the performance of the enterprises in a given sector, it was extremely difficult to refuse them the powers to exercise control as well, and, thus, the first signs of difficulties during the transition period tended to evoke a reflexive response toward creeping recentralization. Resistance to this trend required firm support for the principles of the reform by the Party agencies charged with supervising the implementation of the reform and/or the mobilization of support for enterprise autonomy from other sources.[10]

In those countries that successfully implemented more radical economic reforms, the role of the manager was greatly changed. Under the established, highly-centralized methods of planning and management, the enterprise director's discretion had been relatively limited. In many ways, his role was much more comparable to that of a foreman than that of the general manager in a Western-style firm. With most "managerial" decisions taken on a higher level, the enterprise director concerned himself not with trading off of gains in one area against costs in another, but rather with essentially technical problems of conducting current operations — the reorganization of production lines, setting of maintenance schedules, adjusting production schedules to work around temporary shortages of materials, and so on. Under the new reforms, however, the enterprise directors would be expected to take on a variety of additional functions involving decisions about alternative product lines, possible investment in new machinery, choice of materials and design, improvement of quality so as to ensure sales, and many others. As a "socialist entrepreneur" expected to increase profits by seeking out methods of cutting costs and promoting sales, the director's remuneration and chances for promotion would depend much less on his reliability as an executor of the orders of some superior than on his ingenuity and creativity in autonomous economic decision-making. To his role as "agent of the central authorities" he would also unavoidably add a more substantial role as "guardian of the material interests of the enterprise."

While the challenges of greatly augmented enterprise autonomy and the corresponding increase in managerial responsibilities (and opportunities) were highly appealing to many of the enterprise directors, there is every indication that this was far from a unanimous view. Many incumbent directors of enterprises were uncertain of their own abilities to perform successfully under the new and more demanding arrangements. While the support of the more ambitious and successful enterprise managers was important in getting reforms adopted, the opposition of their less secure colleagues was frequently a source of considerable political difficulties for the advocates of reform.

An important aspect of the social revolutions that had taken place in East Europe during the late 1940's and early 1950's was the nearly universal removal of the "bourgeois" managers from the directorships of the newly nationalized industrial establishments and their replacement by more politically reliable Party members, a rather high percentage of them drawn from the ranks of the working class or peasantry and often possessing only the most rudimentary educational qualifications. Managerial positions were often dispensed in recognition of active and disciplined service to the Party during the transition to power. The criteria for appointment were political reliability coupled with proven leadership ability, and by and large the skills that these men brought to their new careers were those of the agitator and organizer of mass action rather than those of the administrator, the accountant, or the engineer. Still less were they likely to be possessed of the skills and talents of the free-wheeling, profit-seeking entrepreneur. In the late 1950's and early 1960's, it was these same men, now a bit older and considerably more experienced in the routines of administering centrally-developed economic plans, who still constituted the core of the managerial stratum. Their continuing control of the leadership positions in the economy by virtue of their political connections was a continuing source of frustration for the younger and much better educated generation of engineers, economists, and managers trapped below them in the enterprise and ministerial hierarchies, who asserted their own claims to advancement based on superior qualifications for promoting technical innovation and efficiency in production. This phenomenon was sufficiently widespread as to constitute not only a serious practical economic problem but also a serious source of social tension as well.

In Czechoslovakia, as of 1963, only 25 percent of the directors of enterprises and their deputies had more than secondary education.[11] In general, the enterprise deputy directors were much better educated than their bosses. In 1964, it was reported that only 12 percent of the directors had higher education, while 31 percent of them had only an elementary school education.[12] (At the same time, "more than one-half" of all Czechs and Slovaks who possessed university degrees were "not employed in jobs corresponding to their qualifications."[13]) In establishing statutory minimum qualifications for holding managerial and technical jobs in the enterprises, the government had tried to take into account not only formal schooling but also practical experience and on-the-job training; nevertheless, political waivers and grandfather-clause exemptions to even those looser requirements were so widespread that 52 percent of directors and deputy directors were theoretically ineligible to hold their positions.[14]

Data on managerial education and qualifications is less complete for other socialist countries, but enough is available to suggest that the situation was broadly similar elsewhere. That is, the phenomenon of the poorly educated but politically well connected enterprise manager was a widespread one in every East European country, reflecting the essentially similar patterns of political consolidation that occurred in them all during the Stalinist period.

In Hungary, as of 1958, 30 percent of the enterprise directors in the Ministry of Metallurgy and Machine Building had eight years of education or less. The corresponding figures for other ministries were 26 percent in Heavy Industry, 50 percent in Light Industry, and 50 percent in Construction.[15] Hungarian sociologists writing in the 1970's noted that "at present most executives . . . have executive experience of about 15 to 25 years,"[16] suggesting that educational levels of managers could not have been much higher in the early 1960's than in 1958. Moreover, the Hungarian researchers admitted quite frankly that

> In selecting enterprise executives three viewpoints are asserted, with varying weight: political loyalty, professional competence, and leadership talents. The latter two became of almost equal rank to the first only in the sixties.[17]

In Poland, as of 1956, only 15 percent of the enterprise directors in a sample investigated by the Central Statistical Office had any higher education at all, while 10 percent had only an elementary or incomplete elementary education.[18] The level of education of directors rose substantially as the result of the widespread resignations demanded by the Polish workers' councils in 1956-1957 (a sample of forty directors in 1958 included 52 percent with at least some higher education and only 7.5 percent with elementary education [19]), yet nevertheless, by 1966, it was being asserted that nearly 80 percent of the "leading personnel" in Polish industry lacked the stipulated educational qualifications for their present positions.[20]

Figures on the education levels of East German managers are not available, but prior to the building of the Berlin Wall, one of the most serious problems facing the economy was emigration to the West of engineers and experienced industrial managers. Comparison of the 1961 West German census with the 1964 East German census indicates that, by 1961, some 36 percent of all Germans with higher education degrees formerly resident in the Eastern Zone had emigrated to the West, including 75 percent of those with degrees in business administration.[21]

In Bulgaria, despite one of the most extensive programs of higher education in East Europe, the level of managerial qualification seems to have been abysmal. Bogoslav Dobrin, formerly a high-ranking Bulgarian economic official, now in emigration, states unequivocally that

> Managerial staffs were politically appointed without exception. A promotion to managerial level was the reward for some service to the Party, and education, experience, and ability to perform were of lesser consideration. . . . There were thousands of managers with the qualifications of laborers, while thousands of engineers and economists were working as manual laborers. The politically appointed manager concentrated his attention and his contacts on the Party hierarchy rather than on business management.[22]

(Some idea of the magnitude of the problem of underqualification of administrators in Bulgaria may be derived by juxtaposing two figures: while about 35 percent of all Bulgarian Communist Party members were employed in white collar [mainly administrative] jobs during the 1960's,[23] a breakdown of the Party membership by educational attainment reveals that only 9 percent had any higher education and 70 percent had not even completed secondary school.[24])

During the debates of the economic reform proposals in the 1960's, directors of more successful enterprises were often prominent supporters of measures increasing the autonomy of the enterprise. However, it is also rather clear that a great many of the less well educated managers were fearful for their prospects under a new system, and the more radical advocates of reform did little to allay their fears.

The ferocity of the reformers' attack was nowhere greater than in Czechoslovakia. Eugen Lobl warned against the tendency toward leniency and complacency in enforcing managerial standards during the implementation of the reform:

> It is necessary to beware of the illusion that the new type of factory director will emerge naturally from the new forms of management, just as the old type was the natural product of dogmatism in economic thinking. Unfortunately the process is irreversible. . . . Hence we must realize that if we require a new

type of business leader, we must appoint to the leading positions those who are of the required type.[25]

Selucky was even more emphatic:

The reform will not tolerate the retention of anything that is obsolete and that has failed to justify itself in our methods of management.[26]

Under Novotny, the Party line on improving managerial qualifications was more moderate, emphasizing that existing managerial cadres should upgrade their skills, so that "capable *and* politically conscious individuals" will fill the "leading economic posts."[27] The experimentation of 1965-1966 and the snail-like "implementation" of 1967 does not seem to have led to any major turnover among the enterprise managers. An opinion poll carried out by the Research Institute for Economic Planning surveying about 500 "leading executives in industrial enterprises" demonstrated the division within the ranks of the managers. Some 30 percent of the respondents agreed that the "main brake to a faster development of [their own] enterprise" was the limited freedom of decision-making at the enterprise level, while 31 percent opined that the scope and authority of the management under the existing system was "adequate."[28]

The worst fears of "old guard" managers were realized after Novotny's ouster led the Party to adopt many of the attitudes earlier expressed by reformers favoring wholesale dismissals. The Party's new "Action Program," adopted in April 1968, affirmed that

One of the key conditions of present and future scientific, technical and social development is to substantially increase the qualifications of managers. . . . If the leading posts are not filled by capable, educated, expert cadres, socialism will be unable to hold its own in competition with capitalism. This fact will require a great change in the existing cadre policy, in which for years the aspects of education, qualification and ability have been underrated.[29]

At the time that the Warsaw Pact intervention in August interrupted the process, a movement to replace many of the more politically recalcitrant directors was well under way, spearheaded in many instances by the newly-organized enterprise workers' councils, whose members were concerned about management's ability to secure the profitability necessary to qualify the employees for the large year-end bonuses.[30] The struggles over the issue of the "political" directors were bitter and continued even after the Warsaw Pact intervention, at least until the time of Alexander Dubcek's ouster in April of 1969. The process of "normalization" thereafter allowed many of the old Party stalwarts to purge their reformist replacements and to regain leading posts in the enterprises (as in the state and the Party), entailing the removal of some 40 percent of the directors in office when Gustav Husak took over from Dubcek as First Secretary.[31] The intense antagonisms within the Party and within the country as a whole dictated that the new leadership would have once again to subordinate the need for technical expertise to the need for political reliability in the selection of managers.[32]

In Hungary, one of the most fiercely resisted aspects of Janos Kadar's "Alliance Policy" was his insistence that educational and technical qualifications should be given at least even weight with political criteria in decisions on the filling of leadership posts in the economy. This theme was given particular prominence in the Party press from 1962 on, even before the major debates on reforming the system of planning and management began. *Nepszabadsag* identified opposition to this new policy as the characteristic sign of "*petite bourgeois* leftism" and "dogmatism" and declared that

> The Party must never place the advancement of any member of the Party above the interests of the socialist community. . . . . Socialism is the business of all the people. The Party will endeavor to bring into being a situation in which the *apparats* of industry, of agriculture, of the state administration, and of culture are filled with competent men.[33]

Nevertheless, the necessities of maintaining Kadar's "centrist" line and avoiding massive disaffection within the Party cadres dictated that any campaign to uproot the political hacks had to be carried on at no more than a moderate pace. After several articles by reformist economists critical of the Party's slow pace in rejuvenating the ranks of the managers appeared in the press, Vice-Premier Jeno Fock (himself an important supporter of the N.E.M.) defended the gradualist approach:

> Let me establish right at the beginning that I approve of 80 percent of the material contained in these articles. . . . But in one or another of these articles there are paragraphs or sentences which fail to take note of the changes in economic management . . . and do not discriminate between the methods of economic leadership in the 1950's and the 1960's. This opinion is unacceptable.

... This implies that the proposals relating to changes . . . have to be *enforced* with respect to the leading bodies. I would like to ask the economists . . . to depart from the notion that the Central Committee of the H.S.W.P. and the government are not supporting them.[34]

About the time of the 1966 Party Congress, the Hungarian Party leadership seems to have made a fundamental decision that the smooth implementation of the N.E.M. would require a conciliatory policy in order to maintain Party unity and ensure cooperation. The existing managers would be given every chance to prove themselves under N.E.M., and only the most blatantly incompetent would have cause to worry about their continued tenure. (This was, of course, consistent with Kadar's generally "co-optive" approach taken toward the central economic bureaucracy in the elaboration of the final plans for the transition.)

[At the post-Congress meetings of the regional Party organs] there were several debates on the requirements for a Communist economic leader. The question was also raised . . . whether, simultaneously with the introduction of the new economic mechanism, there will be some sort of a "changing of the guard." Our Party organizations rejected this idea unanimously. This does not mean, however, that we shall not suggest that leaders who, on the evidence of many years of service, are unable to fill their leading posts, be relieved of those posts. . . . [B]y being familiar with their work and accepting the responsibility, they may solve the tasks correctly.[35]

Granick's interviews with enterprise managers in Hungary during 1972 elicited the information that attrition was indeed the main mechanism employed for upgrading the level of qualifications of enterprise management under the N.E.M. Changes of general directors of enterprises for reasons other than retirement numbered no more than about 4 percent per annum, a policy which was explained to him as the result of a policy decision in favor of upholding the principle of a "humane" personnel policy and thereby avoiding possible politically harmful resentments. The strategy proved remarkably successful in alleviating managerial fears, for Granick reports that he saw every indication that enterprise directors in Hungary have very few anxieties about being fired or demoted.[36] While Hungary's economy no doubt paid (and continues to pay) a price for Kadar's concessions on this issue, the alternative might well have been the kind of bruising intra-Party struggle that occurred in Czechoslovakia, necessitating the use of more dangerous forms of mass mobilization in order to carry out the removal of entrenched opposition to the reform.

Given the constant presence of the Soviets and their concern for the continued stability of the Hungarian Party's rule, Kadar's preference for limiting the conflict to manageable proportions by making the necessary compromises was probably highly rational.

Economic Reform and the Workers

The fundamental legitimating myth of any Marxist-Leninist regime is that the working class has been elevated by the revolution to the position of ruling class and that the political-economic order of socialism, by giving the fullest expression to the interests of the proletariat, is preparing the way for the ultimate establishment of a classless (and therefore essentially harmonious) society in which the basic material and spiritual needs of all humankind will find their fulfillment. The Communist Party consists of the most enlightened, far-sighted, and active representatives of the working class, and its policies are scientifically designed to bring about the essential political, economic, social, and cultural preconditions for the ultimate transition to "full communism" at the earliest possible date. The party's principal base of support in that endeavor is the working masses, the fulfillment of whose class interests uniquely coincides with the historically necessary steps for the achievement of universal human liberation.

While it is very doubtful whether any very substantial segment of the East European masses supporting themselves by manual labor in the state sector actually understand the complex ideological formulations purporting to demonstrate the "essential" harmony of their material interests with the achievement of long-range Party objectives, it is relatively clear that quite substantial numbers of such people respond positively to the basic symbols evoked in the rhetoric of socialism-as-workers'-state. Diffuse support from the industrial working class constitutes not only the source of abstract legitimacy necessary for the normative integration of the Communist Party cadres but also the practical basis for insuring the smooth day-to-day functioning of the entire society.

The Communist Parties of East Europe have been able to evoke at least the minimum necessary degree of support from their respective working classes most of the time because certain of their important and long-standing policies have in fact provided them important material and symbolic benefits. The combination of the social revolution of the 1940's and early 1950's (which dispossessed the established political, economic, social, and cultural elites and either sent them into exile, physically liquidated them, or at least relegated them to marginal positions under the new order) and the rapid "extensive" development of an urban and industrial economy provided unprecedented opportunities for social mobility to the formerly disadvantaged. Hundreds of thousands of former workers were advanced to positions of administrative authority via their affiliation with the Communist parties. Policies of active discrimination on a class basis sent more hundreds of thousands of men and women of working class and peasant origins into the universities and polytechnics to become the basis for a new "socialist" intelligentsia. Unemployed and underemployed peasants from the countryside flocked into the cities, lured by the carrot of expanding industrial job opportunities and prodded by the stick of brutal methods in agricultural collectivization: for many of them, the transition to unskilled industrial labor (even under the grim conditions of declining average real wages of the early 1950's) represented a measurable step upward from the rural impoverishment they had left behind. While those members of the pre-existing skilled working class who did not move upward into supervisory or administrative positions probably lost ground in their real incomes during the first decade or so of the Communist order, even they acquired certain partially compensating advantages in the form of higher social prestige, improved social welfare benefits, and vastly increased chances for their children to acquire higher education. Moreover, under the conditions of rapid "extensive" growth, the specter of long-term involuntary unemployment had been effectively banished, and the perpetual tightness of the labor market ensured that labor discipline within the work place would be relatively lax, so long as individual workers were careful not to become involved in organized protest or open dissent.

In many respects, therefore, the Communist parties of East Europe enjoyed considerable success in inculcating into the industrial working class a diffuse reverence for "socialist principles" and a feeling that, however much the practice of the regime might depart from the ideal, nevertheless, at bottom, much had been achieved of a positive nature for which they had the Party to thank. In some broad sense, the bulk of the working class accepted a socialist ideology.

The version of socialist ideology current among the less sophisticated, non-vanguard elements of the working class differed, however, from the strict letter of Marxism-Leninism as it was understood by the Party ideologists. For one thing, popular ideology tended to focus much more upon concrete material benefits for the workers in the present period than Party ideologists found congenial, since the latter were often charged with the task of justifying present sacrifices for the sake of rapid growth and future benefits. The workers could be distressingly literal-minded in their interpretations of the content of working class interests. Upward revisions of work norms or downward revisions of piecework rates in order to prevent violation of centrally set wage-fund targets, for example, were a

perennial source of shop-floor disputes (and even more serious distur-
bances, as in Berlin and Plzn in 1953). Exhortations from Party and trade
union activists to speed the pace of production or to "volunteer" extra
unpaid hours of labor for the sake of "building socialism" often provoked
bitter resentment. The familiar tendency of ignorant workers (bemoaned
by Marx in the *Critique of the Gotha Program*) to conceive of socialism
as primarily a matter of equitable *distribution* rather than as a more fully
humanized mode of *production* was much in evidence throughout the
region, reflecting (as the Party ideologists were wont to say) the survival
of an essentially *petite bourgeois* consciousness deriving from the peasant
origins of much of the new working class.

A particularly salient difference between elite and mass conceptions of
"socialism" has to do precisely with the norms governing distribution of
material benefits. The constant exhortations of Party ideologists ever since
the final consolidation of Communist rule against the baleful effects of
"leveling" tendencies testify to the fact that the ethos of the shop-floor
was much more egalitarian than was congenial to a regime bent on rapid
economic development and the systematic harnessing of material incentives
to that end. Party theoreticians were probably partially right in attributing
such manifestations to the survival of a rough-and-ready peasant
egalitarianism, but there were other factors involved as well. In the first
place, Party agitators themselves had often seemed to endorse such notions
during the period of the coalition governments immediately after the war,
when demagogic appeals to primitive egalitarianism constituted a powerful
tool for mobilizing the workers against the privileges of the bourgeoisie,
and when, in any case, the Communists were trying their best to outbid
their rivals, the Social Democrats, for the allegiance of the new working
class. Perhaps more importantly, the operations of the incentive structure
within the factories under the system of centralized planning spontaneously
generated egalitarian responses. Since the plan dictated the enterprise's
wage fund, its staffing pattern, and the expected output per worker, and
since the physical output plans were raised more rapidly every year than
the wage fund, it followed that the new targets could be achieved
simultaneously only if individual work norms or piece rates were periodically revised to require more production in order to attain the same per
worker income. The altogether sensible response of the workers under
these circumstances was to mitigate or forestall further intensification by
concealing possibilities for increasing productivity and by exerting informal
peer pressures against "rate-busters" who threatened to unmask their silent
collusion. Improvements in productivity led not so much to higher wages
as to more demanding quotas, since the ever increasing rate of investment

insisted upon by the Party leadership virtually assured that there could be no visible correlation between success in achieving such productivity improvements and the total wage and bonus funds to be made available. The group pressures and informal understandings with foremen made it possible to avoid ruinous competition among workers so long as everyone respected a rough consensual norm of egalitarianism that would at least insure a comfortable pace of work. And if the factory management got too serious about enforcing a more rigorous labor discipline (as the Party press was constantly demanding), the tightness of the labor market and the prevalence of essentially unskilled labor made it possible for young, single workers to change jobs repeatedly until they found a more congenial boss.

The ending of the era of "extensive" growth in East Europe had a number of effects on the interests of industrial workers. The initial revolutionary displacement of the bourgeoisie and aristocracy from their positions of authority and material privilege was a one-shot opportunity for social mobility that could not be repeated in the future without another revolutionary upheaval against the new "proletarian" elite of the Party (many of whom had attained their new positions of power and privilege at a very young age and therefore long continued to clog the channels of mobility for the generation just behind them). The extremely rapid expansion of the urban, industrial sector of the economy during the 1950's helped considerably to maintain relatively numerous chances for working class upward mobility, but increasingly these opportunities were extended to those who passed through formal educational institutions rather than to rank-and-file industrial workers. The rather sharp deceleration of economic growth in the early 1960's further slowed the rate of social mobility. The slowing of the rural-urban migration also meant that fewer people were experiencing upward mobility from that quarter. As the children of the first wave of the upwardly mobile came of age, they increasingly dominated admissions to the institutions of higher learning. A certain restratification and solidification of the social-economic order was taking place, in short, and people could scarcely fail to be aware of this fact at the lower levels of the pecking order. Heightened resentments of the workers against the "intellectuals" and the "managers" (and of the "intellectuals" and "managers" against the "political hacks" who blocked their advancement) were a natural result of this process and provided much of the dynamic force for the rather turbulent politics of the 1960's.

The economic reforms can be interpreted at one level as the vehicle by which the "technocratic" stratum of slightly younger and better-educated managers and engineers hoped to overcome the blockage of their chances for upward mobility by forcibly displacing the generation of ex-workers and ex-peasants who entered the elite in the 1940's and 1950's and held on to their positions by virtue of their dominance of the Party *apparat* and their sense of solidarity against the challenge of the outsiders. In those countries (such as Czechoslovakia and Poland) where the Party leadership was unwilling to force some sort of accommodation to the aspirations of this "new New Class," the consequences were bitter intra-Party conflicts, while in those countries (such as Hungary and, in their own way, the G.D.R.[37]) where the top leadership was more creative in handling the integration of the new intelligentsia into the elite, the stability of the Party's rule was greatly enhanced.

Yet the specific *form* the reforms took in the various countries was itself of crucial importance, quite apart from the question of intra-elite relations, because of the rather different implications of the terms of settlement for the political, social, and economic standing of social categories and groups outside of the elite. Semi-market socialist approaches to economic reform (along the lines followed in Hungary and Czechoslovakia — and, in a somewhat different form, in Yugoslavia) had a much more pronounced effect upon the positions of the various categories of industrial workers than did the more conservative reforms pioneered by the East German model (with its emphasis on limited decentralization of an essentially administrative character and greater reliance on scientific-technological innovation rather than improvement of operational efficiency as the basic source of further growth). The latter approach seems to lead to a solution of intra-elite conflicts that only marginally broadens the range of interests directly represented in the policy-making process: the former both requires the mobilization of a broader coalition for its successful implementation (because of the greater resistance of established bureaucratic and Party elites) and thereafter continuously stimulates reactive mobilization of working class elements in ways that virtually compel the established elites to devise institutionalized channels for articulation of these interests as part of the price of enhanced economic performance.

Reform of the Wage and Bonus System

Market-style economic reforms affected the interests and opportunities of industrial workers in a variety of highly salient ways. The most important effects had to do with the distribution and absolute level of remuneration for labor and with the balance of risk and security which the workers would be expected to assume. Both of these clusters of issues had important ramifications for the continued "socialist" legitimacy of the political and economic order in the eyes of the workers.

An increased concern for rationalizing material incentives and greater emphasis on the importance of material incentives relative to moral incentives were two of the common characteristics of the movements for economic reform throughout East Europe in the 1960's. The basis for the proper relationship between production and distribution remained the same in theory, however. Marx's formulation in the *Critique of the Gotha Program* continued to be cited, as in the past: "From each according to his ability; to each according to his work."

The implication of the first clause in Marx's slogan was relatively straightforward: everyone should be working very hard to increase the quality and quantity of production. However, remuneration "according to work" has long been subject to varying shades of interpretation. The evidence is strong that many East European workers, especially the less skilled, take this to mean that wages and salaries ought to be proportional to hours put in on the job, the physical effort expended, the degree of hazard involved, the unpleasantness of the task — in short, the degree of "personal sacrifice" made by the individual worker or employee in the everyday performance of his duties. Such a viewpoint tended to suggest rather egalitarian wage structures, at least in terms of differentials between average earnings of different categories of workers and employees, since the biologically determined differences in human capabilities for physical effort are not, after all, extremely great. An often associated attitude is that payment "according to work" involves a kind of moral assessment and presupposes taking into account the level of individual abilities mentioned in the first phrase of Marx's formula. That is, people often assess moral merit, not according to the objective results, but rather according to some rough estimate of the degree to which the individual has "done his best," whatever his physical and mental endowments may happen to be. When a man is thought to have approached rather closely his inherent physical or intellectual limits, people are apt to believe he should be rewarded somehow for his dedication, regardless of the value of the results to other people. (Conversely, when it is believed that even an extremely valuable achievement was due principally to luck or favorable circumstances, there is often a tendency to give little moral credit to the person who brought it all about.) This viewpoint too tends to be associated with belief in relatively egalitarian patterns of inter-category income differentials, on the general assumption that moral merit is relatively equally distributed among various occupational categories.[38]

The economic reformers, on the other hand, generally embraced a more "consequentialist" conception of remuneration according to work, focussing not so much on the subjective costs incurred by the worker in his job or on his moral merits but rather on the externally imputed social importance or value of the net results achieved. For them, wages and bonuses were a tool exploiting self-interest to encourage workers to improve their level of qualification, to attract them into branches of industry where they could be most profitably employed, and to evoke a maximum sustainable degree of diligence in performing the job at hand. The position was summarized by the slogan, "payment according to results," and this was understood to require a considerably more differentiated structure of wage rates and bonuses than previously was in force. For example, the architect of Hungary's N.E.M., Rezso Nyers, expressed it thusly:

> In the field of enterprise management, wage payment should also be criticized; our system of wage payment is based too much on equalitarianism and it does not sufficiently differentiate between the quality of work. In addition, we are using a much too narrow scale of wages. This applies both to workers and directors and restricts incentive. I could also put it this way: the principle of distribution according to work ought to be enforced more effectively and more consistently.[39]

Very similar formulations were common in Czechoslovakia. The 1968 "Action Program" is representative of the reformers' general views:

> The Party has often criticized equalitarian views, but in practice leveling has spread to an unheard of extent, and this became one of the impediments to an intensive development of the economy and to raising the living standard. . . . The harmfulness of equalitarianism lies in the fact that it puts careless workers, idlers and irresponsible people to advantage as compared to the dedicated and diligent workers, the unqualified compared with the qualified, the technically and expertly backward people as compared with the talented and those with initiative.[40]

The principal mechanism for increasing individual and group productivity was a combination of new, more differentiated wage scales with the introduction or augmentation of funds for special bonuses derived from the profits of the enterprise. Thus well-run and profitable enterprises would be able to pay more to their employees than poorly-run and unprofitable ones. Workers would no longer have the old incentives to conceal productive capacities or malinger because they could be sure that improved performance would be reflected in their paychecks.

In designing the new wage and bonus systems, the reformers faced a problem of determining the optimum degree of "bonus intensity" for different categories of workers and employees. On the one hand, where individual incomes are only slightly dependent upon economic results, employees are likely to exert little effort beyond the minimum acceptable and the incentive becomes largely ineffective. On the other hand, if income is too dependent upon the highly variable bonus payments, the employee may resort to desperate action to achieve the bonus at any cost, resulting in uneconomic or even aggressively anti-social behavior. East European policy-makers seem to have designed their bonus systems according to a rough judgment as to the marginal (dis)utility of income shortfalls at various income levels. Lower income workers were presumed to be more concerned with wage stability and predictability, since a high proportion of income must go for necessities, while those with higher incomes were adjudged to be less risk-averse. The reformed bonus systems typically allowed for much larger performance-based bonuses to be paid to those with higher incomes and greater discretion in decision-making (i.e., managerial and technical personnel), while rank and file workers were eligible for bonuses that were much smaller, both absolutely and relative to total income. For example, in Hungary, at the first introduction of N.E.M., the maximum bonus payable to top managerial personnel in the enterprise was 80 percent of base pay, while middle management and engineers could get up to 50 percent of base pay, and ordinary workers might receive up to 15 percent of base pay.

The new wage and bonus systems were expected to increase inequality of incomes in a number of ways that violated widely-held working class notions of socialist morality and exacerbated social tensions. First of all, they tended to widen the disparities in income between the more skilled and less skilled categories of employees within the enterprise, and especially between the managerial or technical staff and the manual workers. Secondly, the bonus systems required supervisors to make invidious distinctions between the contributions of individual workers in the same job category and thereby posed a threat to the solidarity of the work group. (It also left the supervisor vulnerable to accusations of favoritism.) Third, the likelihood that different factories would enjoy different rates of profitability (whether due to better management or simply to a more favorable initial endowment of machinery and materials, neither of which would be within the power of the workers to affect) meant that workers employed in different factories at essentially the same task might be paid substantially different wages, violating the norm of "equal pay for equal work." (Of course this was part of the reformers' purpose: to encourage the migration of workers with transferable skills from less socially profitable industries to more profitable ones.)

The new wage and bonus systems proved to be exceedingly difficult to implement. For significant increases in wage differentials to occur without absolute wage cuts for substantial numbers of people, it would have been necessary for the average of real incomes to grow at a considerably more rapid rate than the customary 1 or 2 percent per annum. But to do this without serious inflationary pressures or shortages this would have required a prior increase in the capacities of the consumer goods-producing sectors of the economy, principally agriculture and light industry, or else a big expansion of imports of consumer goods from abroad. Balance of payments difficulties prevented the latter course from being a fully adequate solution, and the entrenched political power of the heavy industry bureaucracy made it extremely difficult to bring about more than incremental shifts in the allocation of investment funds. In any case, the lag between the new investments and the actual bringing on line of new productive capacities for consumer goods would often be a matter of several years.

The implications for policy were harsh. A relatively rapid rate of increase in productivity would have to take place *before* substantial increases in consumption could take place — yet it was the incentive effects of increasing consumption in pace with productivity increases that had been counted upon to increase the productivity in the first place. The process of "delevelization" would have to occur (if at all) during a period of relative austerity rather than of expansion, which could only intensify the inevitable dissatisfaction such a departure from past income distribution policies would inevitably have brought in any case. There was real danger of a vicious circle in which low morale would lead to lagging productivity and to political pressures to alleviate the plight of the most disadvantaged, which in turn would imply fewer resources available for rationalizing the incentive structure, slower growth, and a consequent need to postpone both further differentiation and the upgrading of the lot of the least advantaged . . . and so on.

In Czechoslovakia, attempts to bring about "delevelization" began with the inauguration of the experimental enterprises in 1965 and 1966, years in which average real wages grew by only 0.8 percent and 1.0 percent respectively. Most of the early schemes for enhancing the role of bonuses and premia in the earnings of manual workers involved expanding the size of the discretionary "foreman's funds," which were distributed by lower supervisory personnel. But the foremen, it soon developed, were quite vulnerable to the informal pressures of their work-mates, and the practice was quickly adopted of paying out the "performance" premia in simple proportion to basic wages. Similar patterns were followed by enterprise directors in the distribution of year-end profit sharing bonuses, as a means of avoiding trouble.[41] (It was later acknowledged by the Czechoslovak trade Union chief that nine spontaneous strikes occurred in connection with efforts to force a more genuinely performance-based incentive system during 1965, one of them involving over three hundred workers who stayed away for two days.[42]) The move toward more differentiated basic wage scales, which was enforced from the ministries by administrative edict, was countered at the level of the enterprise by the simple expedient of reclassifying lower-paid workers into higher skill categories, a new managerial prerogative which had been provisionally delegated to the enterprise director as part of the experiment in order to encourage a more selective, merit-based promotion policy in place of the former reliance on seniority.[43]

The reformers were more successful in increasing the income differentials between white collar employees and the manual workers. Average earnings of "engineering-technical employees" in industry, which were 127 percent of average earnings of manual workers in 1963, increased to 135 percent in 1965, 140 percent in 1966, and peaked at 142 percent in 1967.[44] There was little that could be done by the workers about the centrally set basic wage rates, which were being rather sharply differentiated, but they could and did protest about the more decentralized determination of the formulae for distributing profit-sharing premia. At the "Kablo" enterprise in 1965, the scheme devised by the management involved distributing the premia according to coefficients ranging from .25 to .50 for workers, on up to a maximum of 4.00 for managerial and technical personnel. The resulting thirty-five- to forty-fold differences were successfully protested by the factory trade union committee as "incommensurately high."[45]

The response by the central authorities to protests about excessive differentiation in bonus payments was to decrease the maximum size of managerial bonuses to about 25 percent of base pay, while simultaneously raising managerial base pay to compensate for the pernicious effects of the past leveling tendencies of the 1950's. There is every indication that this increase in the relative incomes of managers continued to provoke worker resentment throughout 1966 and 1967,[46] and the trend was finally brought to a halt during mid-1968, when the differentials declined slightly, as a result of very large wage increases rather than of any absolute decline of managerial salaries. (After the intervention of 1968, part of the policy of "normalization" was once again to diminish the earnings differentials between mental and manual laborers, presumably as an affirmation of the "working-class" character of the new regime: average earnings of engineering-technical workers as a percentage of average earnings of manual laborers, which had been 141 percent in 1968, declined rapidly to 131 percent by 1972.[47])

In Hungary, reformers' efforts to bring personal incomes into better alignment with contribution to profitability also resulted in frustrating resistance from the shop-floor. Hungary had introduced "profit-sharing" in industrial enterprises in 1958, one of the few recommendations of the Varga Commission actually to be enacted. However, from the beginning, the annual profit shares had been distributed routinely in proportion to base pay, without regard to individual performance. The maximum sum payable was four weeks' wages, and the average enterprise was usually able to distribute about eight to twelve days' pay in a given year. By the late 1960's, the profit-share had come to be seen as a routine and almost obligatory payment to be made regardless of individual or collective performance, and consequently it did not have any very great incentive effect, except, perhaps, in promoting generalized feelings of solidarity and loyalty to the enterprise and thus helping to inhibit labor turnover.

The new scheme for profit-sharing bonuses introduced with the inauguration of the N.E.M. in 1968 was designed to have a much more differentiated impact. The enterprise staff was divided into three groups (top management, middle management/technical, and rank-and-file workers). The top category could receive up to 80 percent of their total combined base pay as bonuses (with the total to be divided up among the individuals in the group on the basis of an annual evaluation of relative personal contributions to enterprise success). For middle management and higher level technical personnel, the corresponding maximum figure was 50 percent, and for ordinary workers the maximum was 15 percent. In addition to the payment of these cash bonuses to individuals, enterprise profits were also to finance certain optional fringe benefits supplied by the factories (subsidized meals in the factory cafeteria, sports and cultural activities, free work clothes, housing subsidies or enterprise-constructed staff housing, emergency loans, group vacations, etc.). Certain other benefits would continue to be guaranteed by the state, regardless of enterprise profitability (mainly medical care and pensions).

The large disparities in participation in the cash bonuses between managers and workers produced a great deal of controversy in the factories and were much discussed in the mass media during late 1968 and 1969. Important architects of the N.E.M., such as Rezso Nyers[48] and Matyas Timar,[49] defended the large managerial bonuses in print, on the grounds that the base pay of managers was already far too low relative to that of skilled manual workers (only about 50 percent higher) and that the possibility of gaining large bonuses was a necessary compensatory mechanism. Nevertheless, resistance to the scheme in the factories finally necessitated a retreat from the large differentials, and a new bonus system (increasing maximum workers' shares to 25 percent of base pay) was hurriedly introduced for 1970. In announcing the change, the Party's theoretical journal acknowledged that

> Categorization caused . . . political trouble, since many people — misinterpreting it — considered it a social discrimination and this resulted in the confrontation of workers and leaders. . . . Not even a propaganda campaign and persuasion were able to substantiate the correctness of the categorization. The agitators themselves were not quite sure of the whole matter.[50]

The linking to profitability of many fringe benefits previously guaranteed to workers by the state was also the source of a good deal of grumbling. Evidently there was sufficient concern about the problem to provoke a member of parliament to urge an amendment to the new Labor Code restoring many of these guarantees, on the ground that

> The people consider the various social allocations — day nursery, meal subsidies, recreation — as acquired rights. . . . Special attention should be paid to maintaining the integrity of the acquired rights.[51]

Nevertheless, the Party leadership held firm, and these privileges remained dependent upon profitability.

An attempt at introducing somewhat wider spreads in wage rates predated the inauguration of the N.E.M. by more than one year. Almost no specific information about the progress of this endeavor seems to have been made public. Nyers linked his proposal for "deleveling" wages with a proviso that the overall growth of average wages should be simultaneously accelerated in order to render the changes in relative rates more palatable.[52] Unfortunately, continuing problems with inflationary pressures made it difficult to raise the growth rate of wages in real terms. The wage increases for 1966 amounted to about 1.5 percent in real terms, on the national average. However, Nyers acknowledged in March that the increases, coupled with certain price rises, had been so unevenly distributed that the net impact had been to increase real incomes for about 53 percent of Hungarian households and to reduce them for the other 47 percent.[53] The first weeks after the new wages and prices were announced (in December of 1965) saw considerable protest, leading to eleven arrests of people in widely scattered locations accused of political crimes, mainly attempts at "incitement."[54]

The situation with respect to the growth of real wages did not show much improvement in subsequent years, remaining well below 2 percent per year through 1968, the first year of the full implementation of N.E.M. The years 1969 and 1970 were somewhat better, with average increases of 2.2 percent and 3.9 percent, but 1971 and 1972 were again years of relative austerity, as persistent inflationary pressures and balance of payments difficulties induced the government to intervene repeatedly to restrain the growth of wages and bonuses. As a fairly direct consequence, the new system of differentiation of incomes and the struggle against "egalitarianism" remained the number one topic in public speeches of the chief economic and ideological cadres of the Party. As late as February of 1973, more than five years after N.E.M. came into force, *Nepszabadsag*'s editor declared that the main problem of agitation in the factories was still the campaign to "explain" the principle of differentiating wages according to the work performed.[55]

Prices and the Problem of Unemployment

The wage and bonus "delevelization" programs' challenge to widespread working class conceptions of proper "socialist" distribution was not the only unsettling aspect of the economic reforms from the point of view of manual workers. A particularly troubling implication sprang from the reformers' insistence that enterprise profitability should be the measure of social efficiency and that all enterprises should be expected to support themselves by covering their own costs from revenues earned. One reason for the slowdown in growth performance of the East European economies was believed to be the basically irrational structure of investment that had been created under the influence of Stalinist prescriptions for autarkic growth based upon the expansion of heavy industry, regardless of the endowment of the particular country in natural and human resources. In order to improve growth performance, the reformers argued, it was important not only to improve operating efficiency within the framework of the given structure of the nation's productive plant, but also to modify the basic structure of production itself by shifting manpower and investment away from employment in hopelessly losing ventures and into other areas of production where they could be more profitably utilized. (An excellent example of a losing venture that absorbed enormous resources was Hungary's gigantic steel complex at Sztalinvaros, constructed at great expense in the early 1950's, by planners seemingly oblivious of the fact that Hungary possessed only negligible deposits of both iron ore and coking coal, both of which then had to be imported long distances overland at great expense.)

A major problem afflicting both the Czech and Hungarian economies was the extreme political difficulty of carrying out any such "regrouping of labor" into more profitable lines of production. The older system of economic planning and management, with its monomaniacal emphasis on fulfilling ever-increasing physical output targets and its indifference to financial results, had provided strong incentives for enterprise managers to bargain and plead with their superiors at the ministries for large wage-funds and large labor forces — to hoard labor that was not really necessary but which might prove useful if plan targets were raised by more than was expected. Under earlier conditions of extensive rural under-employment, this policy probably was not especially damaging to economic growth, but as the labor pool became exhausted in the late 1950's, serious labor shortages (especially shortages of highly skilled labor) developed in certain branches which the planners wished to expand particularly rapidly, limiting their growth, while at the same time other, lower efficiency enterprises continued to hoard excess workers, indifferent to the impact of overstaffing on their profitability.

The economic reformers' emphasis on profitability provided incentives for enterprises to dishoard labor which was not contributing to output as much as it cost in terms of wages. The combination of labor dishoarding and the closing down of completely unprofitable operations through some form of socialist bankruptcy promised to improve overall economic efficiency, but at the same time it raised the specter of involuntary unemployment for the unfortunate workers adjudged to be redundant. While the extreme shortages of labor in other sectors made it unlikely that the period of unemployment would be long, nevertheless the transfer to a new job could be highly disruptive for the individuals concerned. They might have to learn new skills, they would have to give up their seniority rights and might take pay cuts, they might have to move to another city or town (which would be no small matter given the chronic and severe housing shortages), social relationships with co-workers would be disrupted, and so on.

The Czech reformer Radoslav Selucky laid out the problem with his characteristic bluntness:

We have a large number of antiquated factories and enterprises which are unprofitable, which produce goods which are not in demand, which employ too many people, or which are, in fact, in operation only to give their employees work. We just cannot afford to preserve an unsatisfactory structure of industrial production, overemployment which slows down technical progress, and production of goods which nobody wants and nobody buys. . . . We shall no longer be able to regard employment as a social question; we shall have to regard it as an economic question governed purely by the purpose it serves.[56]

Selucky was unrealistic in his belief that a socialist state could treat the problem of employment as a purely economic question, and the reason was quite simple. The legitimacy of the regime was at stake. A dominant theme in the Marxist-Leninist critique of capitalism almost from its earliest origins has been an emphasis on the degree to which the workers are constantly threatened with the loss of their very livelihood because of the implacable and impersonal forces of the market. The claim to have abolished this threat to the security of the working class has for years been one of the proudest boasts of Communist Party propaganda and should be recognized as a principal pillar of the legitimacy of the Communist political order throughout the region of East Europe. A characteristically colorful example of the use of the theme of full employment in legitimation of the Communist order was provided by Janos Kadar in 1965:

Comrades! Our Constitution sets down in writing each of our important achievements. . . . According to our Constitution everyone has the right to work. . . . In the past, hundreds of thousands of our working people suffered from hunger and walked around in rags. Workers were the wanderers of the highroads because work was not guaranteed to them. . . . Today there is work and it is honored with decent wages. There are also free sick and old age benefits, paid vacations and many other achievements.[57]

The practical content of the present-day assertion that the East European countries constitute "workers' states," the principal basis for the constant glorification of the "gains of socialism" — at least as far as ordinary workers are concerned — is the overriding principle of social-economic policy that workers (at least so long as they do not become involved in dissident politics) should enjoy near-absolute job security. This has been popularly interpreted to mean that they should be protected not only from prolonged unemployment but also from even the temporary disruptions imposed by *any* involuntary change in occupation or even in place of employment. Dismissal of workers on any grounds other than gross incompetence or continued and serious violations of factory discipline has long been considered by the popular mind and by official ideology to be incompatible with socialist morality.

Policy-makers found themselves in a very difficult situation in trying to deal with the problem of "regrouping labor" in order to streamline the structure of production. Assuring stability and continuity of employment for the labor force was a political imperative, but the costs in terms of economic growth foregone were very high and rapidly increasing.

The Czechoslovak leaders were the first to propose concrete actions, even before the economic reform itself was approved. Although the political sensitivity of the action was underlined by the fact that it was not openly acknowledged in the press until two years later, a Politburo decision was made in 1964 to start closing down the most incurably loss-producing factories. During 1964-1965, a total of 1300 "production units" with 33,000 employees was shut down. The same article that reported these closings for the first time also announced that of the approximately 10,000 production units that remained operational, another 1400 were scheduled for closing during the period of the 1966-1970 Five-Year Plan, affecting another 60,000 employees.[58] As the shift to the new economic system got underway in 1966, the number of closings seems to have been substantially increased.

Since actions with such widespread effects could not effectively be concealed from the public, the authorities began a propaganda campaign giving wide publicity to the more extreme cases of economic waste which were being uncovered and eliminated. For example, at the end of 1966, three rotary furnaces at Mnisek pod Brdy (in central Bohemia) that had previously been used to refine low-grade iron ore were shut down when it was brought to planners' attention that the costs per ton of processed ore were 945 crowns, while the wholesale price of the resulting output was only 535 crowns, even after the substantial price increase obtained in the new price reform.[59] There followed a long series of closings of unprofitable mines and smaller metallurgical plants. In addition to outright closings, considerable publicity was given to especially outrageous instances of featherbedding, such as a coal mine which had recently attempted to reduce its output by discharging a large number of miners, only to discover that output did not subsequently decline at all.[60]

Anxieties and antagonisms arising out of the policy of "labor transfers" were, as one would expect, considerable. Workers' resentments over this issue combined with the concurrent struggles over the new wage and bonus systems to produce a very serious problem of labor morale. The tensions were particularly acute in smaller towns, where a single plant closing or even large-scale layoffs could produce devastating effects on the local economy. Local government and Party officials, who would have to cope with the side effects, usually attempted to mobilize whatever influence they had with the central authorities to secure special dispensations and continued subsidies for the chronically unprofitable plants in their areas. The factory management and the local trade union councils, which would be charged with the task of locating new jobs for the displaced, also had every incentive to fight the closings and layoffs. Workers affected by such decisions were especially adversely affected because there was no government program in existence to provide any kind of unemployment benefits until the middle of 1967, when a system of "allowances" was finally introduced. The allowances came to a maximum of 60 percent of the worker's former pay and were conditional on his willingness to accept whatever temporary jobs might be assigned him by the local authorities (usually seasonal agricultural work).

The unrest generated in the factories appears to have activated the formerly rather passive trade union organizations into pressing for certain safeguards, including the system of unemployment allowances. The new labor code that was enacted in conjunction with the implementation of Czechoslovakia's economic reforms included a provision requiring the director of an enterprise to secure the approval of the enterprise trade union committee before involuntarily discharging any employee. In the event of a veto by the committee, the director could appeal the decision only to the next higher layer of the trade union organization. Since the officials of the trade union apparatus had no stake in enterprise profitability but *were* held responsible both for maintaining enterprise morale and for placing the displaced in new jobs, the trade unions seem to have taken on a genuine protective function.

The mobilization of local and regional organs of the Party and the state administration, as well as the local trade union committees, had a very substantial braking effect on the reformers' efforts to force a more rational deployment of the labor force. By 1967, charges were being aired in the press by hostile critics that certain unnamed "intellectuals" harbored most un-socialist designs for "the creation of a reserve army of the unemployed" for the purpose of tightening labor discipline and repressing the justified complaints of honest workers.[61] By the summer of 1967, the press acknowledged that the policy of labor transfers "has been encountering the greatest embarrassment,"[62] stalemated by "hundreds of interventions from the outside and passive resistance from the inside."[63] Of particular importance in resisting the rigorous application of requirements for enterprise profitability at the expense of layoffs was the role of the Slovak regional Party organizations, since Slovakia was especially hard hit by closings in the first year of the reform. The post-reform decline of 10 percent in the profitability of Slovak enterprises not only had adverse effects on employment, but also threatened to limit the supply of investment funds for further regional development.[64] These alarming developments were a central feature of Slovak regional Secretary Alexander Dubcek's attack on Party First Secretary Antonin Novotny at the September 1967 Central Committee Plenum, which ultimately precipitated Novotny's fall from power.

The continuation of substantial subsidies to keep unprofitable enterprises going was the most direct cost of the effort to maintain full employment, and the stalemating of the process of labor transfers in 1967 resulted in a drain on the state budget for that year of over thirty billion crowns,[65] a figure equivalent to the annual wages of almost 150,000 industrial workers. The additional indirect costs to the economy in terms of economic growth foregone were incalculable but clearly substantial.

During the pre-intervention period in 1968, the major economic reformers, including Sik, Kouba, Turek, and Selucky, actively publicized the economic burden on the general public represented by the continued heavy subsidization of the uneconomic enterprises. Nevertheless, little additional headway actually seems to have been made in closing them down, and in view of the rapid reactivation of the trade unions as representatives of the material interests of the workers that was taking place with official blessings during the Prague Spring, it is very hard to see how anything but an extremely gradualist approach could possibly have received the approval of the governing coalition of Party factions. Had · not the Warsaw Pact invasion intervened, it seems not unlikely that this issue would have emerged as a major source of conflict within the more liberalized order. Under the "normalization" regime of Gustav Husak, the return to centralized methods of planning and management and the exigencies of the political situation also largely prevented any substantial progress in solving the problem of Czechoslovakia's structural maldistribution of the labor force and investments.

In Hungary, structural maldistribution of the labor force was also recognized as a major brake on economic progress. However, Hungarian policies touching upon the "redeployment of labor" were rather more cautious than those which were attempted by the reformers in Czechoslovakia. The Hungarian leadership never spoke about the need for "redeployment" or "regrouping" without including careful reassurance of their unalterable support for a policy of full employment. There was, however, a conscious effort being made to redefine the guarantee of "the right to work" in somewhat less rigid terms than had become customary. Matyas Timar's account of the *in camera* discussions of the preparatory commission for the N.E.M. makes it clear that some more radical economists urged a much more aggressive policy than was in fact followed:

> In order to realize a more efficient employment, one group of economists proposed to tolerate a minimum extent of unemployment — with the simultaneous introduction of unemployment benefits stimulating work — stating that a stricter work discipline and a better organization could be properly secured only in this manner. Another group . . . thought it was correct to maintain full employment but wished to impart a more up to date interpretation.
> . . . By full employment they meant the *overall* balance between demand for labor and the resources of labor. . . . It was clear . . . that the suppression of uneconomical production . . . required . . . the regrouping of the existing labor force, their retraining for other skills with careful circumspection. Finally, the latter view was accepted and implemented, if not with full consistency.[66]

The discussions that occurred around the time of the approval of the N.E.M. often touched upon the possible problems that might be created by the dishoarding of labor when profit would become the chief regulator of enterprise decision-making. Vice-Premier Jeno Fock in his speech to the Ninth Congress acknowledged these fears with unusual frankness:

> At conferences dealing with the reform of the economic mechanism, worries are being voiced that the new mechanism will result in mass unemployment. . . . [T]he people themselves recognize that the enterprises employ a number of people who are not needed and that the trend to make more profit will probably block the hiring of new manpower. . . . We expect the managers . . . to seek the reasonable employment of those people by means of manufacturing new products and opening up new markets. . . . [T]he regrouping of the workers who are not indispensable, even after the expansion of production, should be carried out with the utmost humanity. . . . [N]ew places of employment should be offered and, if it is necessary, chances for retraining. . . . [O]ur goal is still the maintenance of full employment . . . interpreted in a correct way . . . .[67]

The trade union organizations were charged with important responsibilities for softening the impact of the new incentives to economize on labor costs. The Chief Secretary of the Steel and Metal Workers' Union (a union whose workers were apt to be under considerable pressure because of the unfavorable conditions for profitable operation in that industry) declared:

> the trade unions . . . have to use all means to take part in the work to increase productivity. But along with this, the trade unions should also influence the economic managers in such a way that they will not consider reduction of the work force. . . . They should use the means of cutting the work force only at the very worst and they should create adequate new jobs in the interest of employment.[68]

Appreciating the political importance of avoiding any massive dislocations of the labor force, Rezso Nyers laid down the basic strategy to be followed. There was to be very little done toward the regrouping of labor prior to the reform (in contrast to the pattern in Czechoslovakia, where it was undertaken simultaneously with the first experiments and helped to create the adverse political climate that so bedeviled the implementation of the reform). The shifts should be gradual and carefully planned.

> The modification of the production structure is inevitable, but it cannot be realized overnight. . . . We cannot advance by sudden leaps because we would only get into trouble if we wanted to achieve everything at once.
> . . . .
> The correct procedure is for the state, at the beginning, to guarantee the opportunity for uninterrupted operation to every enterprise but, at the same time, to put gradually increasing pressure on the enterprises — by means of the economic mechanism — to manage properly the collective property entrusted to them. [69]

The reasons for such a cautious approach are not difficult to fathom. The problem of uneconomic enterprises (and even whole industries operating at a loss) was of an even greater magnitude than the regime had thus far been willing to reveal publicly. According to Timar, an unpublished study of the Economic Research Institute prepared in connection with the reform of prices produced some dismaying results. The study calculated the profitability of the fifty-eight major sub-branches of Hungarian industry on the basis of 1968 prices. The top twenty-three sub-branches employed 32 percent of the industrial labor force and 32 percent of all fixed assets, and they supplied between 130 and 140 percent of the total net income of industry. The lowest group consisted of nineteen sub-branches operating at a *loss* of 45 to 60 percent of industry's total net income.   These nineteen sub-branches employed *41 percent of the in-dustrial labor force* and 37 percent of all industrial assets.[70]

The very high priority placed by the Hungarian political leadership on maintaining full employment and preventing the closing of the so-called "uneconomic factories" led them to follow policies rather similar to those which emerged in Czechoslovakia in 1967, producing somewhat analogous pressures toward economic recentralization.

If workers are to be kept secure in their established employment and protected from the consequences of their enterprise's inefficiency for their prospects for wage and bonus increases, then the authorities have to depart from the market socialism model and engage in an intervention that has major secondary consequences. High-cost enterprises have to be protected from market-dictated cuts in their output volume (which would make part or all of its staff redundant).   This can be accomplished by some combination of the following three interventionary strategies: (1) The government can devise a special subsidy system to bolster the finances of the weak enterprises. (2) Inefficient enterprises can be protected through a process of merger whereby the new and larger combined body gains monopoly power over its products and their close substitutes.   (3) The prices paid to the enterprises for their output may be fixed in such a way that the costs of even the least efficient enterprise in the industry are covered, while the total volume of demand for the product is artificially maintained at a high level, either by state purchase or by pegging the retail prices for the product below the wholesale prices and making up the difference by a subsidy to the final seller.

All of these forms of direct intervention have a distorting effect on the economy via the price system. Several of the consequences are particularly noteworthy. The fixing of producers' prices at an artificially high level in order to protect the weakest enterprises results in artificially high profits for the other enterprises in the industry. Under both the Czechoslovak and Hungarian economic reforms, enterprises retained a portion of their profits for use as investment funds and as sources for increasing the incomes of their employees. In both countries, the fixing of the new prices in such a way as to protect vulnerable enterprises led to larger-than-planned enterprise profits and, consequently, serious inflationary pressures, which then had to be countered by the imposition of additional controls on the enterprises' supposed freedom of action. Moreover, this same situation led to the maintaining of "sellers' market" conditions generally, with a consequent weakening of the market discipline which was supposed to bring about improvements in quality and enterprise responsiveness to consumers' needs. Finally, the assurance of direct or indirect subsidies large enough to ensure retention of the current labor force removed many of the incentives that the inefficient enterprise would otherwise have had to mend its ways, while the central authorities, concerned about the strain on their budget, were encouraged to exercise "petty tutelage" over the subsidized enterprise in order to cut their losses.

So thorough were the Hungarians in their plans to avoid excessive "shocks" during the first year of the reform due to shutdowns or dishoarding of excess labor that, instead of unemployment, 1968 witnessed a massive labor shortage. The investment boom stimulated by unexpectedly large enterprise profits got under way toward the end of 1968 and accelerated during 1969. The system of wage regulation that the reformers had chosen put a ceiling on the increase in *average* wages in the enterprise, which led to extensive hiring of only marginally needed unskilled laborers so that managers would be able to give raises to their more skilled and valued employees. The total industrial work force increased by about 4 percent, and the number of unfilled job openings in Budapest rose by some 30 percent.

What the reformers had not counted on was the extreme difficulty of carrying out their plans for the gradual shift of workers out of the unprofitable and highly subsidized enterprises. The discontent engendered by the attempts at "develeling" wages and bonuses made it politically imperative that the subsidized industries not merely receive enough to continue operating but also additional sums so that average wages could increase enough to ease the pain. For similar reasons, it was not deemed politically feasible to revise the structure of consumer prices so as to fully reflect actual costs, since the application of the profitability principle in this sphere would have led to substantial increases in the cost of food and hence would decrease the absolute level of real income for a large group of the less-skilled workers (as well as other low income groups within the population). Exemptions and preferences to the basic principles of the N.E.M. were granted on such a wide scale that total subsidies being paid out by the state showed an increasing rather than a decreasing trend. Subsidies increased to thirty-five billion forints in 1968, thirty-seven billion forints in 1969, and by 1973, subsidies had mounted to sixty-three billion forints, or 28 percent of the entire state budget.[71]

While the official evaluations of the N.E.M.'s results continued to be positive, the atmosphere in Hungary seemed to change noticeably in late 1970 and early 1971, as economic policy makers became increasingly concerned at the degree to which the effective and consistent implementation of the reforms was being impeded by the practical political constraints of no major layoffs, no major price increases, and no absolute declines in living standards for any substantial segment of the population. At a conference of economic experts in October of 1971, Premier Fock announced a temporary slowdown in the rate at which the N.E.M.'s principles would continue to be implemented, necessitated by the need to curtail the excessive investment boom and the inflationary tendencies inherent in the too-rapidly increasing wage rates. Administrative curbs were put on investment, wage fund increases, and imports. Four special state committees were appointed to make a critical and thorough review of the N.E.M.'s accomplishments and shortcomings and to make recommendations for its improvement.

A new debate unfolded in the economic journals and the specialized press. By and large, the economists blamed the serious economic difficulties of 1971 on the insufficiently determined and consistent implementation of the N.E.M., especially the rigidities of policies in regard to the labor market, the distortion of the price system caused by the failure to carry out an adequate revision of consumer prices, and the lack of political will to make a determined effort to shut off the subsidies. At the same time, voices within the trade union hierarchy were becoming increasingly critical of the N.E.M. because of its tenuous relationship to what were perceived as basic principles of socialist equality and to the fundamental social policies that these dictated.

The November 1972 Plenum of the Central Committee once again endorsed the basic validity of the N.E.M. in principle but also reaffirmed the necessity of respecting the fundamental political constraints with respect to employment and the living standard. A new departure in policy was undertaken on an *ad hoc* basis, when fifty large "problem enterprises" were in effect removed from the N.E.M. system and placed under close ministerial control as a kind of functional equivalent of going into receivership. While on the one hand this could be seen as a retreat from the N.E.M., on the other it represented a "get tough" policy on the issues of subsidies and over-full employment in much the spirit that was being expressed by the reformers. The N.E.M. was not being abandoned, but it was clearly being placed on hold for an indefinite period, until such time as more vigorous implementation might become compatible with the observance of necessary limits in the areas of incomes policy, price stability, and the avoidance of unemployment.

The Reforms' Impact on the Political Role of Workers

Market-oriented forms of relatively radical economic reform, such as were adopted in Hungary and Czechoslovakia, substantially affect the socio-economic positions, not only of the central economic administration, the Party apparatus, and the enterprise management, but also of the rank and file workers and employees as well. As we have seen, the immediate impact on blue-collar workers is alarming to them because some of the more positively evaluated features of socialism are called into question by the new system of planning and management. Greater reliance upon the market mechanism and the necessity for enterprise management to rationalize for the sake of profitability means that the enterprise must become a more flexible, changing, and hence, less "secure" environment for its personnel. The distribution of rewards undergoes changes which are costly to the less skilled or less ambitious elements of the work force and which threaten the integration of the social system of the enterprise by directly challenging the relatively egalitarian ethos that previously was associated in the popular mind with "the achievements of socialism." Although the intended long-term effects of reforming planning and management were to accelerate the rate of economic growth and thus to make possible a more rapid improvement in the living standards of the entire population, such distant advantages are difficult to grasp under the conditions of austerity and disruption of familiar routines that accompany initial implementation. As a locksmith in a Budapest factory noted in his letter to the editor of *Tarsadalme Szemle*:

> [P]eople started to talk about the new economic mechanism, then, a couple of months later, the price of meat and fuel increased, meals in the factory canteen became more expensive, the rate of old age pension contributions and transit fares increased. All of them meant daily extra expenses. Naturally there also were positive measures. In my case, however, I did not see the balance between plus and minus; at the very best, it could only be noted in the national average.[72]

Thus the first response of many, perhaps most, workers confronted by the uncertainties of the economic reforms in Czechoslovakia and Hungary was one of wariness or even of outright hostility,[73] and the natural sequel was for those who were threatened to seek means to defend themselves. The long, bitter battles over "delevelization" indicate that threatened workers were not without allies and resources for resistance. The devolution of greater discretionary powers to the enterprise management made the makers of important decisions affecting the workers' interests more immediately accessible to them than had been the case under the more centralized system. Managers concerned about the smooth operation of their enterprises often found it expedient to be responsive, at least with respect to matters where the protests were most intense. Moreover, with respect to issues such as factory closings or massive layoffs, the interests of the threatened workers tended to coincide with those of local Party, state, and trade union officials, who would have to deal with the external consequences of managerial or ministerial decisions but who would not themselves derive any appreciable benefits from the increases in profitability or macro-economic efficiency that might result. Such regional officials controlled significant political resources and could often be prevailed upon to intervene on the workers' behalf with the enterprise director or with his ministerial superiors.

With the devolution of greater authority to the enterprise director and with the new, more entrepreneurial role that the director was expected to play, the nature of authority relationships within the enterprise changed considerably. The director no longer appeared in quite the same light. Instead of being merely the agent of the state in charge of the enterprise, deriving his authority essentially from his intermediary role between the staff and "The Highest Authority" as embodied in the state economic plan, the director increasingly derived his authority from his expertise and success in safeguarding and advancing the material interests of his enterprise and of the people who constituted its staff. By that same token, when managerial decisions contradicted the interests of any of the various groupings within the enterprise collective, his relative detachment from the hierarchy above him made him more vulnerable to pressures originating within the enterprise for changes and adjustments.

The destabilizing consequences of the economic reforms for the internal balance of forces and interests that had grown up under the older system led to a search for a new *modus vivendi* in intra-enterprise relations in which the most essential interests of all the participants could be sufficiently protected to ensure the integration and cooperation necessary for the organization in function in its new environment. Because workers saw themselves as threatened with the loss of the basic security they had enjoyed under the old arrangements, both the broader norms of "socialist morality" and the practical necessities of maintaining stable labor relations converged to make legitimate the suggestion that new institutions (or modifications of old ones) with the function of protecting the particularized interests of the work force ought to be an important part of the internal organization of the enterprise. Regularized, institutionalized channels for the "responsible" articulation and representation of interests would be far preferable to the irregular and often extremely disruptive spontaneous efforts at self-defense that tended to arise during the transition to the new systems of planning and management.

One manifestation of such institutionalization that took place in both Czechoslovakia and Hungary was the substantial redefinition of the functions of the trade union apparatus in the socialist enterprise. Under the Stalinist system, the trade unions had been considered to be primarily "transmission belts" mobilizing the labor force for the effective implementation of Party policies, especially the fulfillment and over-fulfillment of the physical targets of the production plan. In Hungary, this "excessively narrow" view of the trade unions' functions was strongly repudiated in 1966 during the preparations for the Ninth Party Congress. Sandor Gaspar, General Secretary of the National Trade Union Council and an important member of the Politburo laid down the Party's new line:

> In 1950, the leadership of the Hungarian Workers Party — by taking an incorrect concept as their point of departure — politically accused the trade unions of syndicalism and social democracy, and limited their function of safeguarding the workers' interests to [the administration of] social benefits. The dogmatic and sectarian political attitude deprived the trade union movement of its historical basic function, its life and soul: the representation and safeguarding of the workers' interests — leaving out of consideration that, even under socialist conditions, the individual interest of the employer and the overall social interest may be in conflict.[74]

Gaspar went on to declare that "the justified increase of the responsibility and authority of the one-man economic leadership" in the enterprise under N.E.M. demanded an increase in the authority of the trade unions.[75] Gaspar's position was basically accepted and affirmed by the resolutions of the Ninth Party Congress.

The new Labor Code, which was drafted during 1966 and 1967 for implementation in conjunction with the N.E.M. in 1968, broke new ground in Communist labor relations by endowing the trade union committees in the enterprises with certain new statutory rights to facilitate the performance of their "protective" function. These statutory rights, five in number, were designated as the "Right of Consent," the "Right of Decision," the "Right of Control," the "Right of Veto," and the "Right of Opinion."

The right of consent applied to certain kinds of decisions at the level of the enterprise which could only be taken in consultation with the trade union committee requiring its final consent to the content of the decision. In general this right was to be exercised through negotiation of the collective contract (concluded annually), which now would specify the basic rules and regulations covering remuneration, labor discipline, and safety precautions. (Formerly, these were largely matters for ministerial regulation.)

The right of decision referred to the right of the enterprise trade union committees to make certain decisions unilaterally, usually after discussion with the management. This right applied mainly to matters of the administration of fringe benefits long under trade union control.

The right of control pertained to the trade union's function of surveillance and checking to ensure enterprise management's compliance with the terms of the collective contract and protective provisions of applicable labor legislation. Violations uncovered were to be reported to higher trade union and ministerial authorities for their decision on further actions to be taken. Rights of access to the books and records of the enterprise were guaranteed.

The right of veto was a radically new experiment. The trade union committees were delegated the right temporarily to block implementation of any managerial decision at the level of the enterprise if such implementation would involve either a violation of the law or would be "contrary to socialist morality." In the event of a veto, implementation would be suspended until the dispute could be adjudicated by the appropriate judicial, ministerial, and/or trade union authorities.

The right of opinion provided that the trade union committee had to be informed in advance of certain kinds of decisions affecting substantial numbers of workers. The union would then have the right to express an official opinion on the matter both to the enterprise management and, if necessary, to higher authorities, before the decision became final.[76]

Under the N.E.M., the Hungarian trade unions seem to have treated their new rights as much more than mere formalities. The right of veto, for example, has been frequently used to prevent or delay both individual firings and mass layoffs.[77] Even more remarkably, the "Directives for the Enforcement of the Right of Veto of the Enterprise Trade Unions" specifically instructed those Party members serving on Trade Union Committees to "decide independently" of the Party organization when considering the question of exercising a veto.[78]

The trade union leadership at the national level, most notably Politburo member and Trade Union Council Chairman Sandor Gaspar, displayed an evident ambition for the trade unions to assume even greater functions than they were in fact assigned by the Party. The most important instance of conflict on this issue occurred during the drafting of the new labor code in 1966. Gaspar took a public stand in favor of making the hiring, evaluation, and removal of the managers of enterprises a matter subject to the decision of the trade unions.

In the [agricultural and artisans'] cooperatives, the members themselves decide who will be their leaders and whether X or Y should stay or be replaced. . . . It is quite natural that, in the form of public property in the state firms, the same principle should be enforced and the appointment or replacement of the leader should depend upon the opinion of the workers as well. . . . This subject will be on the agenda . . . when the Council of Ministers and the secretariat of the T.U.C. will discuss the practical relations between the state and the trade unions.[79]

The resolution of the meeting represented a clear defeat of Gaspar's proposal. Instead, appointment of enterprise directors would remain exclusively a matter of ministerial jurisdiction (in consultation with appropriate Party organs), although the *opinion* of the trade union committee would "normally" be requested during consideration of such matters.[80]

Although many provisions of the N.E.M. were curtailed when the Party leadership decided to put on the brakes in response to the economic crisis of 1971, the active role of the trade unions seems, if anything, to have been enhanced. Gaspar's militant stand against closings and layoffs may indeed have been a principal force behind the restrictive decisions of October 1971 and November 1972. Following the November 1972 Plenum, the trade union apparatus displayed evident satisfaction, and it was even pointedly advocated that the trade union committees should make much more frequent use of the right of veto:

The idea that enterprise trade unions can make use of [the right of veto] only as a last resort must be abandoned.[81]

It is quite clear that the Hungarian trade union movement under the N.E.M. has taken a vigorous role in fulfilling its function as protector of workers' particularized interests. What is much less clear is the extent to which rank-and-file workers can actually exercise effective control over the trade union apparatus. While the Hungarian press provided extensive coverage of the "revival" of factory-level trade union democracy, and it appears that the trade union committees came to be held in much higher regard by the people whose interests they supposedly represent, it is also evident that the higher level trade union committees and Party agencies still exercise decisive control over the selection and promotion of lower-level trade union officials.

What seems to have happened is a result of two somewhat conflicting imperatives. On the one hand, the Party leadership has accepted the idea that labor peace and the demands of socialist morality require the active defense of particularized workers' interests, yet the preservation of the still centralized and monopolistic political order requires that fully autonomous grass roots political forces not be allowed to arise, lest they come to challenge the prerogatives of the Party. The organization of the trade union movement according to the norms of "democratic centralism" under the general supervision of appropriate Party organs at all levels seems to provide a viable mechanism for allowing the expression of workers' grievances and giving them effective channels of access to the decision-making process, without, however, incurring the risks that "extreme" opinions directly contrary to important Party policies will acquire widespread organizational support. Control of recruitment to the trade union committees at the various levels through the Party's "nomenklatura" system gives reasonable assurance that only "sound" Communist Party loyalists will direct the organization machinery and exercise the formidable legal prerogatives of the labor movement.

In Czechoslovakia, efforts to provide channels for workers' interest articulation took a rather different course. There were signs of a certain revitalization of the trade unions as vehicles for worker protection during the period of large-scale experimentation with the new system of planning and management: resistance against excessively large differentiation of bonuses as between managers and manual workers, taking the initiative in pushing through the legal provisions for unemployment "allowances." But the top leadership of the Communist Party (prior to 1968) did not give such enthusiastic encouragement to this trend as their counterparts in Hungary. The May 1965 conference of the Revolutionary Trade Union Movement was instructed on the trade unions' role in the New Economic System by the Central Committee's Secretary for Ideological Affairs Jiri Hendrych, a staunch conservative:

> The point is for the trade unions to free themselves of formalism and to help more than they previously have in educating the working people for greater responsibility and discipline . . . in the application of the new economic thinking.

The unions would continue and intensify their

comradely cooperation in achieving conditions for high labor productivity and plant profitability. On the other hand, a plant council will not be able to interfere with the indivisible authority of managers nor to deprive them of personal responsibility.[82]

Accordingly, at the conclusion of the conference, the Vice-Chairman of the Central Trade Union Council summarized the trade unions' main tasks in the coming years as including only the following:

1.to increase profitability and productivity by encouraging the greater exploitation of science and technology in production;

2.to encourage the improvement of workers' qualifications;

3.to help organize the gradual reduction of the work week to five days;

4.to improve working and social conditions for women; and

5.to facilitate better working conditions, better exploitation of leisure, and better transportation to and from work.[83]

The Czechoslovak trade union movement seems to have begun genuinely revitalizing its protective role only during the course of 1967, as the renewed activism in the factory committees led to substantial changes in the Trade Union Council's leadership. The Central Committee of the TUC that was elected at the February 1967 Congress was composed of new members to the extent of 60 percent, most of them direct from the factory committees rather than from the much more bureaucratized national level trade union *apparats*.[84]

The political upheavals of the Prague Spring led not only to a more revitalized trade union movement but also to something rather different as well: the creation of elected "councils of working people" in the enterprises with general supervisory responsibilities over the management of the enterprise.

Initially, most of the prominent advocates of the economic reform were less than enthusiastic about the scattered proposals for "workers' self-management" that had been put forward by some intellectuals late in 1967 and early in 1968. The economists operated mainly from a "technocratic" or managerial perspective, and it was feared that greater participation of the workers in enterprise management might hamper the director in carrying out the kind of creative, scientific, and long-range decision-making for the development of productivity that the reformers were so very anxious to encourage. Specifically, it was believed by many that a greater voice for the rank and file workers would only reinforce the already strong tendencies toward "leveling" in the wage and bonus system, that measures of rationalization would be resisted, and that workers would push for immediate wage increases at the expense of the long-term commitment to investment and modernization so vital for raising productivity.

On the other hand, the necessity of some mechanism for applying pressure on incumbent directors who were opposed to the reform and/or too closely identified with the old political establishment was readily apparent. The 1965 experiments had often involved creation of a "production committee" within the enterprise, composed of lower-level managers and engineers and charged with advising the director on a variety of basically technical problems of long-term investment strategy. In January and February of 1968, the reformers began toying with the idea of expanding these committees and giving them more important functions in order to use them as a means of upgrading the quality of managerial decision-making. Ota Sik at first proposed an expanded version of the old production committee to function as "a collective expert organ," which would include not only specialists from the enterprise staff but also experts recruited from outside as well (from the banks, from enterprises that were major customers, from local councils, from the universities and research institutes, and so on).[85]   The composition envisaged was one-third management and enterprise experts, one-third outside experts and central organ representatives, and one-third elected representatives of the entire enterprise collective.

The intensification of the political struggles within the Party and the increased activity of the trade unions during April and May seem to have convinced most leading reformers of the need for mobilizing greater working class support for both the economic reforms and the new political leadership. The Party's Action Program adopted on April 5, 1968, already outlined a version of the works council that contained both "technocratic" and "democratic" elements in its conception. While insisting that the councils should be composed in such a way as to ensure "the influence of the interests of the entire society and an expert and qualified level of decision-making," the Action Program went on to describe the councils as part of a program for the "democratization of the economy":

> The economic reform will increasingly place the working communities in the position of bearing the direct consequences of good or bad management. The Party therefore considers it essential that those who bear the consequences should exert an influence. There is need for democratic bodies in the enterprise with well-defined powers in relation to management. The directors and top executives should be responsible to these bodies for overall performance and would be appointed by them. . . . This naturally in no way reduces the indivisible authority and responsibility of the leading executives in managing the enterprise, which, together with their qualifications and managing abilities, is the basic pre-condition of successful enterprising.[86]

By May, Sik had radically revised his original stand. In his speech to the Czechoslovak Economic Society, he endorsed the idea that the majority of the councils' membership should be elected by the workforce from among their own members, with the remainder to be drawn from the "expert" staff and from outside agencies. While the councils still should not attempt to usurp the basic prerogatives of the director, once appointed, Sik nevertheless allowed that it might be appropriate for them under certain circumstances formally to express "lack of confidence" in the director or even to remove him from his position. They would decide the director's salary and the conditions under which his bonuses would be determined (to be agreed in advance by contract). The director was to be assured effective control over production and personnel policies, subject only to a general obligation to report directly to the council periodically and to obtain its general endorsement of the most fundamental long-term policies to be pursued. During the term of his contract, the director would be removable only "for cause," thereby insulating him from possible outbreaks of "demagogic tendencies" within the enterprise collective. Sik's proposals became the basis for the government's provisional "Framework Principles for the Establishment of Working People's Councils" adopted in early June.[87]

Sik's (and the government's) greatly increased emphasis on the "democratic" aspect of the councils seems in good part to have been a reaction to the turbulent conditions which had developed in many of the factories during April and May. Enterprise managers found themselves the targets of a torrent of worker criticism and hostility, as the inhibitions on free speech slipped away and the accumulated frustrations of years of austerity came pouring out. In some cases, managers were blamed for lack of competence or efficiency and therefore for having directly caused the lagging of the employees' bonuses and incomes. In other cases, opposition was more clearly political in nature, being based on the managers' close ties with the conservative local political establishment. There were a number of cases where enterprise directors or plant managers were forced to resign by worker intimidation and even the threat of strike action.[88] In several cases, the reformers in Prague considered the ousted managers to have been efficient and technically competent victims of circumstance, and there was a good deal of concern expressed about the rowdy methods and the extreme egalitarian rhetoric of some of the instigators. Sik's proposals seem to have represented not only democratic idealism but also an attempt to tame the more spontaneous and elemental aspects of working class protest by institutionalizing workers' participation in a setting that would encourage a sense of responsibility and would meld together both "democratic" and "expert" elements in the exercise of general supervision of managerial performance.

Even before official authorization, the organization of enterprise working people's councils had already been undertaken in a number of the larger enterprises during April and May. After the promulgation of the government's preliminary guidelines in June, councils were formed at a rapid pace, numbering several hundred by the end of the month. There seems to have been very little effective central guidance to the formation of the new councils, and many of the organizers paid only casual attention to the provisions of the government's guidelines in the writing of their own charters and by-laws. (A retrospective study of a sample of ninety-five councils determined that the local trade unions had initiated the formation of the councils in about 65 percent of the cases. Communist Party cells were the primary organizers in 17 percent of the cases, and enterprise directors themselves initiated 14 percent.[89])

The enterprise councils tended to go beyond the official guidelines in their stress on the "democratic" aspect of their functioning. The proportion of the membership on the ten- to thirty-man councils directly elected from the factory floor ran as high as 80 percent, with 65 percent being the smallest known proportion. Not all of the councils included any "outside" members at all, and generally those which did include such members chose them themselves by cooptation rather than allow them to be externally appointed or elected. The voting rights of outside members were usually restricted.[90] Moreover, there was a tendency for the councils to claim broader functions for themselves than had been envisioned by the Party leadership. In addition to advisory and supervisory functions, most councils also exercised rights to "co-decision" with the director in certain matters: most importantly, on the division of profits between investment and bonus funds, on proposals for merging the enterprise with some other entity, and on "especially risky" investment undertakings. Most also asserted some sort of veto right pertaining to decisions of the director which might have a major and adverse impact on substantial numbers of the employees.[91]

Nevertheless, even with the high proportions of the councils' memberships that were directly elected (and in multiple candidate, secret ballot elections at that[92]), their overall composition had a distinctly "technocratic" cast. About 26 percent of the council members were university-trained, which made the councilors a considerably better educated group than the nation-wide average for directors of enterprises. About 70 percent of the council members turned out to be either engineers or manual workers skilled enough to be classified as "technicians," while only about 25 percent were ordinary manual workers.[93] Communist Party members constituted at least half the membership in fifty of the ninety-five councils investigated.[94]

The pronounced "technocratic" appearance of the councils' occupational structure and the predominance of Party members within their membership contrasted rather strikingly with the turbulence of the situations that often led to their organization. The goal of increasing the stability of labor-management relations seems to have been well served by their establishment. Moreover, since the councils were utilized as a participatory vehicle in disproportionate degree by the younger professionals and the more highly-qualified manual workers, they were also well-suited to their assigned role of monitoring the performance of the directors and mobilizing support for "rationalization" measures within the enterprises. The trade unions, on the other hand, retained (and increasingly asserted) their role as protectors of the bread-and-butter interests of the worker *qua* employee, conceding to the councils the function of representing the interests of the workers deriving from their participation as co-owners of the social means of production. On certain matters, many of the enterprise charters called for co-decision by union and council (matters of wages and bonus distribution), but, in general, the unions were not considered to be bound by the decisions of the councils or vice versa. The creation of the councils may, however, have acted to moderate the demands of the workers and the trade unions for wage increases: the largest increases and demands for increases came in April and May, and tended to diminish somewhat after June.[95]

Since the rather short period between the formation of the workers' councils and the August 1968 Warsaw Pact intervention had not allowed time for the new organization of authority and influence within the enterprise to fully crystallize, and since the full implementation of the economic reform program had not been accomplished yet either, the long-term implications of the coexistence of both trade unions and workers' councils in autonomous enterprises must remain largely a matter of speculation. Whether the rather close cooperation between the two working-class representative organizations that occurred during the period from the August invasion to the abolition of the councils in 1969 could have continued is questionable, given the rather different interests of the skilled and the unskilled with respect to issues of rationalization and of "delevelization" in wage and bonus scales. However, the institution of the workers' councils clearly did make an important alteration in the structure of power and authority within the enterprise by carrying reactive working class demands for simple self-defense against the vicissitudes of the new socialist market one step further. The workers' councils created opportunities for workers' participation to take on a more positive character and to facilitate the modernization and humanization of the work place simultaneously. Even though the workers in practice tended to elect more educated and skilled men than themselves to carry out the concrete supervision of the performance of enterprise management, this does not necessary imply that the "technocrats" would have felt free to feather their own nests at the expense of their constituents with impunity, given the relative visibility of their actions to the work force at large and the presumption that competitive elections would have continued to occur at regular intervals. The vigilance of the trade union committees might well have provided the necessary checks against such an eventuality.

From the point of view of the economic system as a whole, the institution of the workers' councils represented a very important structural change. The subjection of the enterprise director to the supervision of the council broke the last direct administrative linkage between the enterprise and the central planning authorities. With the power to hire, fire, and remunerate the director taken away from the ministerial bureaucracy, regulation of enterprise decision-making would necessarily have to be either in the form of "financial levers" or of more conventional legislation. Moreover, by subjecting enterprise management to the direct control of their employees, this measure provided "market socialism" with a very important ideological counterweight to charges that decentralization represented essentially "unsocialist" or "unproletarian" and retrogressive change leading to a restoration of capitalism or (at best) the disadvantaging of the manual workers relative to the intelligentsia. As the Yugoslavs have demonstrated, the ideology of "self-management" can compete quite effectively with more conventional Soviet-style Marxism-Leninism for the allegiance of both the working class and the humanistic intelligentsia.[96] Some such normative buttressing is probably necessary to long-term stability of a decentralized, market-oriented socialist economic system.

CHAPTER V

CONCLUSIONS

In summarizing the factors conditioning the outcomes of the economic reform movements in the various East European countries, it is useful to think of the reform process as consisting of a progression of stages or phases, at any one of which part or all of the proposed innovations could be sidetracked or rejected altogether. (In point of fact, the various "stages" historically have often overlapped considerably; nevertheless, ease of explication would seem to justify the simplifications involved in such a sequential account.) Adapting the terminology of the literature on innovation diffusion, we may label these stages of the reform process as follows: (1) Stimulation, (2) Initiation, (3) Persuasion, (4) Decision, and (5) Implementation.[1]

Stimulation of Reform

The immediate stimulus making the general idea of reforming the existing highly-centralized and bureaucratically administered economic mechanisms a live issue in a number of East European countries was the development of economic "performance gaps" — that is, serious and prolonged shortfalls of important indicators of economic performance relative to leadership expectations (with the latter being gauged by the benchmarks of the country's own past achievements and the contemporary achievements of the other communist countries and of the European capitalist countries). In the 1960's, serious problems with economic performance were a *sine qua non* for emergence of a politically potent economic reform movement, and the scope and significance of the reforms undertaken tended to vary directly with the magnitude of the economic debacle. Yet responding to economic difficulties by reforming the system of economic planning and management was neither automatic nor mechanically predetermined.   Serious shortcomings in economic performance (given the strong past commitments of the Communist regimes to a rapid economic growth) in some sense "demanded a response," but the character of the response selected necessarily depended upon the decision-makers' understanding of the causes of the difficulty and their awareness of specific kinds of alternative actions that might reasonably be taken to alleviate the situation.   (For example, the initial response of most East European regimes to the deterioration of capital/output ratios and the consequent retardation of economic growth rates during the mid-1950's was less often institutional reform than a compensating increase in the overall rate of investment at the expense of consumption, as embodied in the return to very ambitious capital construction plans most evident throughout the region from 1959 to 1961.   It was only after the long-term inadequacy of this "more of the same" response became manifest with the crises of the early 1960's that more fundamental remedies began once again to be seriously explored in some of the East European countries.)

Initiation of Reform

The initiative in formulating specific proposals for a degree of economic decentralization and a greater role for market forces in the coordination of economic activities came first of all from professional economists, especially those employed in (or with close connections to) institutions of research and higher education.   Their relative detachment from the planning and administrative bureaucracy meant that they had fewer vested interests in the perpetuation of existing arrangements, while their more "cosmopolitan" professional orientations (in the sense of greater familiarity with both the economic practices of other countries and the theoretical writings of foreign scholars interested in the political economy of socialism) made them more easily capable of perceiving or creating specific alternatives to the status quo than was generally characteristic either of the front-line economic planners and administrators or of the members of the Party's leading organs. In particular, the original architects of the reform proposals were able to draw upon a long suppressed and laboriously rediscovered tradition of "market socialist" thought as a theoretical grounding for their new criticism of the established Stalinist economic orthodoxy.

Yet the initiation of more or less open advocacy of specific reforms required something more than merely intellectual insights by isolated theoreticians.   For an economic reform program to become the basis for a serious movement or tendency with a realistic chance of influencing policy-makers, the new ways of economic thinking had to be diffused more widely among the members of the economics profession and among economic practitioners so that their full implications for practical life could be explored, tested, and elaborated in a comprehensive, consistent form — which necessarily presupposed a prior and significant relaxation of the totalitarian controls of the past over at least this sector of intellectual life. If the political authorities continued to make it physically unsafe to communicate or debate other than strictly orthodox ideas through rigid censorship of scholarly journals, the use of informers, and the consistent imposition of severe penalties for even mild deviations, then the emergence of coherent alternative policy proposals for the consideration of the policy-makers would be greatly retarded or even foreclosed altogether.

Since the elaboration of radically different perspectives on socialist economic institutions and policies in a systematic way was necessarily quite a time-consuming undertaking, it is readily understandable that the most theoretically sophisticated and vigorous schools of reformist economic thought developed in Poland and Hungary, where the early post-Stalin relaxations of political control had been the most dramatic and far-reaching in East Europe. Moreover, the further development and diffusion of reformist economic thinking elsewhere in the region during the early 1960's was closely consonant with the degree of enthusiasm displayed by the various national leadership groups for the second great destalinization campaign that had been launched by Khrushchev shortly before the Twenty-Second Congress of the C.P.S.U. In countries such as Albania and Romania, where the stern enforcement of ideological orthodoxy continued unabated right through the decade of the 1960's, economic reformism was effectively equated with economic "revisionism" and so thoroughly suppressed that it did not become an important intellectual current (an outcome that was no doubt rendered feasible by the continuing relatively high rates of economic growth enjoyed by these relatively less developed socialist economies under an essentially unmodified classical Stalinist system of economic management). The notably hesitant and half-hearted approaches to the lessening of ideological controls over intellectual life in Czechoslovakia, Bulgaria, and the G.D.R. greatly retarded the development of coherent schools of economic thought that could provide a systematic theoretical and practical grounding for the elaboration of workable economic reforms. By their own previous policies that tended to suppress innovative thinking in policy-related academic disciplines, the East European political leadership groups to a greater or a lesser degree limited their own capacities to address the problems of declining economic performance effectively, depriving themselves of the

ready availability of well thought-out alternative policies when the
plausibility of the established orthodoxy should begin to wear thin.

Persuasion

Since the various schemes of economic reform were not initially
conceived within the top policy-making elite, they had to be injected into
the political process from the outside through available channels of
communication and persuasion.   Given the constraints imposed upon
political communications by "unauthorized" persons in these relatively
closed political systems, this was no easy task. The advocates of reform
could not effectively make themselves heard unless at least some members
of the political leadership were first disposed to listen.

Where rigid ideologically-oriented controls on the discussion of policy-
relevant ideas had been partially relaxed, the result was not only greater
communication of innovative ideas among scholars and intellectuals. Such
loosening of the boundaries of acceptable discussion, by expanding the
audience for reformist ideas and improving their quality also made it more
likely that people directly involved in the formation of economic policies
would come into contact with these new ideas through their reading of
technical economic journals and their attendance at professional meetings.
It also became less risky for economists with ideas directly to approach
their more politically well-connected colleagues or even policy-makers
themselves with their proposals.

There was an important international dimension to the increasing
respectability of proposals for decentralization and greater reliance upon
the price mechanism. The demonstration effect of the Liberman debates
in the Soviet Union and the increasing degree of open discussion of similar
ideas in other Communist countries tended to encourage both inde-
pendently-thinking economists and the political leaders in lagging countries
to embark upon similar discussions at home, and the various international
congresses and other meetings of economists from Communist countries
tended to internationalize the debates and to spread reformist ideas from
the more advanced economic schools even to some of the economists from
countries where the domestic opportunities for public discussion of
economic matters remained relatively restricted.

The development of active reformist movements was of course
particularly accelerated in those countries where regime spokesmen issued
public requests for the submission of more, and more innovative, outside
analysis of the economic problems facing the nation,thereby clearly
indicating the desire of political leaders to obtain more varied inputs into
their deliberations than had previously been available from their
subordinates in the economic establishment. In Hungary, the G.D.R.,

and (somewhat later) Czechoslovakia, the regimes opened up important new channels of communication between academic economists and policy-makers with the appointment of large special blue-ribbon commissions or committees explicitly created for the purpose of tapping the advice of economic experts not currently involved in day-to-day economic planning or administration.[2] On the other hand, the political leadership showed little interest in improving their accessibility to outside experts in Albania, Romania, and even Poland, where the more independent stance of national leaders vis-a-vis the Soviet Union tended to nullify the demonstration effect of the Liberman debates and where problems of economic performance seemed less immediately pressing due to favorable demographic and other conditions for the success of classical Stalinist economic methods.

Persuading political leaders that proposals for a more decentralized and market-oriented approach to the economy were worthy of serious consideration was critically dependent upon the ability of the reformers to frame their analysis and to anchor their recommendations in terms that minimized the degree of discontinuity between the new arrangements and the old ones and that emphasized the grounding of the new reforms in the analytical traditions of classical Marxism-Leninism. It was absolutely essential from the outset to differentiate the proposed changes from anything that smacked at all of a restoration of capitalism. The reformers' arguments centered around the propositions that rationalized prices could be an effective tool for more scientific planning by facilitating rational economic calculation, and that effective leadership control of the principle macroeconomic variables would be enhanced rather than diminished by a shift away from administrative methods in favor of economic or "parametric" methods to guide economic decisions at the micro level. The continuing socialist character of the economy would be assured by virtue of the central authorities' continuing decisive control over the allocation of productive resources and the distribution of incomes and by virtue of the fact that private individuals or groups would still be prevented from exploiting other workers through any large-scale private appropriation of the means of production.

From a more ideological perspective, the reformers' analysis of the root causes of decelerating economic growth in the more developed Communist countries was framed so as to legitimize their departures from Stalin's economic dogmas by appealing to a higher authority — the teachings of Karl Marx. Drawing on Marx's characterization of economic growth in industrial societies as being composed of both "extensive" and "intensive" components, the relative significance of which must necessarily shift in favor of the latter as an economy reaches the higher stages of development, the reformers could assert that Stalin's prescriptions for economic growth under socialism constituted an impermissible overgeneralization of the economic laws governing one transitional historical period to the entire era of socialist development. They conceded that the highly centralized system of planning and management and over-riding of market forces characteristic of Stalinist economic policies had indeed been admirably adapted to the maximization of growth in an under-industrialized economy characterized by large-scale unemployment and underemployment of labor and an absolute scarcity of productive capital. But the achievement of a full-employment, urban-based, industrial economy marked the impending exhaustion of the reserves of under-utilized productive resources which in the preceding period had made it possible to achieve rapid growth almost exclusively by "extensive" means. After this point in economic development, further economic growth would necessarily have to be derived from "intensive" sources largely neglected by the Stalinist economic model.

By identifying established economic practices and institutions with the period of extensive growth, East European economic reformers were in the politically enviable position of being able simultaneously to applaud the basic correctness of the Party leadership's past economic decisions *and* to argue for the historical necessity of radical change as the prerequisite for future economic success. The decentralization of microeconomic decision-making, the enhancement of the role of economic calculation in value terms, and the more effective harnessing of material incentives were identified as essential elements of the new economic mechanism that would be best adapted for successful economic development under the new intensive strategy, which must necessarily concentrate on such tasks as the improvement of allocative efficiency in investment, the reduction of waste in production, the stimulation of more rapid technological and managerial improvements, and the more effective utilization of international trade.

Decision for Reform

Comparative examination of the economic reform programs adopted in Eastern Europe during the mid-1960's strongly supports the generalization that the radicalism of the economic reform co-varied with two major variables that were relatively independent of each other, each of which embodied both objective and subjective components. The first factor tending to vary directly with the degree of change in economic arrangements in the direction of greater decentralization and more reliance upon the price mechanism was the seriousness of the "performance gap" in the economy during the immediately preceding period — which is to say, with the extent of the disparity between the actual performance of the national economy and the warranted level of expectations presumptively entertained by the country's political leadership.   The leaders of countries whose economic growth compared unfavorably with formerly achieved rates and with the rates being achieved by either their socialist allies or their capitalist rivals (or both) approved more radical economic reform programs than leaders presiding over economies with more favorable performances by any or all of these criteria.   The second factor conducive to more radical economic reform (given that a performance gap also occurred) was the degree to which the regime allowed the articulation of views critical of currently established economic institutions and policies.   The leaders of countries in which press censorship was more relaxed, in which economists and other social scientists were less inhibited from intellectual contacts with their counterparts abroad, and in which channels of access to policy-makers for economic experts drawn from outside the administrative establishment were provided, were more likely to respond to economic problems with institutional reforms than were the leaders of East European countries pursuing more restrictive policies in the regulation of intellectuals' activity.

An additional background variable of interest in understanding the degree of economic reform undertaken is the impact of the preferences of the Soviet leadership.   In earlier periods, and particularly during the lifetime of Josef Stalin, Eastern European regimes were expected to (and usually did) emulate the Soviet example in the economic field (as indeed in all other fields of policy).   The initial adoption of Soviet-style economic planning and management beginning in 1948 as well as the frequent policy shifts subsequently undertaken in obvious response to Soviet initiatives during the 1950's are impressive evidence for the notion that major economic decisions (such as the decision to undertake modifications in the system of planning and management) in East European Communist systems are apt to be responses to conditions in the Soviet Union rather more than responses to domestic economic circumstances.   This notion, however, is not very useful in furthering our understanding of the politics of economic reform since the 1960's unless it is considerably qualified and placed in the specific context of the period.   While Soviet leaders no doubt had the power to dictate major economic policies to the leaders of many of the East European countries during this period (if they were willing to accept the costs of such an undertaking), there is but little evidence suggesting any such blatant interference in the specific design of the new economic mechanisms adopted during the mid-1960's. The Soviet impact was considerably more subtle than that.

Several important facts about the Soviet attitude toward economic reforms during the 1960's need to be kept in mind. First of all, the Soviet economic system was very much in a state of flux throughout much of the decade, with major modifications of economic institutions and the instrumentalities of control taking place in 1958, 1961, 1965, and 1969 and with a wide variety of limited local or regional "experiments" being announced almost every year after 1962. Under such circumstances, it would have been extremely difficult for anyone, including the Soviet leaders, to specify exactly what "*the* Soviet economic model" consisted of. If there was any implicit imperative for East Europe to emulate their Soviet comrades' approach to economic reform, it could only have consisted of the very general injunction to adopt a somewhat more flexible, innovative, experimental approach to questions relating to economic planning and management (while remaining, to be sure, within the fairly broad limits suggested by the range of topics still considered taboo in Soviet circles). While the Soviet media stepped up its coverage of East European economic experiments during the 1960's, the approach taken was generally upbeat and an openly judgmental attitude was rather scrupulously avoided, at least until after 1968, when open season was declared on certain of the revisionist doctrines of Ota Sik and certain other Czech and Slovak economists whose political activities had made them odious to the Soviet leaders — without, however, extending the condemnations explicitly to the often parallel features of the economic reforms in other Communist countries.

Moreover, in addition to the Soviets' state of uncertainty as to just what kind of economic mechanism would be appropriate to their own needs, it would appear that they were also less sure that their own precise arrangements (whatever they ultimately turned out to be) would necessarily be completely appropriate to the needs of their East European allies. The Soviets, after all, had, and continue to have, an interest in maintaining economic vitality in the region, and it would be strange indeed if Soviet leaders had completely failed to see the adverse consequences engendered in the past when Soviet procedures and policies had been uncritically copied in various East European countries despite very different conditions in their domestic economies.

For these reasons, the direct influence of the Soviet leadership on the East European economic reforms was relatively limited. East European leaders had discretion to experiment (or not) with a rather broad range of economic reforms, and the differences in the reform packages adopted confirm this slackening of the reins that made it possible for them to base decisions primarily upon domestic economic and political considerations.

Nevertheless, the course of events in the Soviet Union was far from negligible in its indirect impact on economic reform in Eastern Europe. The Soviets, particularly Khrushchev, were clearly instrumental in the initial "opening up" of the political process that made the launching of economic reform movements feasible. Soviet pressures for East European Party leaders to emulate Khrushchev's destalinization campaigns were quite formidable in themselves, and in this and other matters, domestic reformers were able to make effective use of the legitimacy bestowed upon their efforts by the Soviet example to undermine the positions of their most dogmatic domestic opponents. Policies which had already been adopted in the Soviet Union had to be viewed as at least subject to discussion as a possible alternative in any of the countries still attempting to maintain close relations with the U.S.S.R. Intellectual trends in the Soviet Union (such as the resurgence of interest in the work of the mathematical economists) lent particular prestige to kindred spirits elsewhere within the bloc and this respectability could be used as a political resource.

Soviet influence also had indirect effects on the economic reforms by virtue of the Soviet leaders' active interest in maintaining political stability within the region, which entailed an effort to exercise a kind of general supervision over the general competence of East European Party leaders to maintain the effectiveness of their Party organizations as the leading political forces of their respective countries. Where Party leaders became embroiled in intense factional struggles, the Party's ability to formulate and implement policy could be threatened, and the decision of the Soviet leadership on whether to back the current leader up could easily prove decisive to the local conflict. The confidence of the Soviet leaders thus constituted a critical asset for actual or aspiring East European leaders in the event of serious disagreements within their Politburos. The issue of economic reform, as we have seen, was often caught up in such internal disputes.

The process by which a sufficient number of top political leaders came to back any given economic reform package usually involved more than simple persuasion to bring about a change of heart in every member of the established Party leadership. In most cases, the adoption of an economic reform came about in good part through changes in the composition of the Party's top leadership group and their circle of close economic advisors and top administrators — changes that had the effect of removing the most implacable foes of the economic reform and replacing them with figures who were more in tune with at least a major portion of the economic reformers' program. Political careers were made, and sometimes broken, on the issue of economic reform, as ambitious members of the Party elite presented themselves as new and dynamic replacements for incumbent policy-makers discredited by the poor performance of the economy under their stewardship. The fate of proposals for economic reform was dependent not so much upon rationalistic calculations of economically optimal arrangements for producing prosperity during the period of intensive growth as upon the outcomes of factional rivalries for power.

In general, the degree to which the decision for economic reform involved changes in the Party and state leadership was determined largely by the degree of elite cohesion already achieved before the issue of economic reform became a serious matter for debate. Where bitter factional rivalries based upon a multiplicity of issues and personal antipathies already had a foothold within the higher Party bodies (as in Poland, Bulgaria, and Czechoslovakia), the attempt to engineer serious changes in the economic sphere rather easily turned into a battle for political survival. Where the factions were fairly evenly matched, the resulting protracted conflict was not only hazardous for the individuals directly involved and their proteges but also for the regime itself, since policy-making in a variety of important areas was likely to remain paralyzed until some resolution of the leadership question could be reached. Since a prolonged deadlock of this sort could scarcely remain a secret from the wider public, such situations always created the danger that either one of the Party factions or, worse, the "enemies of socialism" might mobilize mass support for their cause in ways that could destabilize the existing political order and endanger the Communist Party's dominant position. Therefore, in those countries with a high degree of elite factionalization a combination of enlightened self-interest and Soviet pressures for amicable settlement of differences tended to result indirectly in economic reforms that embodied a great deal of unprincipled compromising and rhetorical papering over of differences. While the slow process of the reforms' elaboration, testing and "final" adoption tended to be accompanied by rather high rates of elite turnover (especially at the level just below the Politburo and Secretariat), the indecisive character of these skirmishes usually prevented the reforms from acquiring the requisite coherence and internal consistency for genuinely successful operation and each shift in the balance of power was reflected in *de facto* modifications of the reform programs' practical operation. Effective implementation of the reforms normally requires a decisive political showdown (which, of course, need never occur at all, as was evidently the case in Bulgaria).

In those countries where the Party's top leadership was otherwise rather cohesive at the time that economic reform appeared on the agenda (Hungary and the G.D.R.), the smooth resolution of differences without major turnovers in elite membership was greatly facilitated, although even in these cases there were still a certain number of irreconcilables who ultimately had to be replaced in the course of the reforms' implementation. Moreover, the economic reform packages which were adopted in these two countries, while very different from each other in their concrete provisions, could still be characterized as having one trait in common that differentiated them both from the programs adopted elsewhere: a relatively higher degree of internal consistency in basic conceptions, which resulted in considerably greater ease of practical implementation.

Implementation of Reform

Two principal facts about the stage of implementation stand out immediately. First of all, if the economic reform process proceeded this far, the sheer numbers of people directly affected increased by several orders of magnitude and ultimately (if all went well) would include virtually the entire economically active population in one way or another. Secondly, although the top Party leadership and the reform's economist advocates heretofore had to concern themselves only with the rather special values and interests of elite groups in advancing arguments and mobilizing power and influence behind their views on reorganizing the socialist economy, the need to secure compliance and cooperation from the general population virtually forced them to take more seriously the values and interests of a much broader cross-section of the citizenry. Decisions earlier taken on the basis of "economic rationality" or of factional political advantage sometimes had to be re-evaluated in the light of difficulties encountered in implementing them on a nation-wide scale. In general, the implementation of economic reforms resulted in considerably less radical departures from previous arrangements than were envisioned in the Party's official statements of principles and reform blueprints.

In theory, immediately following the decision of the leading Party organs in favor of changes in the system of economic planning and administration, the entire membership of a Party organized on Leninist principles would be expected to cast aside previous differences and unite unconditionally for the rapid and full implementation of the Party's current line. In practice, however, this ideal was seldom lived up to in the specific case of the economic reforms of the 1960's. Given the pivotal role of the Communist Party as the initiator and activating force behind policy-making not only in the political sphere but also in the economic, social, and cultural spheres as well, the failure of the Party organization to push resolutely for the fulfillment of leadership decisions effectively meant that they would not be fully implemented, since no other organized political force was (or could be permitted to be) in a position to encroach upon the Party's "leading role."

The responsibility for maintaining Party discipline and mobilizing the Party organization behind Party initiatives rested first of all with the Party's first secretary, and the attitude taken toward the economic reforms by this highest of Communist political leaders (as well as the degree of effective support he enjoyed from his colleagues on the Politburo) was a major factor in determining the fate of the economic reform proposals. The central roles played by Walter Ulbricht and Janos Kadar in first securing the unified support of their Politburos for the economic reform initiatives (which were from the very beginning identified as their own personal policy initiatives) and then closely supervising the work of putting them into practice account in large measure for the high degree of success in implementing these programs more or less as written. Kadar's success in implementing the rather more radical Hungarian reforms evidenced his possession of political skills of a particularly high order, which he employed to co-opt skeptics on both the left and the right fringes of the Party leadership into acceptance of his scrupulously "centrist" program without the necessity for either debilitating compromises on the reform's basic principles or a disruptively large purge of the leadership that might have destroyed the Party's capacity to control the course of political events. At the other extreme, the open negativism of Czechoslovak first secretary Antonin Novotny toward the economic reforms (both before and after their formal adoption as Party policy) not only greatly impeded implementation by allowing hostile bureaucrats in the economic ministries to evade their clear duties with impunity but also contributed directly to the extremely volatile political situation of 1967-1968 by convincing the advocates of economic and political reforms that their basically non-revolutionary goals could not be carried out without a root-and-branch assault upon virtually the entire Party and state apparatus. In a similar fashion, Gomulka's ever-suspicious attitudes toward the Polish economic reform advocates and his unwillingness or inability to take an active role in actually carrying out the already modest proposals approved in 1964 resulted in a policy of economic drift that was ultimately to have tragic consequences not only for Gomulka's personal career but also for his Party and his country. Perhaps the most ambiguous case was that of Todor Zhivkov in Bulgaria. On the one hand, Zhivkov's personal sponsorship of the cause of economic reform against what seems to have been quite formidable leadership opposition was undoubtedly instrumental in bringing about the passage of what was (on paper at least) a surprisingly advanced reform blueprint. Yet within a very short period of time, Zhivkov's political skills (or his nerve?) proved insufficient to overcome bureaucratic opposition at the implementation stage, and he appears to have acquiesced in its reversal in preference to risking a final showdown with those elements in the Party leadership who were deliberately sabotaging what was after all an endorsed element of the Party's program.

Principal sources of powerful opposition to the adoption and implementation of the more radical economic reforms were located within the economic sectoral ministries and parts of the Party apparatus closely connected with economic administration. The decentralizing features of the reforms and the shift to price and incentive manipulations rather than administrative directives as the principal means for securing plan fulfillment, if fully implemented, would deprive many of the central ministerial organizations of many of their former functions and would rationally entail sizable reductions in administrative staffs. Moreover, to the extent that central economic administrative offices become less crucial to the operation of the economy, it would be expected that the material and status rewards for service in such capacities might well diminish over time. On the other hand, the importance of certain of the economic ministries tended to be enhanced rather than diminished by the economic reforms — most notably the Ministry of Finance and the various cabinet-ranked commissions dealing with wage and price determination and the improvement of production technology.

The attitudes of enterprise-level management toward the economic reforms were highly variable. While the reforms increased the scope for managerial discretion and usually offered substantial opportunities for capable managers to increase their incomes, the technocratic overtones of the reform movements foreshadowed a decisive shift in the personal qualities essential for long-term success in a managerial career. Managers who possessed substandard educational credentials but valuable political contacts had good reason to fear dismissal or demotion in a system that would require a higher degree of technical expertise and business acumen. Thanks to the expansion of the educational system during the preceding decades, there was, after all, a substantial pool of aspiring and well-credentialed talent concentrated in middle management and impatient for advancement, which the prospect of economic reform seemed to promise.

Local Party and state officials were also threatened to some degree by the prospect of radical economic reforms. Their prerogatives in supervising local economic enterprises would in many cases be enhanced, yet this too could be very difficult for less educated cadres. Moreover, changes in investment priorities and the drive to reduce subsidies to uneconomic enterprises threatened some of the local economies with disruption and hardships with which the local cadres would have to deal somehow. Enhancing the role of meritocratic criteria in choosing managers not only placed the future careers of less educated cadres in doubt but also diminished the opportunities for local Party bosses to dispense patronage through control of the *nomenklatura*.

The serious threat of radical economic reform to the interests of central economic administrators, local cadres, and enterprise level managers not infrequently resulted in efforts to delay or prevent the implementation of the most unpleasant features of the new system. These members of politically active and influential strata could call upon friends in higher places for special exemptions and protections and could often take advantage of discretionary authority they already enjoyed to further a program of passive resistance. Less individually powerful people, when threatened, had the same natural impulse to defend themselves but generally fewer safe means of doing so.

While the long-range goal of the economic reform was to increase the rate of economic growth and thereby to make possible a more rapid rise in the standard of living, the straightened economic circumstances that provided the stimulus for reform in the first place implied that the immediate sacrifices entailed in the implementation of the new system could not at first be wholly compensated with off-setting improvements, at least not for everyone. Manual workers were confronted with demands for greater effort, yet they would receive about the same pay as before. Meanwhile, they would face both increases in the prices of many common consumer items and an unsettling new possibility of involuntary unemployment. The new emphasis on productivity and upon the value of technical expertise expressed itself in concrete terms at the factory in increased differentiation of incomes between the more skilled and the less skilled labor categories (and especially between the managerial and technical staff of the enterprise on the one hand and the manual workers on the other). Increased authority by foremen and managers to vary the pay and bonuses of individual workers within the same nominal job category on the basis of often subjective evaluations of relative productivity produced additional grievances, and the enhanced importance of the variable bonuses as a proportion of total pay meant that one's income became less predictable and secure.

All of these changes violated widespread notions of fairness and equity, yet the mechanisms available for legitimately expressing these dissatisfactions and for seeking relief were rather limited. The possibilities for collective action were severely restricted because of the "transmission belt" character of existing formal organizations active in the workplace. Nevertheless, forces were soon set in motion that tended to alleviate the situation.

The most obvious (and also the most dangerous) approach for aggrieved workers to attempt to exert some form of countervailing power, at least within the work environment, was the employment of such classical working class sanctions as slow-downs, work stoppages, damaging of machinery, and even the occasional walk-out. Such actions could be extremely costly to the enterprise as well as very embarrassing to the managers or local officials who would have to defend themselves in the inevitable investigations that would follow such disruptions of production. The threat of such extreme actions was a potent inducement for local officials and managers to find ways of avoiding such confrontations whenever possible. Moreover, any large-scale manifestation of discontent by members of the working class constituted a serious problem from the point of view of the Party leadership, since such incidents implicitly called into question the basic formula that legitimated the Communist Party as the party of the workers and the state as a working class state. While repression might do as an immediate response if the situation became truly desperate, it was far preferable all around to try to evolve more effective mechanisms for resolving conflicts of interest that were increasingly being recognized as arising spontaneously but legitimately from the changed economic mechanism.

One such mechanism was relatively informal but often effective — petitioning by employees to officials outside the administrative hierarchy of the factory. In situations where sizable lay-offs seemed to be in the offing, for example, the attendant headaches for the local Party and governmental officials who would be saddled with the responsibility for dealing with the resulting economic crisis were often quite a sufficient motivation for them to bestir themselves on the affected workers' behalf. In such situations, local officials, although they were not precisely "representatives" (since they were not really accountable), found themselves being manipulated as an intermittently available political resource for the otherwise relatively powerless.

The two principal forms of more specifically institutionalized mechanisms for reconciliation of conflicts of interest arising as spinoffs from of the economic reform movements were the (reformed) trade union committees and the workers' councils. The workers' council form of representation for the interests of employees (as it has emerged briefly in

Poland and Hungary in 1956 and in Czechoslovakia in 1968-1969, as well as in Yugoslavia on a more lasting basis) seems to embody the more radical departure from classical Leninist political conceptions, since its natural legitimating ideology invokes the notion that central authorities derive their legitimacy from the councils rather than the other way around. Nevertheless, the deliberate reactivation of the protective function of the trade unions (as occurred to some extent under the Czechoslovak reform and to a much greater extent in Hungary) constitutes in itself a major modification of the traditional Leninist reduction of these organizations to the status of non-autonomous transmission belts for the Party line.

Ironically enough, the acquisition of more effective channels whereby the concrete interests of workers might be more reliably and efficaciously articulated turned out very often (and especially in Hungary) to impede the further progress of the economic reform that was the basic assumption on which the newer, more tolerant view of interest group activities was predicated. Particularistic interests, their vigorous defense made almost ideologically respectable, combined very often to thwart the reformers' efforts to tap new "intensive" sources of economic growth. The efforts to rationalize the structure of consumer prices, to end the subsidization of inefficient enterprises and shift labor to more profitable activities, as well as to link personal incomes more closely to individual productivity all tended to fall victim to the resistance of shifting coalitions of mass and elite influence exerted upon the political leadership.

AN AFTERWORD
ECONOMIC REFORM IN THE GORBACHEV ERA

The Retreat from Reform in the 1970's

The Soviet bloc's wave of experimentation and economic reform crested in the latter half of the 1960's. The potentially destabilizing political side-effects of a thorough-going decentralizing, market-oriented economic reform became all too evident with the turmoil in Czechoslovakia in 1968. Although political rather than economic issues were clearly the paramount consideration in the Dubcek regime's rift with Moscow that ultimately led to armed intervention, the bloc-wide propaganda campaign unmasking the heresies of Czech "revisionism" provided the political opportunity for economic conservatives throughout the region to go on the offensive against domestic supporters of further economic reform. It is not surprising that reformist economists in other socialist countries prudently chose to adopt a lower profile when confronted with vitriolic denunciations of the "reformist economic conceptions of Ota Sik" as tailored to subvert the socialist order and bring about a restoration of capitalism. Clearly the period of purge and "normalization" after the 1968 intervention had a chilling effect on economic policy debates that extended far beyond the borders of Czechoslovakia itself.

Even where moderate economic reformism managed to avoid being stigmatized as politically deviant "revisionism," the administrative headaches encountered in putting into practice the milder reform measures already enacted and the relatively limited improvements in economic performance obtained in the short run tended to dilute the commitment of the political leadership to full implementation of the new system. This was nowhere more apparent than in the U.S.S.R. itself, where the Soviet leadership's diminished zeal for following through on the "Kosygin reforms" of 1965 (which had only begun to be implemented in 1967) was evident by the end of the decade. And with the Soviet reform clearly on hold, the emulation factor in East European policy-making turned once again negative for the cause of economic reform.

For the most part, the East European leaders, like their Soviet counterparts, did not openly repudiate or comprehensively repeal the economic reform packages they had adopted in the mid-1960's. However, with reformist ardor on the part of the Communist Party leadership much reduced, state planning agencies and ministerial bureaucracies throughout most of the region were left free to indulge their natural tendencies for creeping recentralization.

The list of obligatory targets assigned to the enterprises from above again began to expand, the number of materials and supplies to be centrally allocated increased, and self-financed discretionary investment from the funds of the enterprise or repayable bank credits failed to reach the projected proportions. Interest rates charged to the various sectors (and even to particular enterprises) became even more differentiated and *ad hoc* than they had been from the beginning in an effort to assure superficial profitability regardless of real returns to investment, frustrating hopes for improved economic calculation. Managerial discretion in determining the size, composition, and compensation of the enterprise workforce was sharply restricted. Incentive systems basing bonuses and wage increases primarily on enterprise profitability were greatly diluted by the proliferation of special bonuses for meeting quantitative targets and by the practice of imposing multiple physical targets as prerequisites for the actual distribution of profit-sharing funds.

The revisions of wholesale prices carried out in the late 1960's on the basis of "reformed principles of price formation" probably constituted a considerable improvement over former prices in that closer attention was paid to world market prices and to such previously neglected cost factors as interest on capital and land rents, but the general failure to provide for their frequent reworking (as originally projected by the reformers) meant that even these "improved" prices soon would become obsolete as world and domestic market conditions changed. Momentum toward reducing distortions in the retail price structure by sharply cutting budgetary subsidies for foodstuffs was lost throughout most of the region following the December 1970 riots and strikes in Poland, which had been provoked by the sharp retail price increases this policy entailed. The efforts of most East European leaders and economic planners to insulate their domestic economies from the market shocks following the 1973 OPEC price hikes resulted in still further divergences of East European price systems from economically justified relationships.   The failure to establish a flexible price system responsive to changing conditions of supply and demand in turn acted to make the reformers' vision of directing the economy primarily through "financial levers" increasingly impractical and further reinforced Eastern Europe's general trend toward creeping recentralization in economic administration throughout much of the 1970's.

New Substitutes for Economic Reform

The Soviet bloc's retreat from economic reform in the 1970's did not constitute a headlong flight back to the economic theories, institutions and practices of the Stalin era.   Certain elements of the economic reforms of the 1960's survived (albeit in somewhat attenuated form) alongside traditional methods of economic planning and administration.

The economic discussions of the 1950's and 1960's had made their mark.   Many of the more pathological features of the Stalinist economic system had been identified and largely discredited.   It was widely recognized that fiscal and financial levers needed to play a larger role than in the past relative to obligatory physical production targets and that more rational cost accounting and pricing policies were desirable and needed to be pursued.   Creating a better match-up between consumer demand and the output supplied was now acknowledged as a major problem to be overcome.

Perhaps most importantly, Soviet bloc economists and policy makers were still acutely aware that the declining trend in economic growth rates was still very much with them, and most had come to recognize that the possibilities for accelerating economic growth through Stalinist "extensive" strategies were becoming more and more limited.   The pool of underutilized labor in the countryside available for transfer to more productive industrial occupations was nearly exhausted (except perhaps in Poland and Romania), and indeed, shortages of able-bodied younger farmers were becoming an important constraint on agricultural production. The movement of women from the home into the paid labor force had already been largely completed by the end of the 1960's.   Further growth of the industrial labor force would have to come about largely through natural increase in the working age population — and the drastically lowered birthrates of the previous twenty years made the demographic outlook for this unpromising.   At the same time, rapid expansion of the capital stock through a major increase in the already high proportion of national income devoted to investment was deemed to be politically hazardous.   The rate of improvement in popular living standards had already eroded to the point that further austerity could have explosive consequences like those so recently manifested in Poland.

If the rapid increases of labor and capital inputs characteristic of extensive development strategies could not be sustained, then intensive factors improving the efficiency of production would have to contribute a much larger share to reverse the long-term downward trend in economic growth rates. If economic reforms seeking greater efficiency through increased enterprise autonomy, greater market allocation of productive resources, and profit-based managerial incentives were no longer regarded as politically acceptable, then perhaps a strategy emphasizing other approaches to "intensification" of production could be substituted. And this was in fact what mainly occurred in the early 1970's.

The reformers of the 1960's had concentrated on improving economic efficiency primarily through changes in the system of planning and management designed to encourage a more rational allocation of scarce economic resources between sectors by relating investment allocations to profitability and to promote better utilization of resources within the factory by giving management and workers a direct financial interest in raising profits by cutting costs. Policy makers in the 1970's, on the other hand, paid less attention to problems of allocational efficiency and employee motivation, choosing instead to concentrate on the technological determinants of productivity. Economic growth would be accelerated through the much more rapid and widespread replacement of the existing backward productive plant by converting over to the latest, state-of-the-art, labor- and capital-saving technologies.

The historical imperative to adapt socialist institutions for the fullest participation in the "Scientific and Technical Revolution" (STR) was by far the most ubiquitous theme in Soviet and East European ideological writings during the 1970's, and in many respects it dominated economic policy discourse as well. While public discussions of the implications of the STR very often tended toward the abstruse and scholastic, several reasonably straightforward economic policy initiatives were explicitly legitimized by reference to this burgeoning literature.

Adaptation to the imperatives of the STR implied, most obviously, a rapid quantitative expansion of human and material resources made available to existing scientific research organizations and to industrial research, engineering and development units. And indeed, the Soviets and most of the East Europeans markedly increased their expenditures on research and development during the 1970's. But beyond the simple commitment to nurture advancement in scientific and technological knowledge in the abstract, policy makers devoted increasing attention to devising administrative techniques for speeding up practical incorporation of the latest scientific and technological advances into mass production at the factory level.

The characteristic organizational response to this problem of spurring adoption of technological innovations during the 1970's was a centralizing rather than a decentralizing one. In March of 1973, Soviet First Secretary Leonid Brezhnev sponsored a sweeping reorganization of the existing industrial hierarchy. In many respects, Brezhnev's proposals resembled measures successfully employed since the late 1960's in the German Democratic Republic and experimented with on a limited scale in the U.S.S.R. itself, and Brezhnev's wholesale endorsement led to further imitation in other East European countries. The basic plan was to merge existing enterprises producing similar products for various ministries into larger "production associations" (*proizvodstvennie ob'edinennie*) under common operational management. These would replace the enterprises as the basic locus of managerial decision-making, and their directors were authorized and expected to shift production assignments and resources among the subordinate enterprises to bring about more efficient operations through greater specialization and longer production runs. The new production associations would not be supervised by the existing bureaucratic departments (*glavki*) of the industrial ministries. These would be replaced by "all-union industrial associations" (*vsesoiuznie promyshlennie ob'edinenie*), operating on a *khozraschet* basis under the general supervision of the ministries.

Brezhnev's reorganization was supposed not only to reduce the duplication of efforts and red tape formerly involved in poor coordination of production and distribution across departmental and territorial boundaries but also to facilitate the more rapid incorporation of technical progress into production. Industrial associations would have under their control not only production associations and enterprises but also closely related research and design organizations and technical institutes. Even some production associations would encompass their own research and design institutes as well as specialized factories for producing and testing prototypes. Consolidating control over research and development in the hands of directors held rigorously responsible for specific plan targets mandating greatly improved productivity was intended to make the objectives and priorities in R&D more responsive than before to the practical needs of the factories and hence to spur more rapid adoption of technological innovations.

Perhaps the greatest impact of the intensified effort to harness the Scientific and Technological Revolution was in the area of foreign trade.

Both Soviet and East European policy makers were painfully aware that even greatly enhanced scientific and research establishments at home would be insufficient to bring the technological level of their productive plant up to world standards in many economic sectors. Improved coordination and specialization of Soviet bloc R&D efforts and more effective arrangements for intra-bloc technology transfer under the auspices of the CMEA offered one route to improvement, and efforts were made in the early 1970's to pursue improvements along these lines. However, it was still a brutal fact that, in a great many fields of production, it was an industrialized capitalist country rather than a socialist country that was at the cutting edge of technological advancement, and all too often this technological gap seemed insurmountable by socialist research efforts for the foreseeable future. In these sectors, large scale technology transfer from the West seemed to offer the quickest and most practical approach to modernizing production.

Accordingly, the early and middle 1970's saw an enormous increase in Soviet and East European policy-makers' interest in expanding East-West economic cooperation, and there is little doubt that the Soviet bloc's increased desire to overcome political barriers to technology transfer was an important motivating factor in making possible the dawning of the "age of detente" during that period. Measures to accelerate technology transfer did not involve only the traditional approach of increasing direct purchase and importation of the most advanced western tools and machinery, although this was probably quantitatively the most significant component of the policy. More innovative measures included the purchase of Western patents, the conclusion of process licensing and technical assistance agreements with Western firms, "turnkey" factory construction projects carried out by Western contractors in Eastern Europe and the Soviet Union, and even various forms of "co-production" arrangements entailing joint ventures of Western and East European firms.

The large-scale and rapid retooling of Soviet and East European industry entailed in substituting a "technological fix" for the "economic reform" solution to the problem of raising productivity had several clear disadvantages. It would be enormously expensive and would call for maintaining a rather high rate of investment for some years — and this at a time when the recent disorders in Poland had already reminded policy-makers that continuously maintaining and improving popular living standards would be essential to political stability. Large increases in imports from the West would have to be paid for by increasing the flow of exports to earn the necessary foreign exchange, yet the shortcomings in quality of Soviet bloc industrial goods and the physical shortages of their more marketable agricultural commodities and raw materials made it difficult to raise export earnings as rapidly as was thought necessary (although the massive increases in the prices of oil and many other industrial raw materials in the 1970's provided a major improvement in the terms of trade enjoyed by the U.S.S.R. and other net exporters of such products).

For most of the CMEA countries, the answer to the dilemma was found in financing a substantial part of the investment drive from external, rather than domestic, sources. Western governments, newly attracted to the idea that increased East-West economic interdependence would lead eventually to a permanently improved political relationship and anxious to acquire new export markets to combat rising domestic unemployment, not only began easing many of the political barriers to trade with the East but even actively promoted and subsidized it. The interpretation of COCOM restrictions on the transfer of advanced technology to Communist countries were gradually eased. Soviet and East European economic planners found that they were now able to obtain concessionary credit terms from state-owned Western banks and guarantees from Western governments on private bank loans to finance export deals. Western bankers, awash with petro-dollars to be recycled, and manufacturers, hard pressed for profitable sales opportunities in the era of stagflation, scrambled to carve out a share of this enormous and seew risk new market. Because of this ready availability of foreign credit, imports of Western goods — primarily machinery and equipment or other industrial materials — were able to increase at a much more rapid rate than offsetting exports to the West. The Soviet Union's net hard currency indebtedness to the West increased from only about half a billion dollars in 1971 to more than twelve billion dollars a decade later. The Soviets' East European allies boosted their combined hard currency debts from under five billion dollars to over sixty-one billion dollars in the same ten year period.[1] This abandonment of the traditional Stalinist insistence upon equilibrium in the foreign trade accounts made it possible for policy makers throughout the region to have their cake and eat it too for most of the decade. That is, they were able to indulge their tastes for a high rate of growth in investment without suffering the political complications that would have been entailed by the suppression of popular consumption necessary to finance it entirely through domestic savings.

The Persistence of the Performance Gap in Eastern Europe

The decision by Soviet and East European planners to finance so large a proportion of their technical modernization campaigns through foreign borrowing was not inherently an irrational or short-sighted one, in principle. The long-run rate of return from investing the borrowed capital was expected greatly to exceed the interest costs incurred. Boosts in productivity and improvements in product quality derived from a massive upgrading of the capital stock would make it possible rapidly to increase hard currency export earnings in the future. After the necessary time-lag required for bringing the plant and equipment on line, the debt would be serviced and ultimately retired relatively painlessly out of the increased income resulting from the investment.

Unfortunately, the economic payoff for the policies of emphasizing technical modernization over economic reform and relying upon massive Western imports proved to be much smaller than had been expected. Although some of the individual development projects turned out reasonably well, many others were delayed, experienced large cost over-runs, and never reached projected capacities or quality improvement targets. Slow and shoddy construction, material shortages, workforces poorly trained or poorly motivated to use the new equipment, and plain bad planning all made themselves felt. In the end, there was no marked reversal of the adverse trends in growth rates of factor productivity. Although growth rates of national income surged briefly in the first part of the 1970's as the investment boom got under way (classical "extensive" growth), the declining long range trend that had become evident throughout the region in the 1960's continued in effect for the decade as a whole. In short, in the absence of fundamental reforms in the system of planning and management, Soviet bloc policy makers were able to invest borrowed foreign capital no more rationally or success-fully than they had done with domestic savings in the past.

For those countries that relied most heavily upon international borrow-ing during the 1970's, the ultimate constraint on their strategy for economic expansion was the continued availability of further credits. But by the close of the 1970's, it was becoming increasingly evident that neither actual nor prospective growth of East European export capabilities were keeping pace with the growth of East European indebtedness. Servicing even the existing levels of foreign debt was beginning to become a serious burden on many of the East European economies.

Poland, the most seriously overextended of the European socialist countries, found itself laying out nearly all of its hard currency earnings for interest and scheduled repayments of principal on its external debt, with almost nothing left over to purchase the imports of raw materials and spare parts essential to keep many of the shiny new factories in operation. None of the other countries was in such catastrophic straits as Poland, but the debt service ratios of them all were at worrisome levels and rising. Even Czechoslovakia, which had been the most conservative in its borrowing policies, was devoting about one-fifth of its export earnings to debt service in 1980, while the remainder fell in the range of 25% to 45%.[2]

By the early years of the 1980's, the political climate of detente that had led Western governments to favor easy credit for the Soviets and Eastern Europe had seriously eroded. Moreover there was rising (and often well-founded) concern among private bankers about the East Europeans' ability to service their current levels of indebtedness. More and more, creditors became cautious about extending new credits to them, demanding higher interest rates and shorter repayment periods. When Poland and Romania were forced to reschedule their debts in 1981, new loans to the other socialist countries slowed to a crawl. In 1982, bankers moved vigorously to reduce their exposure in the region, creating a severe foreign exchange squeeze for even the less exposed East European economies.

Unable to increase their exports by the necessary margin, East European economic planners necessarily slashed imports, with purchases of Western machinery and equipment taking the deepest cuts. Imports of raw and semi-finished materials were also considerably curtailed.[3] Ambitious investment plans had to be curtailed, with some projects being abandoned and the completion dates of others being considerably delayed, tying up large amounts of capital in non-producing or under-producing plants. Economic growth rates in the region fell to their lowest levels in decades, with Poland and Hungary turning in the worst performances. East Germany and Czechoslovakia managed to weather the storm the best, yet even for them, officially reported growth rates of national income reached only the three to four percent range for the first half of the 1980's.

The Soviet Union's Economic Crisis

The Soviet policy makers had found it neither necessary nor prudent to depend so heavily on Western credit for acquiring Western technology as had the Poles, Hungarians and Romanians. Blessed by nature with large exportable reserves of gold and petroleum, the Soviet Union was in a position to reap large windfall gains from the rapid increases in world market prices for these commodities during the 1970's. The rapid expansion in Soviet arms sales to newly wealthy oil-producing states in the Middle East (such as Libya and Iraq) also helped improve hard currency earnings and further reduced the need to rely upon borrowing to finance the big increases in Soviet importation of Western machinery and equip-ment. The Soviets were able to keep their hard currency debt service ratios in the range of ten to twenty percent throughout nearly all the 1970's and early 1980's,[4] below the corresponding figures for even the most conservative of their East European allies. Consequently, the credit crunch of 1981 and 1982 had much less dramatically negative short-term effects on Soviet economic performance than was the case elsewhere in the region.

Nevertheless, the results of the Soviet economic growth strategy of the 1970's had turned out to be profoundly disappointing. The large gains in productivity that were to have resulted from more intensive exploitation of the Scientific and Technological Revolution never materialized, and, in fact, investment-to-output ratios continued to rise significantly, alarming Soviet economists and planners.   According to one Soviet economist writing in 1984, the return on investment had fallen by half over the previous 30 years and by a third in the previous decade.[5] Officially reported growth rates of Soviet national income trended rather steadily downward, declining from an average annual rate of 7.7% for 1966-1970 to 5.6% in 1971-1975 to 4.3% in 1976-1980 and 3.6% for 1981-1985.

In Chapter II, three different operational criteria for identifying serious "performance gaps" in the economy were used to facilitate the analysis: (1) prolonged (three or more years in a row) underperformance in comparison to the country's own past performance (previous five years' average); (2) prolonged underperformance in comparison to the other European Communist countries; and (3) prolonged underperformance in comparison to the West. Employing the same criteria to evaluate Soviet economic performance since the early 1970's, we can gauge the growing seriousness of the performance gap with which Soviet leaders had to deal.

As already indicated, growth rates of Soviet national income followed a generally declining trend throughout the 1970's and 1980's (see Figure 6.1). In the eighteen years from 1970 to 1987, twelve years featured growth rates of national income below the average rates for the immediately preceding five year periods. The years from 1977 through 1981, however, constituted the only period of underperformance by this criterion uninterrupted for three years or more.

When Soviet growth rates are compared with those attained by the other European Communist countries, no marked or prolonged Soviet underperformance is evident. In the period since 1970, Soviet growth rates have normally been rather close to the average for the rest of the bloc, and, if anything, the U.S.S.R.'s relative performance has tended to improve very slightly since the later 1970's. Whether because of the U.S.S.R.'s windfall gains in the 1970's as a large-scale exporter of petroleum products and gold or for other reasons, the Soviets' economic downturn, while serious enough in its own right, has generally been less pronounced than has been the case for the other Communist countries. In no period since 1970 have the Soviet Union's growth rates fallen below the bloc average for more than two

(Net Material Product at Comparable Prices)

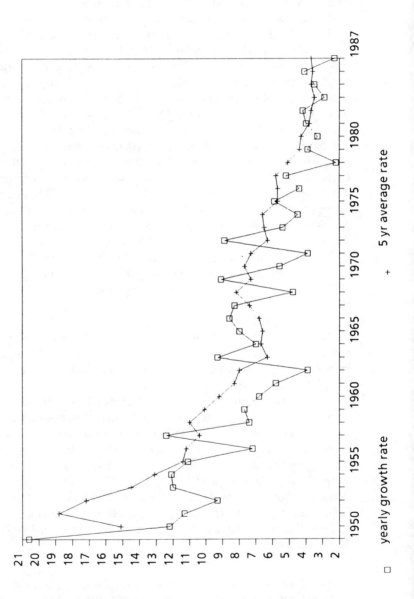

Percentage Growth Rate

□ yearly growth rate   +   5 yr average rate

consecutive years, although, given the general malaise in the East European economies, this probably offered only limited comfort to Soviet leaders.

The U.S.S.R.'s economic performance relative to that of its principal geopolitical rival, the United States, sharply deteriorated, however, and this must have been a cause for considerable concern in the Kremlin. While the computations of Net Material Product released by official Soviet statistical agencies are not directly comparable to Western national accounts based upon the Gross National Product concept, Western intelligence agencies routinely rework Soviet economic reports to calculate fairly reliable estimates of Soviet GNP that are more appropriate for international comparison.[6] Such a comparison shows that the Soviet Union considerably outpaced the United States in economic growth from 1950 through 1975. But in the period from 1976 on, the Soviet Union began to lose ground relative to its rival. In the twenty-five years prior to 1976, American GNP had shown more rapid annual growth rates on only six occasions (just once for as many as two years running, in 1962-1963). During the period from 1976 to 1985, American growth rates exceeded the estimated Soviet figures in eight out of the ten years, including a four-consecutive-year period (1976-1979) and a three-consecutive-year period (1983-1985).

Brezhnev's Response

By the end of the decade of the 1970's, it was abundantly clear that the approved approaches to revitalizing the Soviet economy had failed, and, indeed, the U.S.S.R. was entering the 1980's with its very worst economic growth performance since Hitler leveled much of the country during World War II. Even Communist Party General Secretary Leonid Brezhnev finally began publicly acknowledging the problem. In his unusually somber 1980 address to the Central Committee just before the sixty-fourth anniversary of the Bolshevik Revolution, Brezhnev confirmed that the preliminary results just coming in on the 1976-1980 Five-Year Plan were quite disappointing. As one consequence, already serious shortages of meat, clothing and other essential consumer goods seemed destined to get worse before they got better. In the course of his lengthy recitation, Brezhnev made a confession that was no less remarkable for its understated and turgid phraseology:

> It must be frankly admitted that the mechanism of administration and planning, the methods of economic management and performance discipline, have still not been raised to the level of today's demands.[7]

Despite a growing awareness of serious trouble in the economic sphere, however, the Soviet Union's increasingly aged leadership seemed unwilling or unable to arouse themselves to any form of drastic remedial action. The Brezhnev administration's last feeble gesture in the direction of comprehensive economic reform was embodied in a July 1979 joint decree of the Council of Ministers and the Central Committee of the CPSU.[8]

While the July 1979 decree and its many implementing regulations were less global in coverage than the 1965 reforms and embodied much less radical changes, the 1979 "reform" nevertheless resembled the earlier program in its focus upon improvement of the incentive system as the key to any drastic breakthrough in economic efficiency. Indeed, much of the 1979 decree constituted a kind of compilation or codification of revised bonus schemes already announced with much fanfare over the years since the 1965 reform but evidently never actually implemented on the broad scale originally projected. The overriding goals were reducing excessive usage of scarce labor and materials and stimulation of more rapid adoption of technological innovations in production processes, but, in contrast to the reforms of the 1960's, the improvement of the incentive system was not viewed as a measure to make possible greater independence and initiative by enterprise management. On the contrary, the improved incentive system was to encourage more scrupulous plan fulfilment, while the plans themselves were to become more centralized, "scientific," and detailed than before.

Labor productivity (output per worker) and the proportion of "highest-quality goods" in total output were now to be the two primary indicators determining the size of the bonus funds for enterprises. However, these performance indicators were to be calculated in a new way, substituting "normative net output" (NNO) for the measures of output previously used (most frequently either actual net output or actual gross output). An enterprise's NNO was to be arrived at by multiplying that enterprise's actually achieved net output (value added) by a coefficient mainly determined by the branchwide average of the value added in producing the relevant products. The basic idea was to penalize financially those enterprises that used above-average inputs of scarce labor in meeting their production assignments and reward those enterprises using less than average amounts of labor.

A notable difference between the 1979 decree and the 1965 reforms was the lack of concern for identifying a single summary indicator of overall enterprise performance comparable to the role profitability was supposed to have played. This was consistent with the fact that the designers of the 1979 measures were primarily concerned with inducing enterprise management's adherence to a detailed list of specific authoritative plan targets rather than with stimulating managerial initiative. Although the (normalized) labor productivity and product quality indices were designated as the principal determinants of bonus funds, ministries were also authorized to designate eighteen other compulsory indicators in the enterprise plans and to make actual distribution of the bonus fund to the enterprise workforce contingent upon acceptable fulfilment of these additional targets. Thus the ministerial bureaucracy was still in a position to enforce detailed specifications of output assortment, size and composition of workforce, schedules for installing new equipment or commissioning new plant, introduction of new product lines, limitations on pay increases and so forth.

In addition to the changes in the incentive system, the 1979 decree called for improvements in the process of devising and assigning plan targets to the enterprises. Ministries were ritually enjoined to discontinue the use of the "ratchet principle," whereby managers turning in exceptionally good performance in one year could expect to be penalized by assignment of markedly higher compulsory targets for the following year. Enterprise managers should enjoy "stable norms" over entire five-year planning periods rather than being constantly faced with changing ministerial demands. Greater use of "counterplanning" was advocated, whereby enterprises would be rewarded for adopting annual targets more ambitious than those initially sent down from the ministry in the preliminary draft of the five-year plan.

Perhaps more operationally significant, ministries were urged to make greater use of "progressive" input-output norms in planning the distribution of materials to enterprises in the 1981-1985 Five-Year Plan. That is, guidelines on the permissable quantities of the various raw materials to be provided per ton of planned output should be based, not on the average recorded experience of the industry, but only on the results attained by the most efficient enterprise or enterprises, thereby putting pressure on the less advanced enterprises to update their methods, cut waste, and uncover "concealed reserves."[9]

The measures adopted in the 1979 decree were noteworthy for their non-systematic, ad hoc character. It was not preceded by any unusual public debates or academic discussion, and no theoretical basis for the program was ever elaborated. While the Kosygin reforms of 1965 had never been formally repudiated, there was no attempt to strengthen enterprise autonomy or to reduce the number of often contradictory but still theoretically compulsory directives handed down to management. There was no genuine effort to harnass market forces in support of economic objectives, nor was there any serious attention paid to bringing about greater flexibility in the pricing system. Although different in the specific organizational details, the basic conception was essentially the same as in the Stalinist approach to running the socialist economy. Socialist planning was conceived of as the center's elaboration of a detailed blueprint for microeconomic decisions at the enterprise level, and the role of incentives could only be to encourage conformity to the dictates of the plan, not to sustain a process for continually improving upon it. Persistent shortcomings in plan fulfillment were not to be dealt with by any reconsideration of the character of planning itself but by more familiar techniques, such as devising ever more complex formulae for new plan indicators and additional bonus criteria to be grafted on to the existing system.

New Leadership and New Experimentation in the U.S.S.R.

The death of Leonid Ilyich Brezhnev in November of 1982 and the resulting rapid turnover among Soviet policy makers and top administrators created an opportunity to break out of the policy immobilism that had characterized Brezhnev's declining years. While only two incumbents left the Politburo under Brezhnev's immediate successor, Yuri Vladimirovich Andropov, three men were newly raised to full voting membership in that body and one new candidate member was added. Three new secretaries were appointed to the Secretariat. At a slightly lower level in the policy-making hierarchy, change was also dramatic. During Andropov's fifteen months as General Secretary, one-fifth of all Soviet cabinet ministers and one-third of the heads of Central Committee departments were replaced, along with about one-fourth of the Communist Party's regional and Union Republic first secretaries. [10]

Despite his own relatively advanced age and poor health, as General Secretary, Andropov quickly manifested his conviction that Soviet society suffered from serious problems which the leadership had delayed far too long in facing. In sharp contrast to his predecessor, Andropov openly discussed and expressed indignation at a wide variety of shortcomings in Soviet life that heretofore had usually been considered too delicate to be acknowledged in public. And he demanded strong corrective action. Foremost among these problems was that of inefficiency and unacceptably slow growth of productivity in the economy, as he made clear from his first public speech after assuming the leadership of the Party:

In general, comrades, there are many urgent tasks in the national economy. Needless to say, I have no ready made recipes for accomplishing them. But all of us — the Party's Central Committee — will have to find answers to them, by generalizing Soviet and world experience and collecting the knowledge of the best practical workers and scientists. In general, slogans alone won't get things moving.... I would like to stress that these questions are of paramount, vital importance for the country.[11]

As Andropov himself admitted, although he came into office with a strong determination that something must be done, he clearly did not begin with a well thought-out, integrated program for reforming the economy. The most consistent theme in his many public statements on getting the economy moving again was his stress on the need for increased discipline and conscientiousness on the part of every individual within the party, the state, and the enterprise. The earliest practical measures for reinvigorating economic performance during his administration were the well-publicized police campaigns to punish corrupt or incompetent administrators and managers, to suppress alcohol abuse on the job, and to round up shirkers improperly absent from the workplace. Nevertheless, from the very first, Andropov also repeatedly indicated a cautious openness to structural innovations in the system of planning and management and called for wide-ranging practical proposals in this vein:

A good deal has been said recently about the need to expand the independence of associations, enterprises, collective farms and state farms. It would seem that the time has come to take up the practical resolution of this question.... We must act circumspectly here, conduct experiments if necessary, weigh matters carefully, and take the fraternal countries' experience into account.[12]

Although Andropov's new administration espoused a policy of somewhat greater openness in the public discussion of economic problems, there was no "great debate" in the Soviet mass media comparable in intensity to the Liberman discussions of the early 1960's — or rather, the reformist ideas expressed in public scarcely went beyond those already thoroughly discussed in the 1960's. While a larger number of moderately reformist proposals began appearing in print, especially in the more specialized economic journals, the most lively discussions took place in less visible settings.

Shortly after the November 1982 Central Committee Plenum, a formal commission was set up under the leadership of Gosplan's chairman, Nikolai Baibakov, and charged with the task of analyzing attempts at reforming the economic mechanism in the fraternal socialist countries. The actual research work of the commission was under the direction of its secretary, Academician Oleg Bogomolov, who already headed the Soviet Academy of Sciences' Institute of the Economics of the World Socialist System. Meeting formally about once a month until August of 1985, the commission became a lively forum in which both academic economists and important economic policy-makers debated the merits and demerits of a wide range of possible reform measures.

Although no other special panels of economic experts are known to have been publically commissioned by such high authority in the Andropov period, public criticism of the lack of creativity and progress in Soviet economic science by Andropov and other authoritative Party spokesmen put the academic community and specialized research institutes on notice that new ideas would receive a hearing. Elaboration of reformist proposals became an important preoccupation of the directors and staffs of such organizations as the Central Mathematical Economics Institute in Moscow and the Institute of Economics and Organization of Industrial Production in Novosibirsk. More conservative, yet still innovative, proposals emanated from Gosplan's Economic Science Research Institute and the Council of Ministers' Academy of the National Economy.[13]

At least one special conference of economists drawn from both academia and practical administration was quietly convened (in April of 1983) to discuss questions of economic reform. One paper from that conference found its way into the hands of the Western press and created something of a sensation.[14] The paper was prepared by a group of radical reformist economic researchers in Novosibirsk, evidently under the general leadership of sociologist Academician Tat'yana Ivanovna Zaslavskaya of the Institute of Economics and Organization of Industrial Production.

The "Novosibirsk Report" was remarkable not so much for the essentials of its economic analysis as for its bluntness and political militancy. It asserted as long since established the necessity of a radical economic reform program involving extensive decentralization of authority, greatly enhanced autonomy for profit-oriented enterprise management, the ending of bureaucratic allocation of materials and supplies, and much greater reliance on market forces exerted through a flexible pricing system. The real focus of the memorandum was on the identification of powerful and privileged vested interests who stood to lose by the necessary reforms, coupled with an appeal for vigorous leadership at the highest level of the Party to organize a co-ordinated political struggle mobilizing the potential beneficiaries at lower levels of the political and economic hierarchy in order to neutralize and overcome the predictable bureaucratic resistance to any truly meaningful reform. The report reads very much like a clarion call for class struggle against the New Class. The belated leaking of this outspoken document to the Western press produced a certain embarrassment for regime propagandists and was followed by Zaslavskaya's relative seclusion from the public eye for two years, but it was noteworthy that no public disgrace or formal disciplinary action against the authors was forthcoming.

Although few economists expressed their views with the forcefulness of Zaslavskaya and the Novosibirsk group, the weight of expert opinion consulted was evidently supportive of renewed efforts at economic reform, and Andropov's administration began taking more concrete, though still cautious, steps in that direction. On July 26, 1983, a joint decree of the Central Committee and the Council of Ministers was made public.[15] The decree provided in some detail for the launching of a limited experiment testing new methods of economic management in five selected republic and all-union industrial ministries (later expanded to include an additional five ministries in 1985).

The procedures followed and the economists and other experts consulted in drafting the experimental model have not yet been clarified. A formal commission charged with overseeing the detailed implementation of the experiment was established under the chairmanship of L.A. Voronin, the First Deputy Chairman of GOSPLAN, and it is plausible to suppose that many of the economists and policy-makers who served on this commission were also instrumental in its initial design, including Academician Dzherman Gvishiani, head of the commission's "Scientific Council" and a son-in-law of Alexei Kosygin, and Academician Abel Aganbegyan, Zaslavskaya's boss and protector in Novosibirsk, who succeeded Gvishiani in 1986. Certainly they played a part in its subsequent modification.

Mikhail Gorbachev's responsibilities within the Secretariat expanded rapidly under Andropov, and at the time the experiment was being designed, he was generally believed by Western observers to be the Party *Apparat*'s chief watchdog in the economic policy area, a function he continued to fulfill under Chernenko. Apart from his role in the Secretariat, the best indirect indication confirming that Gorbachev was importantly involved in overseeing the experiment's formulation lies in the fact that many of the lesser officials who clearly were intimately involved received quick promotion as soon as Gorbachev became General Secretary, suggesting that he already regarded them as very much a part of his team — Nikolai Ryzhkov (then Central Committee Secretary for industry), Alexei Antonov (Deputy Premier), S.A. Sitarian (Deputy Chairman of GOSPLAN), and, of course, Voronin himself.

Beginning on January 1, 1984, bureaucratic controls from above were to be considerably relaxed, allowing enterprise directors in the experimenting ministries greater control over important business decisions. Profitability maximization was not to be a major "synthetic index" of performance, but the number of compulsory targets prescribed from above was to be reduced to five — labor productivity growth, cost reduction, the volume of fulfilled contracts for sales, share of highest quality product in total output, and an indicator of scientific-technical progress. Enterprises were to be given discretion over the use of their production development and amortization funds to make autonomously-planned investments to improve quality and productivity. Similarly, enterprises were to have much greater discretion in how to distribute their bonus funds, allowing them to devise their own incentive schemes to better encourage productivity and quality improvement. In order to induce enterprise management to use its newly granted discretion for pursuing the planners' intended purposes, the wage fund was now to be directly tied to the growth rate of normative net output, while the resources provided to the two principal incentive funds were to be mathematical functions of labor productivity and unit cost improvements. The ministries were yet once again enjoined to respect the spirit of the reforms, to provide targets and norms that would be stable and predictable from year to year over the course of the five-year plan, and in general to refrain from the familiar vices of arbitrariness and "petty tutelage."

The "experiment" announced in July 1983 must be seen as an essentially very modest approach to economic reform, in its general scope and ambition much more closely resembling the 1979 decree than the 1965 Kosygin reforms. Since nothing was done either to render the pricing system more decentralized and flexible or to enhance the status of profitability as a goal of enterprise management, the old centralized planning system remained fundamentally intact. The goal was better discipline in fulfillment of the plan designed at the center through more careful specification of plan directives and incentives, not through any substantial alteration in the locus or content of economic decision-making. Indeed, in a great many respects, Andropov's experiment represented little more than a concentrated effort actually to implement (even if only in a few ministries) many of the ad hoc improvements that had nominally been decreed for the whole of industry in Brezhnev's later years but had somehow petered out at the implementation stage due to ministerial antipathy and slack enforcement of Party discipline.

As it turned out, Yuri Andropov did not live to see the results of implementing his reform experiment. Despite early doubts as to his successor's degree of commitment to economic reform when he came to power in February of 1984, Konstantin Chernenko's putatively more conservative "caretaker" administration did not abandon the economic experiment.   Despite occasional testy comments from the General Secretary, reform proposals considerably more radical than those appearing during 1983 began turning up in print during Chernenko's term of office. Moreover, during 1984, the implementation of the economic experiment was carried forward with remarkable continuity and even expanded, doubtless in good part because of Mikhail Gorbachev's new status as "second secretary" and heir apparent and because of the lack of large-scale turnover among economic policy makers overseeing the reform process.

By the end of 1984, some 2300 enterprises were at least nominally operating under the rules of the economic experiment,[16] or about five percent of all Soviet enterprises.   Nevertheless, despite the rather modest character of the reforms, bad faith in ministerial implementation of even the limited decentralization measures was much in evidence. Ministries persisted in specifying obligatory indicators above and beyond those supposedly allowed by the rules of the experiment, repeatedly and arbitrarily changed the "stable norms," blocked the promised discretionary use of enterprise investment funds, and sometimes confiscated and redistributed the resources of wealthier enterprises to subsidize those operating at a loss. Clearly successful implementation of the reforms in the face of bureaucratic foot-dragging would require strong, active and sustained commitment from the highest Party authorities.

Gorbachev's Approach to Economic Reform

As General Secretary, Yuri Andropov had made clear his dissatisfaction at the unacceptable performance of the Soviet economy and had communicated his sense of urgency that something be done about it. He encouraged the presentation of new ideas for revitalizing the economy, and he supported practical testing of somewhat liberalized methods of economic management on a limited sample of Soviet enterprises.   Konstantin Chernenko displayed less personal interest in reformist economists' proposals and less evident enthusiasm about the economic experiment, but he did not seek to roll back the exploratory process initiated under his predecessor. Neither Andropov nor Chernenko, however, ever arrived at a systematic and specific program of comprehensive economic reforms that they were ready to embrace publicly as their own.

Mikhail Sergeivich Gorbachev too had already indicated his profound concern at the poor performance of the Soviet economy in his public statements made during the administrations of Andropov and Chernenko, and the economic experiment begun in 1984 was evidently elaborated under his general supervision. In his first major speeches as General Secretary, Gorbachev reaffirmed his belief that the "extensive" economic strategies relied upon in the past could no longer be effective and made it clear that devising and implementing effective policies for economic revitalization would be the most critical task of his new administration.

At a meeting for managers of production organizations on April 8, 1985, the new General Secretary set the tone for all his early pronouncements on the economy:

Analysis shows that the pace at which we have moved during this five-year plan is inadequate. We will have to step it up, and step it up substantially.... The social and economic development of the country, the strengthening of its defense capability, and the improvement of the Soviet people's lives depends upon how successfully we accomplish this task.

As far as long range tasks are concerned, questions of the resolute switching of production onto the tracks of intensification, the improvement of its structure, the acceleration of scientific and technological progress, the significant heightening of output quality, and the further improvement of the economic mechanism and of management as a whole are coming to the fore.

We must do this — there is no other way. We cannot hope for manna from heaven....

While strengthening centralized planning in the main areas, we propose to continue to expand the rights of enterprises, to introduce genuine economic accountability and, on this basis, to enhance the responsibility, as well as the material interest, of the collective as a whole and of every worker for the final results of work. The economic experiment is also directed toward this end.[17]

Two weeks later, at the Central Committee Plenum, Gorbachev elaborated upon the same theme:

The development of Soviet society will be determined, to a decisive extent, by qualitative changes in the economy, by its switch onto the tracks of intensive growth, and by an all-out increase in efficiency. ...

It is known that, along with the successes that have been achieved in the economic development of the country, in the past few years unfavorable tendencies have intensified, and a good many difficulties have arisen.... [T]he difficulties have by no means been overcome....

What is the reason for the difficulties? ...

Natural and a number of external factors have had an impact, of course. But the main thing, I think, is that the changes in the objective conditions of the development of production, the need for accelerating its intensification and for changes in the methods of economic management were not properly assessed in good time, and — this is especially important — no perseverance was shown in working out and implementing major measures in the economic sphere. Comrades, we must become thoroughly aware of the existing situation and draw the most serious conclusions. The country's historical destiny and the positions of socialism in today's world depend in large part on how we handle matters from now on.[18]

Gorbachev was clearly and explicitly identifying himself with the cause of economic reform and positioning himself in such a way that his leadership would have to be evaluated by his success or failure in revitalizing the Soviet economy through the promised policy innovations. Yet he was also too shrewd to commit himself prematurely to any specific economic reform model without first assuring himself of the political support that would be necessary for its adoption and effective implementation. The strategy for generating this political support had at least two important components — the policy of *glasnost* and the "renewal of cadres."

The policy of *glasnost* or "publicity" entailed relaxation of previously quite rigorously enforced censorship guidelines designed to prevent any disclosure of "downbeat" social or economic data deemed embarassing or uncomplimentary to the regime. *Glasnost* also entailed a somewhat more selective easing of the ban on attributing blame for such unsatisfactory facts of Soviet life to the mistaken or self-serving decisions of powerful regime policy-makers (almost exclusively during previous administrations) or to fundamental features of the economic mechanism. In the atmosphere of increased toleration for unconventional economic thinking, several individual Soviet economists went so far as to endorse explicitly in print the idea of adopting new economic rules of the game based on Hungary's N.E.M.[19] Economic debate for the first time became even livelier than in the early 1960's.

Shocking revelations and dramatic exposes made possible by *glasnost* served Gorbachev's political interests precisely through the sense of crisis and the fear of possible disaster that they aroused. Ugly facts and ominous trends were the necessary substantiation for the new General Secretary's fervent and repeated exhortations that personnel, policies, habits and institutions could not remain as they were. Through *glasnost*, Gorbachev and his allies sought to nullify the predictable rationalization for complacency: "If it ain't broke, don't fix it." *Glasnost* not only would help mobilize broad-based popular support for change but also would undermine the credibility and morale of the vested interests most inclined to resist it.

The "renewal of cadres" has been a recurrent feature of succession periods in Soviet history. The new leader, having once acquired his position through a process of oligarchic bargaining and coalition-making among his Politburo comrades, finds his power limited by resurgent norms of "collective leadership." To become more than "first among equals" and to put his own stamp on policy, the General Secretary then characteristically has sought wherever possible to use his influence over personnel assignment to substitute new policy-makers and executives who are personally beholden to himself for the incumbents who were held over from the old administration and whose personal loyalties and policy commitments may be questionable. Historically, post-succession periods have normally involved above average turnover rates among the regional Party secretaries, the Central Committee Secretariat, the membership of the Central Committee, the Council of Ministers, and (ultimately) within the Politburo itself.

Gorbachev's efforts at consolidating his power through personnel changes were unusually vigorous during his first year or so in office. By the middle of 1986, turnover in the Secretariat stood at 68 percent, while that of the Council of Ministers had reached better than 40 percent (including the Premier and more than half of the deputy premiers). About one-third of the Party's regional first secretaries and top officials of the union republics had been replaced under Gorbachev.[20] Some 40 percent of the incumbant members of the old Central Commitee were excluded from the membership of the new Central Committee elected at the 27th Congress of the CPSU in March 1986.[21]

Although Western Kremlinologists are by no means united in their views as to the completeness of Gorbachev's success in consolidating his personal preeminence over the rest of the Party's top leadership,[22] during the Spring of 1986, the General Secretary clearly began showing much more willingness to go beyond generalities and link his own name with highly controversial proposals. In his report to the Party Congress in February, Gorbachev gave a foretaste of the specific recommendations soon to come:

> Comrades! Accomplishing the new tasks in the economy will be impossible without a thoroughgoing restructuring of the economic mechanism and the

creation of an integral, efficient and flexible system of management that enables us to more fully realize the possibilities of socialism.

Economic management — and this is obvious — needs constant improvement. But now the situation is such that we cannot restrict ourselves to partial improvements — a radical reform is necessary.[23]

His choice of words was politically significant. For the first time, Gorbachev went beyond the relatively neutral term "restructuring" (*perestroika*) in describing his plans for the economic mechanism to call for "radical reform" (*radikalnaya reforma*). The term "reform" had been pointedly excluded from official Soviet rhetoric regarding the economy ever since the 1968 invasion of Czechoslovakia.

While Gorbachev's report for the Congress was largely couched in terms of generalities, he said enough to indicate the main drift of his thinking in several areas for economic reform. Referring to Lenin's enthusiasm for the "tax in kind" that inaugurated the NEP in the 1920s, the General Secretary endorsed the idea of state delivery targets for collective farms that would be unchangeable over five year periods, with the management to be left free to market above-target output at uncontrolled prices. He wanted further encouragement of family work-teams operating as independent subcontractors for state and collective farms. He suggested that popular living standards could be cheaply and rapidly improved through legislation reflecting a more permissive attitude toward private and small-cooperative economic activities in the services sector of the urban economy.

Gorbachev's initial proposals for reforming the management of state industry were less detailed. Essentially he reaffirmed the principles of the economic experiment begun in 1984, calling for their implementation in a larger and larger proportion of Soviet enterprises. The principles of enterprise self-financing and strict economic accountability were depicted as the key to linking improvements in plan fulfillment and efficiency to the financial interests of both management and rank-and-file workers. He called for a "systematic restructuring of the price system as a whole" to give prices greater flexibility, and he noted that greater use might be made of negotiated contract prices. Ministries were once again urged to refrain from exercising "petty tutelage" over their enterprises, although the impact of this exhortation was somewhat diluted by the injunction "to enhance the effectiveness of centralized management and to strengthen the role of the center in realizing the basic goals of the Party's economic strategy."

Although the 27th Congress obligingly provided a generalized endorsement of the need for economic "restructuring," no basic "blueprint" analogous to those of the 1960's was formally adopted. The task of enacting a more precise and detailed statement of basic concepts and principles to guide the drafters and framers of economic reform legislation was to be taken up by the next plenary session of the Central Committee, originally scheduled for the fall of 1986.

It is perhaps indicative of the political delicacy of this task that the meeting to approve the economic reform had to be rescheduled several times. The intellectual task of working out a coordinated program was itself a formidable one, and securing something like a consensus among the spokesmen for the affected economic agencies must have been a maddeningly time-consuming assignment, especially since the Central Committee's Economic Department had had to function without an effective Chief for nearly all of 1986. Finally, in January of 1987, Nikolay Slyun'kov was appointed a Central Committee Secretary and given charge of the drafting of the reform, assuming leadership of the Economic Department.[24]

Gorbachev explained that "we postponed the beginning of the plenary session three times, since we could not go ahead with it without having clarity on basic questions."[25] While denying the existence of organized opposition, the General Secretary became even more explicit in later public speeches in acknowledging that "specific exponents [of resistance to *perestroika*] are at the level of the Central Committee and the government and in the ministries . . ."[26]

It was not until June of 1987 that the Central Committee finally convened to consider a systematic pronouncement on the subject of economic reform — and even then the General Secretary declined to submit most of the promised draft decrees for their inspection, contenting himself with a more generalized endorsement of the main directions for change.[27] (Nevertheless, Western analysts generally agreed that the June Plenum was a landmark in Gorbachev's consolidation of personal authority, since he was able to have four new full members added to the Politburo, including Aleksandr Yakovlev, regarded as the General Secretary's closest advisor on domestic policy, and Nikolay Slyun'kov, the man who supervised the actual drafting of the reform documents.) About two weeks after the Plenum, nearly a dozen detailed reform decrees were adopted in the name of the Central Committee and Council of Ministers on the authority of the Party and state leadership,[28] without evidence of prior consideration or specific endorsement by the full Central Committee.

Gorbachev's Reform Blueprint

With the publication of the June Plenum's resolution "Basic Provisions for Radical Restructuring of Economic Management" and the subsequent decrees, as well as the Supreme Soviet's passage of the final version of the new "Law on the State Enterprise,"[29] the basic features and schedule of implementation for Gorbachev's economic reform program were finally made specific, although certain important ambiguities remained to be clarified.

If Gorbachev's reform package is assessed according to the criteria earlier applied in Table 2.5 to rank order the East European economic reforms of the 1960's,[30] the 1987 blueprint registers as clearly more "radical" than the Kosygin reforms of 1965. Moreover, Gorbachev's program also turns out to be rather more "radical" by this measure than the 1960's economic reforms in East Germany and Bulgaria, which had often been discussed by Western commentators speculating in the early 1980's as to the most likely prototype for a moderate Soviet economic reformer to rely upon in the coming post-Brezhnev succession period. However, Gorbachev's economic reform proposals were still clearly less "radical" than the 1960's reforms in Hungary and Czechoslovakia.

One principal theme of the 1987 reform documents is the need for a stricter interpretation and much more rigorous enforcement of the long-established principle of *khozraschet* in order to control costs and stimulate greater efforts to raise productivity. The enterprise is to be held more effectively responsible for seeing to it that its sales revenues cover all its labor and capital costs. According to the "self-financing" principle, smaller investments for purposes of modernization or renovation would be paid for out of amortization accounts or special reserve funds derived from enterprise profits, while larger investments would be financed through interest-bearing bank loans. Enterprises are to be assessed a sort of rental fee (levies on capital) to the state budget for the continuing right to use existing capital assets, based upon a percentage of their valuation. Free provision of capital investment from the state budget is supposed to become very rare — to be reserved primarily for the establishment of new enterprises in sectors deemed especially crucial to long-range national development (and, one would surmise, for struggling enterprises in the defense sector whenever rigid insistence on self-financing might delay or obstruct the military procurement process). Permanent subsidies for enterprises unable to meet their basic operating expenses are no longer supposed to be a common option, with procedures for enterprise receivership or bankruptcy now being available as a last resort when management proves incapable of correcting recurrent losses.

Since the payroll represents for most enterprises a very large share of operating costs, effective enforcement of the self-financing principle in individual enterprises necessarily entails some mechanism to fine-tune wage rates and/or to adjust the numbers of employees on staff. Under the reform, enterprise management is supposed to have much greater freedom to determine staffing levels and more discretion in allocating the existing wage fund among remaining employees. Under one optional pay system provided for in the new statute on the enterprise, not only employee bonuses but also the rate of increase in basic wage rates are evidently to be made dependent upon enterprise profits, which would seem to imply an end to the long standing Soviet system of nationally standardized pay grades.

The measures to enforce *khozraschet* and "self-financing" more strictly and to tie managerial and employee incomes more meaningfully to the bottom line of the enterprise balance sheet, if actually adhered to, would represent an important departure in Soviet economic administration. However, there is little here that was not projected earlier in the 1965 reforms and then later reneged upon. Gorbachev has generally articulated this portion of the reform less in terms of new opportunities for managerial autonomy and creativity and more in association with the rhetoric of "strengthening discipline." Indeed, evoking the prospect of diminished incomes and perhaps involuntary unemployment for slackers in the fight to raise productivity clearly entails a strong element of motivation through fear.

Linking incomes with stricter financial accountability clearly has potential for restricting the incidence of careless waste of materials on the shop floor. It perhaps may be made effective against extremes of overstaffing, as in the well-publicized Shchekino experiments. But for such enterprise-level incentives to induce cost-saving technological innovation and a more rational allocation of resources and tasks among enterprises and among branches of production, the enterprise would require greatly increased authority to determine product assortment and production levels, raw materials specifications, choice of production technology, and long range investment plans.

The degree of practical autonomy actually to be enjoyed by the enterprise remains one of the major imponderables of current Soviet economic reforms, despite fervant rhetorical endorsement of the general principle. According to the "Basic Provisions," direct and detailed instructions from above in the form of an obligatory annual enterprise plan are supposed to be eliminated with the shift to five-year plans linking enterprise financial incentives to a variety of technical and financial performance norms, including profitability. Administrative techniques for exercising central control over enterprise activities are supposed to be displaced by "economic" methods. Yet Gosplan, the ministries, and even republic-level authorities will retain the right to issue compulsory orders to ensure fulfillment of production targets for designated "high priority" products. Even for lower priority items, ministries will also have the right to send their enterprises advisory "control figures" on virtually the entire range of production indicators formerly dictated by binding plan directives. Since Gorbachev himself has made it clear that ministers will be held strictly accountable for the detailed fulfillment of their portion of the national economic plan, it is not unreasonable to expect attempts by the ministries to exploit their considerable discretionary powers so as to render "non-binding" control figures effectively compulsory for enterprises when enterprise production decisions seem to threaten the ministry's plan fulfillment.

A principal practical barrier to effective enterprise autonomy in the past has been the supply system for raw materials and machinery. Innovative enterprise directors itching to deviate from their accustomed assortment of raw materials or to install new equipment not already assigned from the center found themselves largely unable to carry out their independent initiatives, regardless of the rubles in their discretionary accounts, because the physical materials needed were simply not available for purchase, supplies having long since been fully committed through a rigid system of bureaucratic rationing that did not hold back reserves for unplanned uses. The 1987 reforms call for making supply more responsive to demand through partially replacing the centralized system of planned material balances with a new system of "wholesale trade" in the means of production. This would be based on direct negotiation of the terms of delivery contracts between the consumer enterprise and either the producer enterprises themselves or *khozraschet* wholesale dealerships to be created by the State Committee for Technical Supply (*Gosnab*) to act as middlemen. However, both the materials required for enterprises to fulfill mandatory state orders and "particularly scarce" goods would continue to be administratively rationed in the old way.

Clearly the practical autonomy actually to be enjoyed by the enterprise under the reform will depend heavily upon the self-restraint of Gosplan and the ministries. If the central authorities choose to designate a large proportion of enterprise production as "highest priority" commodities, then enterprise management will have little of the promised freedom for maneuver, since practically all energies and resources will have to be devoted to fulfilling mandatory state orders and little room will be left for freely negotiated contracts.   And indeed, if necessary machinery and materials for enterprise activities include any of the items officially designated as in short supply, probably the enterprise will actively lobby to fill its order books with mandatory state orders, since it may otherwise be extremely difficult or impossible to secure rationed supplies through the wholesale trade network.   If enterprise autonomy in production planning is allowed to flourish only where central administrators perceive "slack" in the economy, then the next even moderately ambitious five-year plan can be counted upon for enough "tautness" to strangle this aspect of the reform in the cradle.

The rhetorically endorsed principle of allowing enterprises much greater autonomy in making investment decisions presents a particularly difficult test for the self-restraint of the central planners.   The rule that investments should normally be self-financed by the enterprise concerned (either directly from accumulated sales revenues or through bank loans carefully screened for repayability) will tend to concentrate the wherewithal to purchase capital goods (and thereby expand production) in the hands of the most profitable enterprises and economic sectors.   Under the assumptions of neo-classical economic analysis in a market economy, this would be generally a good thing, since it tends automatically to direct scarce capital to those areas of the economy promising the maximum rate of return for society as a whole.   However, both Gorbachev himself and virtually all prominant Soviet economic reformers have repeatedly indicated their conviction that the sectoral allocation of investment is among the essential macroeconomic proportions that no authentically socialist economy may leave to be determined by the spontaneous workings of the market mechanism.   Even after the reform, the central authorities will insist on allocating investment among sectors according to political rather than economic criteria.   This must entail a continuing temptation for *ad hoc* administrative interventions either to redistribute the profits of successful enterprises or to nullify their effective purchasing power through rationing of capital goods.   Such interventions may be expected to undermine the incentive effects and even the credibility of the reform itself for both workers and enterprise management.

Finally, the very workability of the economic reform is heavily dependent upon what is to be done about the reform of the pricing system. Enterprise revenues are determined in great part by the prices at which the output can be sold.   Enterprise costs are similarly dependent upon the prices at which the factors of production can be obtained.   Greater incentive for the enterprise to pursue profitability can stimulate the economic rationalization only if the enterprise accounts and financial planning projections that guide managerial decision making incorporate economically sound prices for final products and the various factors of production potentially employable in creating them. That is to say, the pricing system needs to be flexible enough to reflect actual supply and demand conditions. The 1987 economic reform documents call for a comprehensive revision of wholesale, procurement and retail prices preparatory to full implementation of the reform during the 1991-1995 five year plan. Yet the principles on which the new prices are to be based remain basically the same as are professed under the existing system. That is, essentially an "average cost plus" methodology is to be followed for wholesale and procurement prices. Retail prices too are to be brought into somewhat closer correspondence with production and distribution costs, but they will still in many instances (foodstuffs, alcohol, etc.) be substantially modified by means of various taxes and subsidies designed to serve both social welfare values and the practical need to manipulate the population's effective demand into at least rough conformity with planned supplies of consumers' goods. Repeated pledges that elimination of food subsidies will take place in such a way as not to lower living standards suggest that reform of retail prices will at best require many years to complete.

The most important potential for improving the flexibility of the price system lies in new provisions for many procurement and wholesale prices to be negotiated between enterprises during the contracting process rather than decreed by central planning agencies. However, even for such negotiated contracts, state lists of "base prices" and "normative parametric prices" are supposed, in some as yet unspecified way, to constitute the reference point for "negotiated" pricing agreements. Even to the extent that genuine bargaining over price is allowed to take place in the negotiation of delivery contracts, serious price distortions are still likely to emerge due to the monopolistic and/or monopsonistic positions of the enterprises, which will continue to be organized into compulsory industrial associations that will be tempted to function as cartels to maximize their members' bargaining power. In any case, since both state prices and contract prices will normally be required to remain fixed for at least five year terms, it seems doubtful that the overall rationality of the price structure will be improved for very long by the one-shot price reform. If the reform model is to be permanently institutionalized, some method will have to be found for prices to be more frequently realigned to reflect changing conditions of supply and demand.

Prospects for Implementing Gorbachev's Economic Reform

While the practical implementation of some aspects of Gorbachev's reform blueprint has already begun in 1988, the announced timetable for full completion of the reform is a more protracted one. Most of its provisions are supposed to be at least provisionally in effect by the beginning of the 1991-1995 five year plan. It is therefore still too early to evaluate directly either the extent of active opposition to implementing the reform or the degree of economic success the reform may be able to achieve once implemented. Eastern Europe's experience in the 1960's suggests, however, that among the crucial determinants of success in the implementation stage will be the degree of commitment to the reform exhibited by the Party's General Secretary and the degree of cohesion or factionalism within the Party's top leadership.

By laying such enormous stress on the seriousness of the economic crisis and by publicly identifying himself so closely with *perestroika* as the only possible solution, Mikhail Gorbachev has already placed himself in a position where the success or failure of his economic reforms will very likely determine whether he can hold on to political power. If Gorbachev's economic reform should be neutralized in the implementation stage, it seems highly unlikely that it will be through any lack of vigorous effort by the General Secretary to mobilize the full resources of the Secretariat to overcome ministerial foot-dragging.

It is virtually certain, however, that even in the absence of bureaucratic sabotage, there will at least be some fairly serious difficulties of a transitional nature. The creation of whole new organizations (such as the wholesale trade network) and the redefinition of the functions of existing organizations (such as the ministries and the industrial associations) is bound to result in a great deal of initial confusion and disruption. Beginning to enforce the principles of cost accounting and self-financing on the many Soviet enterprises that have operated at a loss for years must inevitably force policy makers to confront the unpleasant realities of imminent pay cuts, large-scale lay-offs, disruptive reorganizations or mergers, and even bankruptcy and liquidation for whole enterprises. The likely political and social consequences of such "transitional problems of adjustment" are bound to create genuine dilemmas for even the most sincere reformers. At a minimum, strong pressures for special exceptions and "temporary" subsidies to cushion the impact of sudden change are sure to arise.

The question is, when the pressure is really on, will Gorbachev be able to maintain the necessary level of support for his economic program from his Politburo colleagues? Will the Soviet leadership remain unified enough to leave Gorbachev the freedom of maneuver to accept the short-term concessions most necessary for averting a popular backlash while still maintaining enough momentum and consistency in the reform to secure its eventual consolidation?

During his relatively brief tenure at the head of the Soviet leadership, Mikhail Gorbachev has already demonstrated formidable talents as a political strategist. Although Western Sovietologists still differ as to the degree of Gorbachev's predominance within the Soviet leadership, he has removed his most obvious rivals from the Politburo and has succeeded in adding several close supporters to that group. He has been able to bring about wholesale personnel changes at the Republic and regional levels of the Party and state organizations. Through the policy of *glasnost* he has successfully mobilized much of the Soviet *intelligentsia* in support of his reforms. The provisions promising at least the forms of greater industrial democracy added on to the new Law on the State Enterprise seem designed to reconcile the more activist elements in the industrial workforce to the rigors of the new economic model by extending greater opportunities to participate in preparations for the changeover. While implementing such major changes is always bound to be a messy and conflict-provoking business, it would seem that the odds now favor a relatively thorough implementation of the basic features of Gorbachev's economic reform. For the reform to be successfully institutionalized over the longer term, however, the changes will of course have to produce noticeable improvement in economic performance.

Eastern Europe's Prospects for Reform

The economic difficulties of the late 1970's provoked a revival of reformist economic discussions in much of Eastern Europe, and the rather mild economic experimentation embarked upon by the Soviets in 1978-1979 helped to reinforce a certain renewal of interest in going at least a little beyond the normal levels of institutional tinkering among the region's political elites.

Hungarian policy makers became particularly vocal about the need for greater consistency in applying the principles of the 1968 reform in day to day practice, and a number of rather intriguing measures were introduced for the further extension of the N.E.M., including provision for a greater role for private enterprise and small cooperatives in the services sector. The Bulgarians adopted a number of measures designed to re-emphasize the importance of the principles of *khozraschet* and to link bonuses more closely to effective cost-cutting. The East Germans concentrated their efforts on reorganizing existing enterprises and V.V.B.s into still larger and more internally integrated managerial units known as *Kombinate*, incorporating not only production activities but also research institutions and foreign trade organizations.   Even the staunchly anti-revisionist leadership in Czechoslovakia took steps to reduce slightly the number of obligatory plan targets handed down to industrial enterprises. Only neo-Stalinist Albania and Romania seem to have remained relatively untouched by the trend toward experimentation with at least mild economic reform.

As would be expected because of the extreme severity of its economic crisis and the virtual breakdown of censorship accompanying the rise of the Solidarity movement, Poland was the scene of Eastern Europe's most thorough-going economic debates in the first half of the 1980's.   Quite radical economic reforms involving substantial movement in the direction of "market socialism" were widely promoted, usually in conjunction with recommendations for greatly increasing the authority of revitalized and democratized organs of workers' self-management at the factory level to prevent managerial abuses, to protect the operational autonomy of the enterprise from the central bureaucracy, and to safeguard the material security of the workforce amid the dislocations of the transition to the new model.   The economic reform program actually adopted in principle by the regime fell short of the most radical proposals aired in the debate but constituted nevertheless the most radical economic reform blueprint formally endorsed in any Soviet bloc country since those of Hungary and Czechoslovakia in the late 1960's.   Even after martial law and the suppression of Solidarity, the Jaruzelski government remained formally committed to the implementation of most of the earlier economic reform package, although progress in actual implementation has been slight for reasons connected largely with persistent factionalism within the Party leadership and the seemingly well-founded fear that civil unrest may result from the necessary alterations in the retail price structure and the sectoral distribution of incomes.

Since the accession of Mikhail Gorbachev and his fervent embrace of the cause of economic *perestroika*, the "emulation factor" has become considerably more favorable to the cause of economic reform in Eastern Europe, although the gradual increase over the last two decades in the degree of internal autonomy enjoyed by the smaller member states of the Soviet bloc may have somewhat attenuated the potency of this influence.

The most openly critical East European evaluations of Soviet *perestroika* have certainly come from the countries least closely aligned with the Soviets. Albania under its new leader Ramiz Alia has thus far shown no inclination whatever to modify the late Enver Hoxha's flat repudiation of all attempts to adulterate classical Stalinist economic practices with market socialist elements. The Albanian Party organ *Zeri i Popullit* recently compared Gorbachev's policies unfavorably even with those of the arch-revisionist Leonid Brezhnev and charged that *perestroika* represented nothing less than "a frontal attack against Marxism-Leninism."[31]

Romania has refrained from explicit criticism of Gorbachev and *perestroika* by name. However, Romanian General Secretary Ceausescu's frequent references to "rightist deviations" as the currently most dangerous threat to socialist construction, his condemnation of "so-called market socialism," and his recent indignant protest that it is "impossible to speak about socialist renewal . . . and perfecting socialism through the so-called development of small private property"[32] leaves little room for doubt as to his views on Soviet *perestroika*. Because of the vigilance of Ceausescu's censors, Romanian news media coverage of Gorbachev's economic and political reforms has been scanty and lacking in detail. In any case, although Ceausescu has been content to criticize Gorbachev's economic policies only obliquely, he has not been at all shy about reiterating his long-standing position that each ruling Communist Party has the sovereign right to interpret the laws of socialist construction for itself, and consequently that Romanian socialism will not be redesigned "according to foreign patterns and models."[33] Despite Romania's increasingly desperate economic situation, President Ceausescu seems thus far to have successfully prevented any coalescence of opposition to his leadership through his techniques of rigorous censorship, periodic purges, and frequent transfer of his subordinates, and any program of even relatively moderate economic reform for Romania will have to await his departure from the scene.

The remaining, more closely aligned East European Communist Parties, however, have displayed widely varied degrees of enthusiasm in their applause for Gorbachev's economic reforms. While all of them more or less readily endorse the notion that *perestroika* is a rational and creative response to serious difficulties faced by the Soviet economy, Party positions differ considerably as to the desirability of adopting the Soviet reforms in their own countries.

The Hungarian leadership has been most enthusiastic about the Soviet economic reform and emphasizes its similarity to their own N.E.M. Rezso Nyers, the economist who was the principal architect of the N.E.M., has been coopted once again into the Party leadership. Hungary's N.E.M. is being revitalized and extended, a process that seems to have accelerated following the retirement of Janos Kadar and his replacement as General Secretary by Karoly Grosz at the May 1988 Party Congress. While N.E.M. concepts already had a strong basis of support in Hungary and a movement toward their more consistent application had already reemerged during the last years of the Brezhnev era, it seems clear that Gorbachev's reformism has strengthened Hungarian economic reformers and accelerated the reform's renewed progress.

Poland's Party chief Wojciech Jaruzelski has been among the most fervent public endorsers of Gorbachev's economic reform, and for good reason. For the first time in many years, Poland's Communist leaders are able to pursue greater domestic legitimacy through endorsement of significant reforms without endangering their amicable relationship with their Soviet protectors. Poland's history of repeated failures to implement formally adopted economic reforms, the deep-seated lack of trust in their government on the part of Polish citizens, the economy's desperate imbalances, the Party's factionalism and Jaruzelski's partial political dependence upon hard-liner supporters all suggest that the probability of thoroughly implementing Poland's economic reform is not remarkably high. Nevertheless, a positive attitude toward economic reform by the Soviet leadership has undoubtedly improved the reform's chances for survival considerably beyond what they would otherwise be.

The political implications of Gorbachev's economic reformism in Czechoslovakia provide an interesting contrast to the Polish case. Whereas most of the existing Polish leadership can reasonably hope to gain in personal stature and collective legitimacy by disassociating themselves from the economic policies of their discredited predecessors, Czechoslovakia's Party leadership is composed almost entirely of men who came to power in the wake of the 1968 Warsaw Pact intervention and whose principal career accomplishments have consisted precisely in the ruthless extirpation of the "revisionist" political and economic reforms of the Dubcek era. Any dramatic movement toward emulation of Gorbachev's economic reforms and steps toward political liberalization cannot help but be interpreted as a comprehensive repudiation of the past two decades of Czechoslovak policies, virtually necessitating considerable turnover in the composition of the Party leadership and creating strong pressures for the return of literally thousands of victims of the post-invasion purges to active political life. That is, the political situation could become very similar to that which precipitated the factionalism and civil disorders of the mid-1960's.

Because of Czechoslovakia's slightly better-than-average economic performance in recent years and because of the special political sensitivity of reformism in that country, it is not surprising that much of the generally hard-line Czech and Slovak leadership has been highly skeptical of Gorbachev's reformism, yet Soviet pressure is particularly hard for this

reflexively pro-Soviet group to resist effectively. The recent retirement
of long-time Party Chief Gustav Husak (itself a development not unrelated
to Gorbachev's pressures for reform) has created a more fluid situation of
elite competition as the new pecking order is sorted out within the Party
leadership and the various contenders for power seek to mobilize support
from both the broader population and their Soviet allies. According to
reports in the *Frankfurter Allgemeine Zeitung*,[34] Prime Minister Lubomir
Strougal has taken the lead in advocating a thorough-going emulation of
Soviet *perestroika* and *glasnost*, while fellow Politburo members Vasil
Bilak and Jan Fojtik oppose this and actively campaign to maintain the
status quo. The Party's new General Secretary, Milos Jakes, has attempted
to stake out a centrist position between them. Lacking a stable consensus
within the top political leadership, Czechoslovakia's already pronounced
susceptibility to Soviet pressures is probably still further enhanced, so
some further movement toward serious economic reform may very well
be imminent in that country. If this turns out to be the case, it will require
extraordinary political skill for the incumbent Party leadership to limit the
political fallout to survivable proportions.

Although Bulgaria suffered no such massive public trauma as
Czechoslovakia in the sputtering out of its late 1960's economic reforms,
the issue of renewed economic reform seems to have again become a
highly contentious one in the Bulgaria of the mid- and late 1980's. As
has been the pattern throughout the history of Bulgaria's Communist
regime, each of the various Soviet movements in the direction of moderate
economic reform or experimentation in recent years has rather quickly
resulted in a parallel gesture from Bulgarian policy makers, widely
regarded as the Soviet Union's most reliable allies. Yet despite the
customary immediate and enthusiastic endorsements for new Soviet
policies always forthcoming from Party Chief Todor Zhivkov, and despite
the Party's formal approval in principle of quite a number of domestic
reform measures during 1986 and 1987, the increased radicalism of
Gorbachev's more recent economic and (especially) political initiatives
has clearly dismayed a sizable share of Bulgaria's political elite.

Although official Party spokesmen have taken unusual pains recently to
deny the existence of any serious conflict within the Bulgarian leadership,
Western analysts have been citing indirect and circumstantial evidence that
the opposite is in fact the case and that conflicts over both policy issues
and the leadership question have become unusually intense during 1987
and 1988.[35] One manifestation of this situation is that practical measures
to implement reforms putatively already approved by the highest Party
authorities have not been forthcoming at all, despite prior announcements

by Zhivkov himself of early deadlines for their drafting and enactment. The new Code on Self-Managing Organizations and the new Law on Regional People's Councils, which were to have been enacted in January 1988 have not yet appeared as of this writing, more than seven months late, despite their importance for the reform program formally approved at the July 1987 Central Committee plenum. 1988 meetings of the National Assembly and of the Central Committee have been indefinitely delayed. That Zhivkov himself is in danger of losing control is suggested by several recent instances in which Zhivkov's own seemingly authoritative pronouncements have been "corrected" or even contradicted by other official spokesmen or even in Politburo resolutions. Substantively important and critical portions of at least one Zhivkov speech have been cut from the version published in the official Party newspaper. Measures have been taken to remove Zhivkov's portrait from display in public places, while institutions renamed in memory of Zhivkov's late daughter Lyudmila have recently had their original names quietly restored.

If, as now seems likely, Todor Zhivkov soon follows his fellow Party Chiefs Gustav Husak and Janos Kadar into retirement, a transitional period of intensified leadership factionalism and competition seems unavoidable before the current policy deadlock over reform questions can be resolved. While conservative, anti-reform elements seem to occupy important positions within Bulgaria's power structure, other prominant likely contenders for Zhivkov's mantle, such as Prime Minister Georgi Atanasov and Secretariat member Chudomir Aleksandrov, have in the past made strongly reformist speeches signaling their willingness to follow in Gorbachev's footsteps.[36] Predicting the outcome of a struggle in which information about the participants and their alignments is so scarce is not an easy proposition, but, on the basis of past experience, we may at least speculate that the evident lack of consensus within the Bulgarian leadership will tend to enhance the already extensive influence of the Soviet leadership in Bulgarian affairs and (assuming Gorbachev's policy initiatives are not blocked at home) thereby increase the chances for eventual successful implementation of Bulgaria's economic reforms.

The German Democratic Republic, as one of the most deeply penetrated of the regimes in Eastern Europe and one of the U.S.S.R.'s closest allies in foreign affairs, might be expected to be among the most willing to emulate Gorbachev's economic reforms. This has not proved to be the case, however. This is partly to be understood in the light of the G.D.R.'s relatively less severe economic "performance gap." While the G.D.R., like its other East European allies, has undergone a certain economic decelleration since the late 1970's, it has not been so marked as elsewhere, and the G.D.R. has recently enjoyed about the most satisfactory growth performance in the region. Moreover, the SED's General Secretary Erich Honecker has displayed little interest in further measures either to promote economic reform or to extend *glasnost* to permit critical public discussion of economic policies. His political position does not seem to be threatened by any pronounced degree of factionalism within the Party leadership that might provide leverage for would-be advocates of more radical economic reform at home or in the Soviet Union.

Honecker's stance on the Soviet economic reforms has been approving but distant. That is, Honecker has demonstrated his fidelity to Socialist Internationalism by heartily endorsing Gorbachev's economic reforms as an inspired response to the problems that have unfortunately developed in the Soviet economy in recent years, while at the same time he has been at some pains to emphasize that conditions are very different in the G.D.R. and should not be addressed in precisely the same way.   Sounding incongruously like the much denounced national deviationists of an earlier period, Honecker now calmly asserts that, on the subject of reform, it is up to each socialist country "to analyze and determine according to its own means what the next tasks are."[37] He blandly asserts that since the East German economic system has already been incrementally reformed as changing circumstances demanded over the years, the G.D.R.'s economic performance has remained basically satisfactory, and therefore no drastic changes are now necessary or appropriate. Up to now the Soviet leadership seems to have accepted this argument, and there has been no sign of any particular pressure on the G.D.R.'s leadership to revise its thinking on the matter of economic reform. Unless this situation should change, the likelihood of significant economic reforms in the G.D.R. would seem to be remote.

To summarize, as we look across Eastern Europe in these last years of the 1980's, the short- to medium-term prospects for a substantial shift toward a more decentralized, market-oriented form of socialist economic organization have never been brighter in the past forty years.   Sharp declines in economic performance have led at least a significant minority of the Communist leadership in virtually every country in the region to have serious doubts about the long-term viability of the command economy after once completing the early "extensive" stage of industrialization. The gradual loosening of the straight-jacket of ideological dogmatism and rigid censorship within the economics profession has made it possible to carry on rational dialogues about the strengths and weaknesses of alternative models of socialist economic organization and to formulate realistic proposals for institutional improvement in almost every country of the region, with the exceptions of the neo-stalinist enclaves of Albania and Romania. The new ascendancy of reformism in the Soviet Union has largely removed a previously serious external obstacle to change in the dependent countries of the region and may in fact act as an additional positive stimulus to reform for some otherwise conservative East European politicians.

Although the chances for economic reform in the region are better than ever before, we should nevertheless avoid excessive optimism. As we have seen, large and powerful segments of the Party and state bureaucracies still have every reason to regard economic reform as contrary to their basic interests, while many among the general population can expect to experience at least short-term disruptions and disquieting changes in their way of life. Previous historical experience suggests that only rather severe crises normally can tempt Communist leaders to take on such well-entrenched vested interests, precisely because victory is less than certain. We must remember that two of the most far reaching Communist economic reforms in recent history — Yugoslavia in 1966 and Czechoslovakia between 1966 and 1968 — each required a massive purge of the top and middle ranks of the party and the government and ushered in periods of considerable popular unrest and political instability.

It is little wonder that Communist political leaders have so often found it expedient to compromise on more limited economic reforms during the most severe economic downswings — and then to quietly backtrack as the first signs of cyclical economic recovery relieve the sense of urgency and crisis. Paradoxically enough, the very success of the reforms in bringing about early economic improvement may work to undermine the reforms themselves, unless those political leaders most strongly committed to the cause of economic reform are able promptly to consolidate their positions and reduce the power not only of their opponents but also of their less committed allies. Transforming experimental economic arrangements, however successful, into stable and valued institutions will eventually require far reaching political and ideological struggle, the outcome of which may well remain in doubt for the balance of this century.

NOTES

Chapter 1

1. Karl Kautsky, *Die Soziale Revolution* (Berlin: Vorwarts, 1906). For an excellent account of Bolshevik prerevolutionary assumptions about socialist economic arrangements, see Laszlo Szamuely, *First Models of the Socialist System* (Budapest: Akademiai Kiado, 1974), especially pp. 23-79.

2. *Ibid.* See also Stephen Cohen, *Bukharin and the Bolshevik Revolution* (New York: Alfred Knopf, 1973); Alexander Erlich, *The Soviet Industrialization Debate* (Cambridge: Harvard University Press, 1960); and Adam Kaufman, "Origins of the Political Economy of Socialism," *Soviet Studies* IV, No. 3 (1953), pp. 243-272.

3. It should also be noted that certain economic activities did not fall under the administrative control of the central ministries but rather were subordinated to local and regional councils for purposes of planning and administration. This applied especially to small-scale production of consumer items and services for local consumption with largely local materials.

4. Ludwig von Mises, "Die Wirtschaftsrechnung im sozialistischen Gemeinwesen," *Archiv fur sozialwissenschaften*, vol. 47, 1920. Translated and reprinted in Friedrich A. von Hayek, ed., *Collectivist Economic Planning* (London: George Routledge and Sons, 1935), pp. 87-130.

5. Friedrich von Hayek's "selected" bibliography of the major contributions to the debate as of 1935 ran to more than forty entries. (*Ibid.*, pp. 291-293.)

6. Oskar Lange, "On the Economic Theory of Socialism," *Review of Economic Studies* IV, Nos. 1 and 2 (October 1936 and February 1937); Hayek, *op. cit.*; Fred M. Taylor, "The Guidance of Production in a Socialist State," *American Economic Review* XIX (March 1929); H.D. Dickenson, "Price Formation in a Socialist Community," *Economic Journal* XLIII (June 1933).

7. See Dobb's review of Lange's *On the Economic Theory of Socialism* in *Modern Quarterly*, 1939, and Dobb's own book *Political Economy and Capitalism* (New York: International Publishers, 1945), pp. 270-338.

8. See his review of *On the Economic Theory of Socialism* in *Economica* VII, No. 26, New Series (May 1940).

9. With considerable success. By the mid-1960's, many of his mature theoretical works had been translated into Serbo-Croation, Czech, Hungarian, German, and even Russian. He is among the most frequently footnoted authors in East European economic literature, albeit not always with approval, and his intellectual influence was also considerably enhanced by his regular and active participation in international meetings of socialist economists. His continuing contacts with Western former colleagues also made Lange an important intellectual "transfer agent" and reinterpreter of such "bourgeois" techniques as econometrics, input-output analysis, and linear programming.

10. "Economic Reforms: A Balance Sheet," *Problems of Communism* XV, No. 6 (November-December 1966), p. 44.

11. For example, skepticism about the Yugoslav model (tinged with general good will, however) is quite apparent in the much translated and highly influential reformist tract by Wlodziemierz Brus, *Ogolny problemy funkcjonowania gospodarki socjalistycznej* (Warsaw: PWN, 1964), *passim*. That this skepticism was not simply simulated for the censors is evident by the even stronger reservations Brus expressed after his forced emigration in *Socialist Ownership and Political Systems* (London: Routledge and Kegan Paul, 1975), especially pp. 62-93.

12. For accounts of the origins of economic reform proposals in Hungary and Poland during the mid-1950's see, respectively, Bela A. Balassa, *The Hungarian Experience in Economic Planning* (New Haven: Yale University Press, 1959), and John M. Montias, *Central Planning in Poland* (New Haven: Yale University Press, 1962). Both emphasize the home-grown character of the critical literature, while making passing references to interest in Yugoslavia's experiences.

13. *Ekonomika i polityka Jugoslawii* (Warsaw: PWN, 1957). Also influential in the Polish discussions was Czeslaw Bobrowski's on-the-scene analysis - *Jugoslawia socjalistyczna* (Warsaw: PWN, 1957).

14. See Deborah D. Milenkovitch, *Plan and Market in Yugoslav Economic Thought* (New Haven: Yale University Press, 1971), and J.M. Fleming and V.R. Sertic, "The Yugoslav Economic System," *I.M.F. Staff Papers* IX, No. 2 (July 1962), pp. 202-203.

15. For some useful accounts of Marxian value theory and its relationship to both classical political economy and post-classical developments in economic thought, see Murray Wolfson, *A Reappraisal of Marxian Economics* (New York: Columbia University Press, 1966); Ernest Mandel, *Marxist Economic Theory* (New York: Monthly Review Press, 1970), two volumes; Joseph Schumpeter, *A History of Economic Analysis* (New York: Oxford University Press, 1968).

16. Bukharin first won his spurs as a major economic theoretician in 1917 for his lengthy tome attacking marginal analysis, *The Economic Theory of the Leisure Class* (New York: Monthly Review Press, 1972).

17. For several excellent summaries and commentary on the significance of these debates, see Gregory Grossman, ed., *Value and Plan: Economic Calculation and Organization in Eastern Europe* (Berkeley: University of California Press, 1960). For a detailed history of the development and significance of Soviet mathematical economics, see Michael Ellman's *Soviet Planning Today* (Cambridge:

Harvard University Press, 1971), and G. Hardt *et al.*, *Mathematics and Computers in Soviet Economic Planning* (New Haven: Yale University Press, 1967).

18. For the most famous and influential example of this soft-sell approach, see Oskar Lange's much translated textbook *Introduction to Econometrics* (London: Pergamon Press, 1959).

19. Oskar Lange, *Political Economy*, Vol. I, trans. A.H. Walker (New York: Macmillan, 1963), p. 185. Similarly, much was later made of the fact that Kantorovich had invented linear programming in the 1930's before it was independently discovered and popularized in the United States by G.B. Dantzig and his associates during World War II.

20. For a discussion of the economic significance of such interpretations of linear programming, see R. Dorfman, P. Samuelson, and R. Solow, *Linear Programming and Economic Analysis* (New York: McGraw Hill Co., 1958). See also Lange's 1959 textbook *Introduction to Econometrics*, previously cited.

21. An early and influential example of this genre was produced in Hungary by Janos Kornai. Cf. *Overcentralization in Economic Administration: A Critical Analysis Based on Experience in Hungarian Light Industry*, trans. John Knapp (Oxford: Oxford University Press, 1959).

Chapter 2

1. See *Current Soviet Politics*, Vol. II, p. 87, for an English translation.

2. *Ibid.*, pp. 138, 153-154. See also R.W. Davies, "Economic Aspects of the Twentieth Congress," *Soviet Studies*, October 1956.

3. I have been unable to locate any account of the Czechoslovak commission's history, but scattered remarks in various writings of Ota Sik indicate that such a body was created in the Spring of 1956, that he was an active member, and that its proposals in watered-down form were the basis for the decentralizing "mini-reform" approved by the Central Committee in February 1958 and inaugurated in April 1958.

4. The most far-reaching discussions in the G.D.R. were occasioned by published proposals by Fritz Behrens (the Director of the Central Statistical Institute) and his associate, Arne Benary. They called for much greater autonomy for the enterprises, a larger role for the workers' collectives in managing them, and the use of "economic levers" rather than "administrative levels" to ensure enterprise conformity to the central plan. See Fritz Behrens, "Zum Probleme der Ausmitzung oekonomischer Gesetze in der Ubergangsperiode," and Arne Benary, "Zu Grundprobleme der politischen oekonomie des Socialismus in der Ubergangsperiode," both in the journal *Wirtschaftswissenschaft* (3. Sonderhefte, 1957). Although both finally lost their positions and were forced to recant in early 1958, they moved into rather good jobs at the Institute of Economic Sciences of the Academy of Sciences, where they quietly continued to spread their views among like-minded or at least sympathetic colleagues. Thomas Baylis notes that in the early 1960's, the Institute was something of a revisionist stronghold and provided personnel who were active participants in the design of the New Economic System

(*The Technical Intelligentsia and the East German Elite* [Berkeley: University of California Press, 1974], p. 217).

5. Based on conversations with several leading Polish economists in Warsaw in 1973, with two Czech economists interviewed in the U.S.A. in 1969, and with two prominent Hungarian economists interviewed in the U.S.A. in 1972 and 1978. All had participated in the elaboration of the reform proposals of their respective countries.

6. The Polish Economic Council's "Theses" and much of the debate were published in multiple languages by the Polish authorities. The Varga Commission's findings were widely circulated in both German and Russian translations among foreign economists. For an account of the Polish efforts, see Andrzej Brzejski, "Poland as a Catalyst of Change in the Communist Economic System," *The Polish Review* XVI, No. 2 (1971).

7. See Abraham Katz, *The Politics of Economic Reform in the Soviet Union* (New York: Praeger, 1972), pp. 45-80.

8. *Ibid.*, pp. 58-64.

9. The Czechoslovak reform of 1959 was a bit of a hybrid. Having originally been conceived as an enterprise-oriented decentralization, it was modified drastically at the last minute to emulate Soviet geographical decentralization in many respects. The results of eclecticism and half measures were evident in the poor showing of the new system, which was quickly abandoned.

10. A former vice-chairman of the Polish Economic Council later revealed that objections by "other socialist countries" were cited to him as the government's principal reason for nullifying the Council's 1957 "Theses." See the comments by Wlodzimierz Brus in *Gospodarka Planowa* (Warsaw), November 1966, p. 11.

11. See, for example, Carl Linden, *Khrushchev and the Soviet Leadership, 1957-1964* (Baltimore: Johns Hopkins Press, 1966), and Michel Tatu, *Power in the Kremlin from Khrushchev to Kosygin* (New York: The Viking Press, 1970).

12. See Francois Fejto, *A History of the People's Democracies*, trans. Daniel Weissbort (New York: Praeger Publishers, 1971), chapter 8, and J.F. Brown, *The New Eastern Europe: The Khrushchev Era and After* (New York: Praeger Publishers, 1966), pp. 3-74, for accounts of the interaction between Khrushchev's maneuverings and specific national political alignments in the leadership changes of the 1961-64 period.

13. *Current Soviet Policies*, Vol. IV, p. 100.

14. *Ibid.*, p. 20.

15. O. Antonov, "For All and For Oneself," *Izvestiia*, November 22, 1961.

16. *Pravda*, September 7, 1962. Liberman's articles and the main contributions to the vigorous debate that followed are available in English translation in Myron Sharpe, ed., *Planning, Profit and Incentives in the U.S.S.R.*, Vol. I (White Plains, N.Y.: International Arts and Sciences Press, 1966).

17. *Pravda*, November 20, 1962.

18. The "performance gap" concept seems to have been coined by Anthony Downs in his *Inside Bureaucracy* (Boston: Little, Brown, 1967), although the underlying notion is a very old and almost commonsensical one.

19. In Czechoslovakia in 1964, the total value of unsold inventories reached a quarter of the year's total output. *Hospodarske Noviny* (Prague), No. 12, 1964, cited in Harry Shaffer, "Out of Stalinism," *Problems of Communism* XIV, No. 5 (September-October 1965), p. 32. In Hungary in 1967, it was acknowledged that aggregate stockpiles in industrial enterprises had reached such a scale that they "considerably exceeded the volume of a full year's domestic trade in manufactured articles." *Nepszabadsag*, July 9, 1967. Translated in Radio Free Europe Research Dept., *Hungarian Press Survey* # 1846 (September 11, 1967).

20. For a leading Hungarian economist's lucid survey of these problems, see Janos Kornai, *Rush Versus Harmonic Growth* (Amsterdam: North Holland Publishing Co., 1972).

21. See Paul Marer, *Soviet and East European Foreign Trade, 1946-1969* (Bloomington: Indiana University Press, 1972); also, U.S. Congress, Joint Economic Committee, 93rd Congress, 2nd Session, *Reorientation and Commercial Relations of the Economies of Eastern Europe* (Washington, D.C.: Government Printing Office, 1974).

22. See Josef Goldman and Karel Kouba, *Economic Growth in Czechoslovakia* (Prague: Academia, 1969); Curtis Harvey and John I. Hincke, Jr., "Central Planning and Economic Growth in a Mature Socialist Economy," *Jahrbuch der Wirtschaft Osteuropas*, V (Munich: Gunter Olzog Verlag, 1974), pp. 345-360; I.N. Beliaev and L.S. Semenova, *Strany S.E.V. v mirovoi ekonomike* (Moscow: Mezhdunarodnye otnosheniia, 1967), pp. 43-45; M. Usievich and V. Shabunina, "Puti povysheniia effectivnosti obshchestvennogo proizvodstva v strannakh-chlenakh S.E.V.," *Voprosy ekonomiki* (Moscow) XX, No. 11 (November 1967); Ernst, *op. cit.*, p. 892.

23. See the statistics collected by Bogdan Mieczkowski in *Personal and Social Consumption in Eastern Europe* (New York: Praeger, 1975).

24. Radoslav Selucky, "People and Plan," *Kulturni Tvorba*, February 7, 1963.

25. A. Miloshevsky, "On the Question of Strengthening Economic Incentives in Our Country," *Novo Vreme*, No. 11, 1963. Summarized in Bogoslav Dobrin, *Bulgarian Economic Development Since World War II* (New York: Praeger, 1973), pp. 119-122.

26. *Neues Deutschland*, August 24, 1962, cited in Martin Janicke, *Der Dritte Weg* (Koln: Neuer Deutscher Verlag, 1964), p. 178.

27. "Interview with Fritz Behrens," *Sonntag*, November 18, 1962, reprinted in *SBZ-Archiv* XIV, Nos. 1-2 (1963), pp. 29-30.

28. Walter Ulbricht, "Speech at the 17th C.C. Plenum," *Dem VI. Parteitag entgegen* (Berlin: Dietz Verlag, 1962), p. 38.

29. For an excellent summary of the development of Kalecki's thought, see George R. Feiwel, *The Intellectual Capital of Michal Kalecki* (Knoxville: University of Tennessee Press, 1975). Kalecki's most mature formulation of his theory of growth is now available in English translation as *Outline of a Theory of Growth in a Socialist Economy* (London: Oxford University Press, 1969). Kalecki's works were also widely read in East European economic circles, and they were translated into Czech, Hungarian, German, and Serbo-Croatian. His views were given still

further circulation by virtue of their influence on other widely translated Polish economists such as Wlodzimierz Brus and Oskar Lange.

30. The German Democratic Republic, of course, had an additional demographic problem due to the steady exodus of the most skilled and physically vigorous portions of the industrial work force to the West, until the building of the Berlin Wall in 1961.

31. This description of demographic and labor force trends really applied most accurately to the G.D.R., Czechoslovakia, and Hungary by the 1960's. Bulgaria's "reserves" were still somewhat greater, but the trend was already obvious to demographers. Poland and Romania (and evidently also Albania) were (and are still) in a quite different situation. These two countries appear to have still such abundant reserves of labor power in rural areas (and such rapid rates of natural population increase) that a primary problem has been the creation of enough new jobs to go around. See Paul F. Myers, "Population and Labor Force in Eastern Europe: 1950 to 1996," in U.S. Congress, Joint Economic Committee, *Reorientation and Commercial Relations of the Economies of Eastern Europe*, pp. 421-478. See also Marie Lavigne, *The Socialist Economies of the Soviet Union and Europe* (White Plains, N.Y.: International Arts and Sciences Press, 1974), pp. 150-152.

32. For the most elaborate presentations of this rationale in English translation, see Ota Sik, *Plan and Market Under Socialism* (Prague: Academic Publishing House, 1967); Rezso Nyers, "Problems of Profitability and Income Distribution," *New Hungarian Quarterly* (Budapest), No. 40 and 41 (Winter 1970 and Spring 1971), pp. 11-29 and 21-41; and Radovan Richta *et al.*, *Civilization at the Crossroads* (Prague: Academia Publishing House, 1969). For a Western account of the East German rationale, see Thomas Baylis, "Economic Reform as Ideology," *Comparative Politics* III, No. 2 (1971), pp. 211-229.

33. Goldman and Kouba *op. cit.*, p. 142.

34. Yevsei Liberman, "Planning, Productivity and Standards of Long-Term Operation," in Sharpe, *op. cit.*, p. 67.

35. *Novo Vreme*, November 1963, as cited in Dobrin, *op. cit.*, p. 120.

36. Baylis, *The Technical Intelligentsia*, pp. 202, 203, 217.

37. William Robinson, *The Pattern of Reform in Hungary* (New York: Praeger, 1973), p. 57.

38. Vladimir Kusin, *Political Groupings in the Czechoslovak Reform Movement* (New York: Columbia University Press, 1972), pp. 113-114.

39. Dobrin, *op. cit.*, p. 119.

40. *Ibid.*, p. 122. J.F. Brown, *Bulgaria Under Communist Rule* (New York: Praeger, 1970), pp. 160-172.

41. Nicholas Bethell, *Gomulka: His Poland, His Communism* (New York: Holt, Rinehart, and Winston, 1969), pp. 241-245. For some revealing (though biased) accounts of the increasing concentration of policy-making power in the hands of Gomulka and a few cronies, see the special issue of *Nowe Drogi* for May 1971 (containing the texts of the new leadership's statements on the circumstances necessitating Gomulka's removal), especially Jan Pajestka's account of Gomulka's private disdain for the economic profession.

42. See the "Theses of the Economic Council Concerning Certain Changes in the Economic Model," *Zycie Gospodarcze* (Warsaw), No. 22 (June 2, 1957), and "Theses on Determining the Principles of the Price Structure," *Zycie Gospodarcze*, No. 51 (December 22-29, 1957), as well as the less official proposals put forth in *Dyskusja o polskim modelu gospodarczym* (Warsaw: PWN, 1957).

43. Raymond B. Nixon, "Factors Related to Freedom in National Press Systems," *Journalism Quarterly* XXXVII (1960), p. 21, and "Freedom in the World's Press: A Fresh Appraisal With New Data," *Journalism Quarterly* XLII (1965), pp. 6 and 13.

44. Additional evidence supporting the validity of the measure for purposes of the present hypothesis is the fact that it correlates highly with a number of other independent measures of degree of "liberalization" in East Europe. See Jan F. Triska and Paul M. Johnson, *Political Development and Political Change in Eastern Europe* (Denver: University of Denver Monograph Series in World Affairs, 1975), p. 15.

45. The correlation coefficients cited in the text and displayed in Table 2.8 are based upon data from eight countries only, including the USSR but excluding Yugoslavia on the grounds that many of the reforms referred to in Table 2.5 had already been approved in principle in Yugoslavia considerably before the new reform package of the mid-1960's was adopted. Thus the mid-1960's reform package in Yugoslavia arguably did not represent *change* from the previous status quo as the other reform packages elsewhere in Eastern Europe did. Nevertheless, it is also arguable that earlier Yugoslav reforms had not been well-implemented in practice, and therefore the mid-1960's reforms there in fact did represent as radical a change as the score suggests. If Yugoslav data are included in the correlations of Table 2.8, the relationships hypothesized are still confirmed, in most cases even more strongly. The correlations of economic reform with performance gaps and with censorship become .74* and .58 respectively, with the latter correlation now significant at the .03 level. The partial correlations (controlling for the other independent variable) become .99* and .99** respectively, and the multiple correlation coefficient for economic reform with both performance gaps and censorship becomes .99** as well.

46. Jan F. Triska and Paul M. Johnson, *op. cit.*, pp. 22-28.

47. Henry Teune and Sig Synnestvedt, "Measuring International Alignments," *Orbis*, volume 10 (Spring 1965), pp. 171-189.

48. Katz, *op. cit.*, pp. 53-77, 105-123.

49. See, for example, *Pravda* for February 5, 1965; March 2, 1962; April 9, 1965; April 25, 1965; and May 9, 1965; *Izvestiia* for January 5, 1965, and June 5, 1965; and *Ekonomicheskaya Gazeta* for November 25, 1964.

50. For example, *Izvestiia*, February 18, 1969: "If one compares the Hungarian economic reform with our own, the concrete outlines . . . do not coincide in all respects. Nevertheless, it is precisely the economic reform which opens up new possibilities in the field of Soviet-Hungarian economic cooperation."

Chapter 3

1. One unusual kind of "in-and-outer" perhaps deserves special mention: economists who held important posts in the 1940's but were jailed when they were slow to go along with the rapid "sovietization" of the economy after 1948. E. Lobl and J. Goldman were two prominent examples of such reformers in Czechoslovakia. Petko Kunin played a similar role in Bulgaria after his release from a fifteen-year jail term and his restoration to the Central Committee in 1962.

2. "Report to the 22nd. Congress," *Current Soviet Policies*, Vol. IV, p. 100.

3. For the most comprehensive and authoritative statement of the 1965 Soviet economic reform blueprint, see Alexei Kosygin, "Report to the September 1965 Plenary Meeting of the Central Committee C.P.S.U.," *Reprints from the Soviet Press* I, No. 2 (October 21, 1965), Supplement, pp. 3-52.

4. As noted in the previous chapter, Poland's economic management team also underwent a considerable shake-up in 1961-1963. In this case, however, it was largely the reformers of 1956-1957 who had managed to hang on in secondary positions who were getting the pink-slips in the aftermath of the serious difficulties of 1962, not the old-line administrators of the Stalinist era, who were making a definite comeback.

5. For example, just before the inauguration of the New Economic Model in Hungary in 1968, the industrial ministries employed about 7000 people in their central offices. This figure was supposed to be reduced to about 5000 with the full implementation of the reform, a reduction in force of about one-fourth. Michael Kaser and Janusz Zielinski, *Planning in East Europe* (London: The Bodley Head Ltd., 1970), p. 32.

6. Walter Ulbricht, "The Preparations of the Sixth Congress of the German Socialist Unity Party," in *Dem VI. Parteitag entgegen* (Berlin: Dietz Verlag, 1962), p. 38.

7. The East German discussions are summarized in Karl Thalheim, *Die Wirtschaft der Sowjetzone in Krise und Umbau* (Berlin: Duncker und Humbolt, 1964).

8. Walter Ulbricht, *Das Program des Sozialismus und die geschichtliche Aufgabe der S.E.D.* (Berlin: Dietz Verlag, 1963).

9. Thomas Baylis, *The Technical Intelligentsia and the East German Elite* (Berkeley: University of California Press, 1974), p. 237. Apel and Mittag assumed the leading roles in the more formalized working group.

10. The basic documents were published as *Richtlinie fur das neue okonomische System der Planung und Leitung der Volkswirtschaft* (Berlin: Dietz Verlag, 1963).

11. Walter Ulbricht, "The New System of Planning and Management of the National Economy in Practice," *Die Wirtschaft* (Berlin), June 28, 1963, pp. 1-21.

12. For a fuller and more detailed account of the economic arrangements embodied in the N.E.S. in its various stages, see Gert Leptin, "The German Democratic Republic," in Hans-Hermann Hohmann et al., *The New Economic Systems of Eastern Europe* (Berkeley: University of California Press, 1975), pp. 43-78. For an account emphasizing the degree to which the emphasis shifted away from decentralization toward more "scientific" approaches to centralized man-

agement based on huge, vertically and horizontally integrated V.V.B.s and on the re-reduction of the autonomy of the enterprise (a process that got underway after Erich Apel's suicide in December 1965 and accelerated in 1968), see Michael Keren, "The New Economic System in the G.D.R.: An Obituary," *Soviet Studies* XXIV, No. 4 (1973).

13. A major shift took place in the composition of the Central Committee in January of 1963: over 30 percent of the incumbent members were not re-elected, and the new CC was substantially younger, better educated, and more likely to be directly involved in economic management functions. (Peter Ludz, *The Changing Party Elite in East Germany* [Cambridge: MIT Press, 1968], p. 321.) The local S.E.D. organizations were substantially revamped according to the "production principle" in 1963, only to be returned to the "geographical principle" in 1966. The year 1965 saw the appointment of seventeen new Cabinet members, only one of whom was over 45 years old. The number of demotions and forced retirements of enterprise and factory managers found incapable of handling their new responsibilities under N.E.S. was evidently the highest of any of the East European reforms. (David Granick, *Enterprise Guidance in East Europe* [Princeton: Princeton University Press, 1975], p. 483.)

14. It has sometimes been suggested that Ulbricht had been specifically ordered by the Soviet leadership to undertake the N.E.S. so that East Germany might serve as a sort of experimental laboratory for reforms being discussed in the U.S.S.R. See, for example, J. Nawrocki, "From the NES to Computer-Stalinism," *Deutschland Archiv* IV (April 1971), p. 348; and Ilse Spittman, "East Germany: The Swinging Pendulum," *Problems of Communism* XVI, No. 4 (1967), p. 15. There is no direct evidence for this, other than anonymous but allegedly "well-informed" sources and the indisputable fact that Ulbricht's sudden conversion to the cause of reform came, evidently, during a one-month vacation in the Soviet Union. If he did, in fact, receive such a commission, this also would help to account for the lack of Politburo resistance to so seemingly radical a turnabout. It seems more likely, however, that he received encouragement of a relatively unspecific nature rather than a detailed "assignment." The N.E.S. did not closely resemble *any* of the publicly discussed Soviet "models," except in the very general sense of emphasizing material incentives, profitability as a measure of efficiency, and a reduction in the number of compulsory physical targets to be handed down to enterprise management.

15. Baylis, *The Technical Intelligentsia*, p. 247; Welles Hangen, *The Muted Revolution* (New York: Alfred A. Knopf, 1966), pp. 3-9.

16. For a detailed account of the impact of the Twenty-Second Congress and of Khrushchev's personal intervention in Bulgaria, see J.F. Brown *Bulgaria Under Communist Rule* (New York: Praeger, 1970), pp. 96-142.

17. Ibid, pp. 137-142, 173-195.

18. On the economic matters discussed at the Eighth Congress, see Bogoslav Dobrin, *Bulgarian Economic Development Since World War II* (New York: Praeger, 1973), p. 119; and Wolfgang Eggers, "Economic Reform in Bulgaria," in Karl Thalheim and Hans-Hermann Hohmann, eds., *Wirtschaftsreformen in Osteuropa*

(Koln: Verlag Wissenschaft und Politik, 1968), pp. 212-216. On the significance of Kunin's rehabilitation, see Dobrin, op. cit., p. 120, and Brown, op. cit., pp. 47 and 140-141.

19. Michael Gamarnikow, *Economic Reforms in Eastern Europe* (Detroit: Wayne State University Press, 1968), p. 60; J.F. Brown, "Reforms in Bulgaria," *Problems of Communism* XV, No. 3 (1966), p. 49.

20. For extensive summaries of the principal positions put forward in the Bulgarian public economic debates, see Dobrin, op. cit., pp. 119-122; Eggers op. cit., pp. 213-216; and Brown, "Reforms in Bulgaria."

21. Brown, "Reforms in Bulgaria," p. 19.

22. Brown, *Bulgaria Under Communist Rule*, pp. 162-163.

23. Brown, "Reforms in Bulgaria," p. 21.

24. See his interview in *Die Presse* (Vienna), July 17, 1965.

25. Finally published in *Rabotnichesko Delo* on December 4, 1965.

26. Ibid., April 29, 1966, as cited in Gamarnikow, op. cit., p. 62 (emphasis supplied).

27. The following summary of the Bulgarian reforms is necessarily schematic. For fuller descriptions, see Heinrich Vogel, "Bulgaria," in Hohmann et al., op. cit., pp. 199-222; Eggers, op. cit., pp. 217-229.

28. *Novo Vreme*, October 1968, as cited in L.A.D. Dellin, "Bulgaria," in L.A.D. Dellin and Hermann Gross, eds., *Reforms in the Soviet and East European Economies* (Lexington, Mass.: Lexington Books, 1972), p. 43

29. Ibid., p. 49.

30. Ibid., p. 44.

31. Brown, *Bulgaria Under Communist Rule*, p. 171.

32. *Rabotnichesko Delo*, November 15, 1967, cited in ibid., p. 171.

33. Cited in Dobrin, op. cit., pp.. 141-142.

34. The best account in English of the changes in Bulgarian economic arrangements since 1968 is Heinrich Vogel, "Bulgaria," in Hohmann et al., op. cit., pp. 199-222.

35. Brown, *Bulgaria Under Communist Rule*, pp. 173-195.

36. The results of the Ninth Party Congress in November of 1966 (barely six months after formal approval of the economic reform blueprint) rather graphically indicated Zhivkov's vulnerability and his strong desire to avoid intra-Party conflict. Instead of purging those who had so vigorously resisted his major policy initiative, he acquiesced in a clear retreat. The only member dropped from the Politburo was his own protege, Mitko Grigorov (who had earlier spoken up for the reform), while the two new members added were septuagenarians who had been relatively unprominent since the days of Stalinism, Todor Pavlov and Tsola Dragaicheva, both of whom subsequently showed themselves to be extremely conservative in matters both cultural and economic.

37. Cited in Dellin, op. cit., pp. 52-53.

38. Ibid., p. 53.

39. See for example, Theodore Frankel, "Economic Reforms: A Tentative Appraisal," *Problems of Communism* XVI, No. 3 (1967), pp. 29-41; Keith Bush,

"The Reforms: A Balance Sheet," *Problems of Communist* XVI, No. 4 (1967), pp. 30-41; and Alec Nove, "The U.S.S.R.," in Dellin and Gross, op. cit., pp. 19-38.

40. *Novo Vreme*, No. 10, 1968. Cited in Dellin, op. cit., p. 54; Vogel, op. cit., p. 217; and Dobrin, op. cit., p. 140.

41. The purges in Czechoslovakia in 1949 to 1954 resulted in the removal of fifty of the ninety-seven members of the Central Committee and six of the seven members of the Secretariat, and the execution of the Party's General Secretary (along with ten other top cabinet officials). At least 16,000 people were arrested and over 200 of them were executed. (Jiri Pelikan, ed., *The Czechoslovak Political Trials, 1950-1954* [Stanford: Stanford University Press, 1971], pp. 56-57.) Some 550,000 Party members were purged, most of them also losing their posts of authority in non-Party economic and mass organizations. (Zbigniew Brzezinski, *The Soviet Bloc: Unity and Conflict* [Cambridge: Harvard University Press, 1967], p. 97.)

42. *Kulturny Tvorba*, February 7, 1963.

43. Speech to the regional Party aktiv in Ostrava, *Rude Pravo*, March 24, 1963, as cited in Zdenek Elias and Jaromir Netik, "Czechoslovakia," in William E. Griffith, ed., *Communism in Europe, Volume II* (Cambridge: M.I.T. Press, 1966), p. 259.

44. For an account of the effects of destalinization in Czechoslovakia during 1963, see ibid., pp. 257-265, and H. Gordon Skilling, *Czechoslovakia's Interrupted Revolution* (Princeton: Princeton University Press, 1976), pp. 45-89.

45. Vladimir Kusin, *Political Groupings in the Czechoslovak Reform Movement* (New York: Columbia University Press, 1972), pp. 113-114.

46. Ota Sik, "The Survivals of Dogmatism in Political Economy Must be Overcome," *Nova Mysl*, No. 9, 1963, cited in George Feiwel, *New Economic Patterns in Czechoslovakia* (New York: Praeger Publishers, 1968), p. 142.

47. As recently as June, Novotny was charging that those "who are looking for a new model in the sphere of socialism" were also and inevitably "looking for a new model in the sphere of ideology." *Rude Pravo*, June 13, 1963, as cited in Elias and Netik, op. cit., p. 260.

48. Feiwel, op. cit., pp. 141-142.

49. Ibid., p. 143.

50. *Rude Pravo*, March 18, 1964, as cited in Edward Taborsky, "Where is Czechoslovakia Going?" *East Europe* XVI, No. 2 (1967), p. 7.

51. *Rude Pravo*, April 6, 1964, as cited in Feiwel, op. cit., p. 144.

52. *Rude pravo*, May 29, 1964, as cited in Feiwel, op. cit., p. 144.

53. *Rude Pravo*, May 29, 1964, cited in Elias and Netik, op. cit., p. 264.

54. The published version is available in English in *Eastern European Economics*, No. 3 (Summer 1965), pp. 3-18. In 1968, Sik revealed that the principal change had been the removal of an extended section analyzing the necessary political, social, and institutional changes required for the effective implementation of the proposed economic reforms. ("Interview with Ota Sik," *Prace*, March 5, 1968, cited in Feiwel, op. cit., p. 541.) Sik's subsequent writings

specify more concretely that the draft called for the very substantial reduction of employment in the central ministry offices, the merger of most of the sectoral ministries into a single Ministry of Industry, and the combatting of monopolistic tendencies by the effective dissolution of the branch associations as bodies with compulsory powers over the member enterprises. (Ota Sik, "Czechoslovakia," in Dellin and Gross, op. cit., p. 65.)

55. *Rude Pravo*, January 3, 1965, cited in *East Europe* XIV, No. 2 (1965), p. 30.

56. Feiwel, op. cit., p. 197.

57. Novotny made major speeches stressing the need for strengthening the central direction of the economy on October 28, 1965, and November 3, 1965. As late as December of 1966, he was still denouncing those who took "an over-critical attitude" toward "the old, so-called system of management by administrative directive," stressing the essential role of compulsory plan indicators: "Not even by applying the perfected system of management do we renounce this basic instrument of direction." *Rude Pravo*, December 20, 1966, as cited in *East Europe* XVI, No. 2 (1967), p. 43.

58. *Prace*, September 10, 1965, as cited in Michael Gamarnikow, "The Reforms: A Survey," *East Europe* XV, No. 1 (1966), p. 18.

59. "Interview with Ota Sik," *Kulturny Noviny*, March 29, 1968, translated and reprinted in *Studies in Comparative Communism* I, No. 1 (1968), pp. 7-16.

60. Feiwel, op. cit., p. 322.

61. For a detailed account of the September 1967-January 1968 crisis that led to Novotny's ouster, see Skilling, op. cit., pp. 161-182.

62. Janos Kadar, "Report to the Ninth Congress of the H.S.W.P.," - *Nepszabadsag*, November 29, 1966, available in English translation in Radio Free Europe Research, *Hungarian Press Survey*, No. 1770, December 12, 1966. On Kadar's prolonged struggle against "dogmatist" elements in the Party *apparat*, see William Robinson, *The Pattern of Reform in Hungary* (New York: Praeger Publishers, 1973), especially pp. 70-96.

63. For accounts of the Varga Commission's proposals and the political opposition to them, see Robinson, op. cit., pp. 22-23; and Ivan Berend, "The Historical Background of the Recent Economic Reforms in East Europe: The Hungarian Experiences," *East European Quarterly* II, No. 1 (1968).

64. As quoted in Bennett Kovrig, *Communism in Hungary: From Kun to Kadar* (Stanford, CA: Hoover Institution Press), 1979, p. 353.

65. See the unflattering assessment by Oldrich Kyn (one of the original participants) of the adequacy of economic education in Czechoslovakia before the middle 1960's. For example, Kyn notes that virtually none of his colleagues had been familiar with the concept of "externalities" and relatively few were acquainted with the chief conclusions of the inter-war "socialist calculation" debates (except at second-hand, from the writings of Polish economists). "The Rise and Fall of Economic Reforms in Czechoslovakia," *American Economic Review* LX, No. 2 (1970), p. 301.

66. Robinson, op. cit., pp. 55-56, citing Nyers' 1968 account of the origins of the N.E.M., exact source not cited. That the political divisions within the Central Committee at the time were pronounced and bitter was indicated by the fact that the editor of *Nepszabadsag* on May 16, 1963, found it necessary to reiterate once again that Leninist norms of Party life were fundamentally incompatible with the existence of "separate platforms" or organized "factions" within the H.S.W.P. (editorial excerpted in H. Gordon Skilling, "Opposition in Communist East Europe," in Robert Dahl, ed., *Regimes and Oppositions* [New Haven: Yale University Press, 1973], p. 9).

67. For example, Miklos Ajtai, the Chairman of the Planning Commission (and an advocate of the reform very early on), gave a talk to a select group at the Party's Political Academy, which was partially reported in the Party daily *Nepszabadsag*, January 14, 1965. He did little more than reveal the vague outlines of the scheme and let drop that commissions of experts were being formed.

68. The various panels were specialized according to such substantive matters as planning methodology, price formation, wages and material incentives, foreign trade, taxation and finance, investments, and other subjects. Their make-up was deliberately diverse and their discussions were detailed, vigorous, and exhaustive, lasting in all over about three years of regular meetings. Every effort was made to generate a consensus view before finalizing official recommendations. For a principal participant's inside account of some of the more important debates within the panels, see Matyas Timar, *Reflections on the Economic Development of Hungary, 1967-1973* (Budapest: Akademiai Kiado, 1975), pp. 40-58.

69. *Nepszabadsag*, November 21, 1965.

70. *Tarsadalmi Szemle* III, Nos. 7 and 8 (1966), as cited in Peter Toma and Ivan Volgyes, *Politics in Hungary* (San Francisco: W.H. Freeman and Co., 1977), p. 33.

71. "Report on the Addresses Delivered by Janos Kadar and Rezso Nyers at the Closing Conference of the Preparatory Committee on the Reform of Economic Management," *Tarsadalmi Szemle*, July-August 1966, translated and reprinted in Radio Free Europe Research Department, *Hungarian Press Survey*, No. 1729, July 19, 1966, pp. 2-3.

72. Quoted in ibid., p. 7. This strategy of including potential opponents in even the initial stage of deliberations as a method of building confidence found application in another way as well. According to the private remarks of at least one participant in the drafting process, multiple copies of all the literally hundreds of internal memoranda and working papers of the eleven preparatory committees were transmitted routinely to the Soviet government and the economic commissions of the Community Party of the Soviet Union, to avoid any appearance of secretiveness that might arouse anxiety or suspicion.

73. Ibid., p. 8.

74. *Tarsadalme Szemle* XXII, No. 12 (1967), p. 24, as cited in Robinson, op. cit., p. 91.

75. Radio Free Europe Research, *Hungarian Situation Report*, February 6, 1967, p. 3.

76. *Nepszabadsag*, August 28, 1968, cited in Radio Free Europe Research, *Hungary*, No. 25, 1969, p. 5.

77. *Magyar Nemzet*, August 31, 1968, cited in ibid., p. 5.

78. See B. Rodionoz, "Gathering Speed," *Izvestiya*, September 16, 1968; M. Tiurin, "Steps of Growth," *Izvestiya*, November 14, 1968; V. Gerasimov, "With the Participation of Millions," *Pravda*, February 13, 1969; M. Timar, "A Country's Reform and Economic Development," *Pravda*, April 22, 1969.

79. *Nepszabadsag*, November 29, 1966, translated and reprinted in Radio Free Europe Research, *Hungarian Press Survey*, No. 1770, December 12, 1966, pp. 46-47.

80. The two documents are "Theses of the Economic Council Concerning Certain Changes in the Economic Model," *Zycie Gospodarcze*, No. 22, June 2, 1957; and "Theses of the Economic Council on Determining the Principles of the Price Structure," *Zycie Gospodarcze*, No. 51, December 22-29, 1957.

81. Stefan Jedrychowski (head of the Planning Commission), as quoted in an interview of *Trybuna Ludu*, November 21, 1957.

82. "Increased Tasks and Prerogatives of the Planning Commission," *Trybuna Ludu*, January 5, 1960.

83. Kazimierz Secomski, a vice-chairman of the Planning Commission, noted in *Rocznik Polityczny i Gospodarczy* that "anti-inflationary measures required that many intended economic steps, e.g., changes in the model, had to be limited or postponed" (Warsaw: Panstwowe Widawnictwo Economiczne, 1958), p. 442. The figures on nominal wage increases are derived from *Rocznik Statystyczny* (Warsaw: Glowny Urzad Statystyczny, 1974), pp. 8-9.

84. See the reports on the Plenum in *The New York Times*, March 2, 1958, and the *Neue Zurcher Zeitung*, March 3, 1958.

85. *Gospodarka Planowa*, November 1966, p. 11.

86. On Gomulka's style of leadership, see Zbigniew Pelczynski, "The Downfall of Gomulka," in Adam Bromke and John W. Strong, eds., *Gierek's Poland* (New York: Praeger, 1973), pp. 1-24, especially pp. 9-13.

87. See *Polityka*, No. 48, 1961.

88. Polish national income grew by only 2 percent in 1962, mainly due to retrenchments made necessary by a balance of payments crisis and bottlenecks in the construction industry. Both were the consequences of an overambitious investment drive.

89. *Trybuna Ludu*, November 27, 1962. See also Gomulka's discussion of current economic policies in the Party theoretical journal *Nowe Drogi*, No. 1, 1964, where Gomulka's rather traditional preferences for extensive growth strategies were made crystal clear.

90. "The Key Problem for the Plan for 1964," *Nowe Drogi*, No. 12, 1963.

91. *Theses of the Central Committee of the P.U.W.P. for the IV Party Congress* (Warsaw: Kziazka i Wiedza, March 1964).

92. *Trybuna Ludu*, June 25, 1964.

93. The two principal documents setting forth the reform are the Council of Ministers' Decree No. 224 "Concerning Economic Progress in the National

Economy and the Organization of Economic Services," *Monitor Polski*, August 18, 1964; and the Report of the Politburo to the IV Plenum of the Central Committee, "Directions of the Changes in the System of Planning and Management of the National Economy in 1966-1970," *Nowe Drogi*, No. 8, 1965, and the accompanying Central Committee Resolution of endorsement (ibid.).

94. For an analysis of the adverse consequences of this eclectic approach to reform, see Janusz Zielinski, "On the Theory of Economic Reforms and Their Optimal Sequence," *Economics of Planning* VIII, No. 3 (1968), pp. 195-215.

95. Jan Pajestka and Kazimierz Secomski, *Doskonalenie planowania i funcjonowania gospodarki w Polsce Ludowej* (Warsaw: Kziazka i Wiedza, 1968), pp. 5, 6, 13.

96. Jozef Wilczynski, *Socialist Economic Development and Reforms* (London: Macmillan Press, 1972), p. 162.

97. *Zycie Gospodarcze*, No. 4, 1967, p. 5.

98. *Trybuna Ludu*, July 27, 1965.

99. See Jedrychowski's speech closing the Central Committee debate at the July 1965 Plenum, reprinted in *Nowe Drogi*, No. 8, 1965.

100. "Resolution of the IV Plenum of the C.C.-P.U.W.P.," *Nowe Drogi*, No. 8, 1965, pp. 82-99.

101. *Zycie Gospodarcze*, No. 17, 1966.

102. *Gospodarka Planowa*, No. 8-9, 1966, pp. 28-29.

103. Janusz G. Zielinski, *Economic Reforms in Polish Industry* (London: Oxford University Press, 1973), p. 256.

104. J. Glowczyk, "The Reform and the Men," *Zycie Gospodarcze*, No. 31, 1967.

105. For assessments of Gomulka's attitudes toward economic reform and the intellectuals, see Nicholas Bethell, *Gomulka: His Poland, His Communism* (New York: Holt, Rinehart and Winston, 1969), pp. 229-273; J.F. Brown, *The New Eastern Europe* (New York: Praeger, 1966), pp. 50-64; Pelczynski, op. cit., pp. 5-8.

106. For a representative sampling of Gomulka's thinking on economic growth strategies, see his article in *Nowe Drogi*, No. 1, 1964.

107. For discussions of the ins-and-outs of the factional rivalries in the P.U.W.P., see Adam Bromke, *Poland's Politics* (Cambridge: Harvard University Press, 1967), pp. 178-212; Brown, *The New Eastern Europe*, pp. 50-64; Jerzy Ptakowski, Political Maneuvers in Warsaw," *East Europe* XIII, No. 4 (1964), pp. 3-9; and A. Ross Johnson, "Poland: End of an Era?" *Problems of Communism* XIX, No. 1 (1970), pp. 28-40.

108. A. Bromke, op. cit., p. 199.

109. The pamphlet has been translated into English and published in *East Europe* XIV, No. 3 (1965), under the title "The Stalinist Underground in Poland."

110. See Bromke, op. cit., pp. 199-201, and Ptakowski, loc. cit.

111. In addition to *Trybuna Ludu* and *Zycie Warszawy*, a principal purveyor of thinly-veiled anti-semitism was *Slowo Powszechne*, the organ of the pro-regime

"progressive" Catholic organization "Pax," headed by the veteran prewar fascist and anti-semite Boleslaw Piasecki.

112. *Prawo i Zycie*, April 7, 1968, as cited in Johnson, op. cit., p. 31.

113. W. Iskra, "Ideological Backbone of the Economy," *Trybuna Ludu*, April 23, 1968, as cited in Michael Gamarnikow, "The Polish Economy in Transition," *Problems of Communism* XIX, No. 1 (1970), p. 42.

114. M. Krajewski, "Socialist Democracy and Market Socialism," *Trybuna Ludu*, March 29, 1968.

115. B. Fick, "The System of Incentives," *Zycie Gospodarcze*, February 7, 1971. See also Antoni Marek, "The Draft of a New Wage System in Poland," Radio Free Europe Research, *Poland*, April 1, 1970.

116. Measures to halt the excessive expansion of the industrial labor force led to mass lay-offs involving some 200,000 workers during 1970, and the draft of the 1971-1975 plan provided for residual unemployment of about 500,000. (H. Krol, "Intensive Development versus Employment," *Trybuna Ludu*, February 15, 1971.) The former figure amounted to about 2 percent of total employment in the socialist sector in 1970.

117. Price increases were first made public in *Trybuna Ludu*, December 13, 1970. The impact on working class living standards can be inferred from Polish studies of working class family budgets, which have shown that food expenses already accounted between 40 and 50 percent of average working class family incomes (depending mainly on family size). See *Budzety rodzin pracownikow zatrudnionych w gospodarcze uspolecznionej poza rolnictwem i lesnictwem, 1958 r.* (Warsaw: Glowny Urzad Statystyczny, 1969).

118. For an account of the reshuffling and purging of the Party leadership carried out by Gierek in his first year of power, see Adam Bromke, "A New Political Style," *Problems of Communism* XXI, No. 5 (1972), pp. 1-19.

119. And indeed, when the Polish government tried once again in the summer of 1976 to end the five-year freeze in consumer prices, the result was quite similar — massive strikes and demonstrations followed by a complete rollback of prices to restore the status quo ante.

120. Gierek's speech was reprinted in full in *Trybuna Ludu*, February 8, 1971.

121. "Interview with Jan Pajestka" (Co-chairman of the Commission), *Zycie Gospodarcze*, January 2, 1972.

Chapter 4

1. During the height of the Stalinist terror, in the late 1940's and early 1950's, failure to achieve plan targets was sometimes construed as deliberate sabotage and led to imprisonment or even the death penalty for the unfortunates deemed responsible. Although such affairs were widely publicized for their deterrent effects, the use of criminal penalties for purposes of economic management was relatively infrequent even then and became much more so by the 1960's.

2. "Material incentives" consisted primarily of monetary transfers in the form of wages, piece-work rates, and bonus payments. However, various forms of individual consumption administratively allocated as "perks" or as special rewards

were also of some importance: for example, use of recreational facilities, free vacations, special allotments of theater tickets, administrative permission to enjoy priority of access to scarce or unusually high quality consumer goods in times of rationing, etc.

3. "Moral incentives" refers to a variety of manipulative techniques appealing to the non-material interests of the individual in order to encourage desired performances: appeals to the moral values of the individual and the effort to instill the belief that one's work furthers "higher ends"; efforts to mobilize peer group pressure so as to make achievement of esteem dependent upon good work performance; holding up individuals for praise before the general public by awarding medals, ribbons, and titles to exemplary performers, etc.

4. Each position of leadership in the state, the economy, and the mass organizations was entered under the *nomenklatura* of some Communist Party committee. This meant that recruitment to that position and supervision of the incumbent's performance was the responsibility and prerogative of the corresponding Party organ. By means of the *nomenklatura* the Party was able to exert discipline and control over all legitimate organized activity in the society, directing it in accordance with Party policies and objectives. The more important the position, naturally, the higher the Party organ within whose *nomenklatura* it falls.

5. Ota Sik, "Czechoslovakia: Prohibitive Odds," in L.A.D. Dellin and Hermann Gross, eds., *Reforms in the Soviet and Eastern European Economies* (Lexington, Mass.: D.C. Heath and Co., 1972), pp. 64-65. (For his remarks on the projected functions of the branch associations, see pp. 65-66.)

6. *Nepszabadsag*, December 25, 1966, featured a Christmas message that must have brought cheer to the hearts of many a worried bureaucrat or factory manager:

> The Party attitude is clear: the reform of the economic mechanism is not some sort of changing of the guard. There is no need for such a thing. Those people — and they are in a majority among the leaders and employees — who were able to keep going under the old mechanism . . . can be sure that they will continue to do so . . .

(Translated and reprinted in Radio Free Europe Research, *Hungarian Press Survey*, No. 1790, February 13, 1967, p. 5.)

7. Michael Kaser and J. Zielinski, *Planning in East Europe* (London: The Bodley Head, 1970), p. 32.

8. David Granick, *Enterprise Guidance in Eastern Europe* (Princeton: Princeton University Press, 1975), p. 295.

9. Ibid, p. 37.

10. In Czechoslovakia's case, Sik notes that the battle was being lost until 1968, when the mobilization of new political forces in favor of the reforms became possible because of the revival and reinvigoration of political life generally (op. cit., p. 65). In Yugoslavia, a fundamental aspect of the official ideology, the principle of enterprise self-management, provided an essential basis for organizing

resistance to bureaucratic recentralization, and the basing of political organization on the self-management principle ensured that forces favoring autonomy would be prominent in the decision-making centers. In the case of Hungary, relative success was attributable to the relatively smooth economic transition, which provided fewer excuses for recentralization, and to the firmness of the Party leadership.

11.*Statistika Rocenka CSSR*, 1966, as cited in Radovan Richta et al., *Civilization at the Crossroads*, trans. Marian Slingova (White Plains, N.Y.: International Arts and Sciences Press, 1968), p. 230.

12.*Mlada Fronta*, November 21, 1964, as translated in *East Europe* XIV, No. 2 (1965), pp. 18-20.

13.*Rude Pravo*, May 13, 1965, as cited in Michael Gamarnikow, *Economic Reforms in Eastern Europe* (Detroit: Wayne State University Press, 1968), p. 115.

14.Pavel Machonin, "The Social Structure of Contemporary Czechoslovakia," *Czechoslovak Economic Papers*, No. 11, 1969, p. 158.

15.*Figyelo*, May 27, 1958, as cited in Zbigniew Brzezinski, *The Soviet Bloc: Unity and Conflict* (Cambridge: Harvard University Press, 1967), p. 143.

16.Zsuzsa Hegedus and Marton Tardos, "Some Problems Concerning the Role and Motivation of Enterprise Executives," *Kozgazdasagi Szemle*, No. 2, 1974, translated and reprinted in *Eastern European Economics* XIII, No. 2 (1974-1975), p. 91.

17.Ibid., p. 91.

18.*Polityka*, September 1957.

19.H. Najduchowska, "Directors of Industrial Enterprises," in Adam Sarapata, ed., *Przemysl i spoleczenstwo w Polsce Ludowej* (Warsaw: PWN, 1965), p. 94.

20.Z. Kwiatkowski, "The Right Man in the Right Place," *Zycie Literackie*, August 21, 1966.

21.Russell Hardin, "Western Approaches to East German History," *New German Critique* I, No. 2 (Spring 1974), p. 120.

22.*Bulgarian Economic Development Since World War II* (New York: Praeger, 1973), p. 28.

23.See Richard Staar's compilation of the figures on class composition of the Party released at the various Congresses in his *Communist Regimes in Eastern Europe*, 3rd ed. (Stanford: The Hoover Institution, 1977), p. 36.

24.Paul Cocks, "Retooling the Directed Society," in Jan F. Triska and Paul M. Cocks, eds., *Political Development in Eastern Europe* (New York: Praeger, 1977), p. 76.

25."Not by Bread Alone," *Kulturni Zivot*, January 16, 1965, as cited in Gamarnikow, op. cit., pp. 115-116.

26.*Piroda a Spolecnost*, No. 11, 1967, translated and reprinted in *East Europe* XVI, NO. 9 (1967), p. 23.

27.Novotny's formulation in his New Years message, *Rude Pravo*, January 1, 1965, cited in Harry Shaffer, "Out of Stalinism," *Problems of Communism* XIV, No. 5 (1965), p. 40.

28.Jan Lipavsky, "Anachronisms — and Chances?", *Literarni Noviny*, January 6, 1968, translated and reprinted in Radio Free Europe Research, *Czechoslovak Press Survey*, No. 2001, February 2, 1968, pp. 3-4.

29."The Action Program of the Communist Party of Czechoslovakia," in Paul Ello, ed., *Czechoslovakia's Blueprint for Freedom* (Washington, D.C.: Acropolis Books, 1968), p. 108.

30.The most publicized incident occurred in August, when the director of the Skoda Works, the largest industrial complex in the country was forced by the Council into resigning in favor of his better-educated and more popular deputy. See R. Vitak, "Workers' Control in Czechoslovakia," in Jaroslav Vanek, ed., *Self-Management* (London: Penguin, 1975), pp. 284-285.

31.*Christian Science Monitor*, January 29, 1975, p. 3.

32.As of 1972, only 34 percent of enterprise directors and deputy directors had had higher education, as compared to 31 percent in 1966. The training of 57 percent did not meet the theoretical minimum requirements for holding their positions. *Statistika Rocenka C.S.S.R.*, 1973, p. 127.

33.*Nepszabadsag*, June 3, 1962, cited in Francois Fejto, "Hungarian Communism," in William E. Griffith, ed., *Communism in Europe, Volume I* (Cambridge: M.I.T. Press, 1964), p. 268.

34.*Figyelo*, June 2, 1965, translated and reprinted in Radio Free Europe Research, *Hungarian Press Survey*, No. 1610, June 12, 1965.

35."Interview with Gyula Varga, Secretary-General of the Zala County Party Committee," *Nepszabadsag*, December 10, 1966, translated and reprinted in Radio Free Europe Research, *Hungarian Press Survey*, No. 1777, December 28, 1966.

36.Granick, op. cit., pp. 243-244.

37.See, inter alia, Peter Ludz, *The Changing Party Elite in East Germany* (Cambridge: M.I.T. Press, 1972), and Thomas Baylis, *The Technical Intelligentsia and the East German Elite* (Berkeley: University of California Press, 1974), for an account of the striking success of the top East German leadership in advancing the "technocratic" elite to positions of prestige and even influence without fundamentally altering the basic features of the political order.

38.See K. Doktor, "Research on Behavior and Opinions of Workers in a Polish Factory," *Polish Sociological Bulletin*, No. 3-4, 1962; Vaclav Holesovsky, "Labor and the Economic Reforms in Czechoslovakia" (Amherst: University of Massachusetts Labor Relations and Research Center, 1968), mimeographed; J. Kordaszewski, *Place wedlug pracy* (Warsaw: Ksiazka i Wiedza, 1963); Sandor Lakos, "Questions of Social Equality," *New Hungarian Quarterly* XVI, No. 57 (1957); B. Levcik. "Wages and Employment Problems in the New System of Planned Management in Czechoslovakia," *International Labor Review*, No. 95, 1967; Alexander Matejko, *Socjologia pracy* (Warsaw: PWE, 1968).

39."Problems Connected with Our System of Economic Management," - *Tarsadalmi Szemle*, July 1965, translated and reprinted in Radio Free Europe Research, *Hungarian Press Survey*, No. 1621, July 16, 1965, p. 19.

40.Ello, op. cit., pp. 107-108.

41. *Podnikova organizace*, No. 8, 1965, p. 337, as cited in George Feiwel, *New Economic Patterns in Czechoslovakia* (New York: Praeger, 1968), p. 204. See also *Odborar*, No. 6, 1967, p. 267, for a report that some factory managers had even been pressured into distributing the entire profit-sharing fund in *equal* shares in order to prevent work stoppages. Cited in Alex Pravda, "Some Aspects of the Czechoslovak Working Class and the Economic Reform in 1968," *Soviet Studies* XXV, No. 1 (1973), p. 107.

42. Karol Polacek, interviewed in the West German monthly *Der Gewerkschafter*, September 1967, as cited in Radio Free Europe Research, *Czechoslovak Background Report*, September 27, 1967, p. 3.

43. *Svobodne Slovo*, January 18, 1968, as cited in Feiwel, op. cit., p. 346.

44. Calculated from data in *Statisticka Rocenka C.S.S.R.*, 1963 and 1967, p. 165 and p. 206, respectively.

45. *Hospodarske Noviny*, No. 40, 1965, as cited in Feiwel, op. cit., p. 203.

46. Holesovsky, op. cit., pp. 19-21.

47. *Statisticka Rocenka C.S.S.R.*, 1973, p. 243.

48. *L'Unita* interview in issues for June 28 and July 1, 1969, summarized and excerpted in Radio Free Europe Research, *Hungarian Situation Report*, No. 35, July 22, 1969.

49. *Nepszabadsag*, April 4, 1969, translated in Radio Free Europe Research, *Hungarian Background Report* No. 27, April 17, 1969.

50. *Partelet*, January 1970, as cited in Radio Free Europe Research, *Hungary*, No. 5, February 17, 1970.

51. "Speech of Eva Radnai to Parliament," *Nepszabadsag*, July 13, 1967, cited in Radio Free Europe Research, *Hungary*, August 31, 1967.

52. "Reform of the Economic Mechanism in Hungary," *Problems of Peace and Socialism*, November 1966.

53. *Nepszabadsag*, March 13, 1966, as cited in Radio Free Europe Research, *Hungary*, March 18, 1966, p. 3.

54. Robinson, op. cit., p. 82.

55. *Npeszabadsag*, February 11, 1973, cited in Radio Free Europe Research, *Hungary*, No. 8, May 21, 1973.

56. *Piroda a Spolecnost*, No. 11, 1967, as translated and reprinted in *East Europe* XVI, No. 9 (1967), pp. 23-24.

57. Janos Kadar, "Constitution Day Speech in Bekescsaba," *Nepszabadsag*, August 23, 1965, translated in Radio Free Europe Research, *Hungarian Press Survey*, No. 1632, August 27, 1965, pp. 3-4.

58. *Rude Pravo*, March 24, 1966, cited in Pravda, op cit., p. 106.

59. *Rude Pravo*, December 9, 1966, summarized in *East Europe* XVI, No. 2 (1967), p. 44.

60. *Nova Mysl*, No. 25, 1967, p. 31, cited in Holesovsky, op. cit., p. 9.

61. *Nova Mysl*, No. 21, 1967, p. 17, cited in ibid., p. 10.

62. *Nova Mysl*, No. 25, 1967, p. 31, cited in ibid., p. 10.

63. *Odborar*, No. 19, 1967, p. 1041, cited in ibid., p. 10.

64. Robert Dean, *Nationalism and Political Change in Eastern Europe: The Slovak Question and the Czechoslovak Reform Movement* (Denver: University of Denver, 1973), p. 24.

65. Ota Sik, interviewed in *Prace*, March 6, 1968, as cited in Pravda, op. cit., p. 108.

66. Timar, op. cit., p. 73.

67. *Nepszabadsag*, December 1, 1966, translated in Radio Free Europe Research, *Hungarian Press Survey*, No. 1774, December 21, 1966, p. 4.

68. Tivadar Nemeslaki, interviewed in *Nepszabadsag*, October 16, 1966, translated in Radio Free Europe Research, *Hungarian Press Survey*, No. 1757, November 3, 1966.

69. *Tarsadalmi Szemle*, July 1967, translated in Radio Free Europe Research, *Hungary*, August 31, 1967.

70. Timar, op. cit., p. 63.

71. Radio Free Europe Research, *Hungary*, No. 18, December 10, 1973, and Rezso Nyers, "Problems of Profitability and Income Distribution II," *New Hungarian Quarterly*, No. 41 (1971), p. 23.

72. Joszef Polgar, "Letter to the Editor," *Tarsadalmi Szemle*, January 1967, translated in Radio Free Europe Research, *Hungarian Press Survey*, No. 1796, March 1, 1967, p. 2.

73. A public opinion poll reported in *Hospodarsky Noviny*, No. 27, 1967, found that more than one-quarter of the blue collar workers in the sample were "completely lacking in confidence" in the new reforms. The members of the "technical intelligentsia" in the sample, in contrast, included only 10 percent who were so pessimistic. (Cited in Radio Free Europe Research, *Czechoslovakia*, August 18, 1967, p. 3.)

74. "The Increased Role and Tasks of the Trade Unions in Our Country," *Tarsadalmi Szemle*, September 1966, translated in Radio Free Europe Research, *Hungarian Press Survey*, No. 1745, September 24, 1966, p. 2.

75. Ibid., p. 4.

76. Radio Free Europe Research, *Hungary*, No. 1, January 15, 1967.

77. In 1973, the widely cited figure was that the right of veto had been used 150 times. Radio Free Europe Research, *Hungary*, No. 17, December 10, 1973.

78. *Munka*, July 1968, translated in Radio Free Europe Research, *Hungarian Press Survey*, No. 1941, June 25, 1968.

79. *Nepszabadsag*, June 19, 1966, translated in Radio Free Europe Research, *Hungarian Press Survey*, No. 1724, July 8, 1966, p. 6.

80. *Nepszabadsag*, July 3, 1966, summarized in Radio Free Europe Research, *Hungary*, November 11, 1966.

81. *Munka*, December 1972, cited in Radio Free Europe Research, *Hungary*, No. 2, March 8, 1973.

82. *Prace*, May 21, 1965, as cited in *East Europe* XIV, No. 7 (1965), p. 40.

83. Ibid.

84. *East Europe* XVI, No. 3 (1967), p. 41.

85.Sik's speech on Radio Czechoslovakia I, March 27, 1968, translated and reprinted in Ota Sik, *Czechoslovakia: The Bureaucratic Economy* (White Plains, N.Y.: International Arts and Sciences Press, 1972).

86.Ello, op. cit., pp. 138-139.

87.See Skilling, op. cit., pp. 434-435; and Vitak, op. cit., pp. 281-283.

88.Pravda, op. cit., pp. 113-114. Stoppages of work to secure the removal of unpopular managers occurred in Pisek, Tiplice, Zilina, and Trinec, among other places.

89.*Odbory a spolecnost*, No. 4, 1969, as summarized in Vitak, op cit., p. 283.

90.Vitak, op. cit., p. 284.

91.Ibid., p. 285; Pravda, op. cit., p. 119.

92.Vitak, op. cit., p. 284. In the sample of 95 councils Vitak examines, there were 3622 candidates for the 1421 seats. Some 85 percent of the employees above the age of eighteen cast ballots.

93.Ibid., p. 286.

94.Ibid., pp. 286-187.

95.Feiwel, op. cit., pp. 470-471; Pravda, op. cit., pp. 112-113.

96.See Bogdan Denitch, *The Legitimization of a Revolution* (New Haven: Yale University Press, 1976), for the best account of the role of the "self-management" ideology in stabilizing the Yugoslav political and economic system.

Conclusion

1.The labeling scheme is slightly adapted from that employed by Everett M. Rogers and F. Floyd Shoemaker to analyze innovation processes generally. *The Communication of Innovations: A Cross-Cultural Approach* (New York: The Free Press, 1971), pp. 99-134, 275-281.

2.An especially important role was played, both on the various "committees of experts" and through less formal channels of consultation, by economists whose careers had encompassed both academic positions and stints of practical experience in the Party or state economic apparatus and who therefore enjoyed a certain respect in both milieus.

Afterword

1.U.S. Central Intelligence Agency, Directorate of Intelligence, *Handbook of Economic Statistics, 1982*, (Washington, D.C.: U.S. Government Printing Office), pp. 54, 77.

2.Analysts of the Central Intelligence Agency, "Eastern Europe Faces Up to the Debt Crisis" in U.S. Congress, Joint Economic Committee, *East European Economies: Slow Growth in the 1980's. Volume 2: Foreign Trade and International Finance* (Washington, DC: U.S. Government Printing Office, 1986), p. 180.

3.Ibid., p. 159.

4.Joan F. McIntyre, "The U.S.S.R.'s Hard Currency Trade and Payments Position," in U.S. Congress, Joint Economic Committee, *Gorbachev's Economic Plans*, Volume II (Washington, DC: U.S. Government Printing Office, 1987), p. 484.

5.V.I. Kushlin, "Razvitie proizvodstvennogo apparata i investitsionye protsessy," *Ekonomika i organizatsiia promyshlennogo proizvodstva*, November 1984, p. 70, as cited by Stanley H. Cohn, "Soviet Intensive Economic Development Strategy in Perspective," in U.S. Congress, Joint Economic Committee, *Gorbachev's Economic Plans*, Volume I (Washington, DC: U.S. Government Printing Office, 1987), p. 15.

6.See U.S. Congress, Joint Economic Committee, *U.S.S.R.: Measures of Economic Growth and Development, 1950-1980* (Washington, DC: U.S. Government Printing Office, 1982); and U.S. Congress, Joint Economic Committee, *Gorbachev's Economic Plans*, Volume I (Washington, DC: U.S. Government Printing Office, 1987), pp. 126- 165.

7."Comrade L.I. Brezhnev's Speech at the Plenary Session of the Central Committee on October 21, 1980," *Pravda* and *Izvestiia*, October 22, 1980, p. 1, as translated in *Current Digest of the Soviet Press*.

8.Decree No. 695, *Sobraniye postanovlenniy pravitel'stva SSSR*, No. 18, 1979, pp. 390-431].

9.For more detailed description and analysis of the 1979 measures, see Morris Bornstein, "Improving the Soviet Economic Mechanism," *Soviet Studies*, Vol. 37, No. 1 (January 1985), pp. 1-30; Philip Hanson, "Success Indicators Revisited: The July 1979 Soviet Decree on Planning and Management," *Soviet Studies*, Vol. 35, No. 1 (January 1983, pp. 1-13; Gertrude Schroeder, "Soviet Economic Reform Decrees: More Steps on the Treadmill," U.S. Congress, Joint Economic Committee, *Soviet Economy in the 1980's: Problems and Prospects*, Part 1 (Washington, DC: U.S. Government Printing Office, 1982), pp. 65-88.

10.Timothy J. Colton, *The Dilemma of Reform in the Soviet Union*, revised and expanded edition (New York: The Council on Foreign Relations), 1986, p. 91.

11."Speech by Yu. V. Andropov at the Plenary Session of the CPSU Central Committee on November 22, 1982," *Pravda* and *Izvestia*, November 23, 1982, pp. 1-2, as translated in *Current Digest of the Soviet Press* Vol. XXXIV, No. 47 (December 22, 1982), p. 5.

12.Ibid., p 4.

13.For an excellent "who's who" among influential Soviet economists in the early 1980's, see Anders Aslund, "Gorbachev's Economic Advisors," *Soviet Economy*, Vol. 3, No. 3 (July-September 1987), pp. 246-269.

14.Dusko Doder's summary of the contents appeared in the Washington *Post* on August 3, 1983. The complete text was reprinted in *Survey*, Volume 28 (Spring 1984), pp. 88-108.

15.*Ekonomicheskaya gazeta*, No. 31 (July 1983).

16.Tsentralnoe statisticheskoe upravlenie, *Narodnoe khoziaistvo v 1984 godu*, p. 130.

17."Initiative, Organization and Efficiency: Speech by M.S. Gorbachev," *Pravda* and *Izvestia*, April 12, 1985, as translated in *Current Digest of the Soviet Press*, Volume XXXVII, No. 15 (May 8, 1985), pp. 1-3.

18."On Convening the regular 27th CPSU Congress and the Tasks Connected with Preparing and Holding It — Report by M.S. Gorbachev, General Secretary of the CPSU Central Committee," *Pravda* and *Izvestia*, April 24, 1985 as translated in *Current Digest of the Soviet Press*, Volume XXXVII, No. 17 (May 22, 1985), p. 3.

19.See, for example, B.P. Kurashvili, "Kontury vozmozhnoi perestroiki," EKO, No. 5 (1985), pp. 59-80.

20.Timothy J. Colton, *The Dilemma of Reform in the Soviet Union*, revised and expanded edition (New York: The Council on Foreign Relations), 1986, p. 91.

21.Jerry F. Hough, "Gorbachev Consolidating Power," *Problems of Communism*, Volume XXXVI, No. 4 (July-August 1987), p. 28.

22.See, for example, the sharply contrasting evaluations in Thane Gustafson and Dawn Mann, "Gorbachev's Next Gamble" and Jerry Hough, "Gorbachev Consolidating Power" (both in *Problems of Communism*, Volume XXXVI, No. 4 (July-August 1987), pp. 1-43.

23.*Pravda* and *Izvestia*, February 26, 1986, p. 4, as translated in *Current Digest of the Soviet Press*, Volume XXXVIII, No. 8 (1986), p. 15.

24.Aslund, *op cit*, pp. 248-249.

25."*Perestroika* — A Vital Concern of the People," *Pravda*, February 26, 1987, translated in *Current Digest of the Soviet Press*, Volume XXXIX, No. 8 (1987), p. 8.

26.M.S. Gorbachev, "Youth — the Creative Force of Revolutionary Renewal," *Pravda*, April 17, 1987, translated in *Current Digest of the Soviet Press*, Volume XXXIX, No. 16 (1987), p. 11.

27."Osnovnyye polozheniya korennoy perestroiki upravleniya ekonomiki," *Pravda*, June 27, 1987.

28.*O korennoy perestroike upravleniya ekonomiki — sbornik dokumentov* (Moscow: Gospolitizdat), 1987.

29.*Pravda*, July 1, 1987.

30.If Gorbachev's reform were to be added into Table 2.5, the column entries would be coded as follows: (1) +, (2) +, (3) +, (8) +, (5) +, (6) +, (12) + /-, (9) + /-, (10) + /-, (11) -, (4) -, (7) + /- .

31.As quoted in *Radio Free Europe Research*, RAD BR/121 (June 29, 1988), p. 1.

32.*Scinteia*, January 27, 1987, as quoted in *Radio Free Europe Research*, RAD BR/95 (May 30, 1988), p. 2.

33.*Radio Free Europe Research*, RAD BR/121 (June 29, 1988), p. 2.

34.*Frankfurter Alllgemeine Zeitung*, June 23, 1988.

35.See, for example, Stephen Ashley, "Can Todor Zhivkov Survive as Bulgaria's Leader?," *Radio Free Europe Research* Bulgarian SR/6 (July 14, 1988), pp. 3-7.

36.Ibid., p. 5.

37.Reuters dispatch, June 15, 1988, as cited in *Radio Free Europe Research* RAD BR/121 (June 29, 1988), p. 2.

SELECTED BIBLIOGRAPHY

Books

Baykov, Alexander. *The Development of the Soviet Economic System*. Cambridge, Eng.: Cambridge University Press, 1947.

Baylis, Thomas. *The Technical Intelligentsia and the East German Elite*. Berkeley: University of California Press, 1974.

Bergson, Abram. *Economics of Soviet Planning*. New Haven: Yale University Press, 1964.

Bornstein, Morris, ed. *Plan and Market: Economic Reform in Eastern Europe*. New Haven: Yale University Press, 1973.

Brown, J.F. *Bulgaria Under Communist Rule*. New York: Praeger, 1970.

Brus, Wlodzimierz. *The Economics and Politics of Socialism: Collected Essays*. London: Routledge and Kegan Paul, 1973.

_____. *The Market in a Socialist Economy*. Trans. Angus Walker. London: Routledge and Kegan Paul, 1972.

Csikos-Nagy, Bela. *Socialist Economic Policy*. Budapest: Akademiai Kiado, 1973.

Dellin, L.A.D., and Gross, H., eds. *Reforms in the Soviet and East European Economies*. Lexington, Mass.: Heath, 1972.

Dobrin, Bogoslav. *Bulgarian Economic Development Since World War II*. New York: Praeger, 1973.

Douglas, D.S. *Transitional Economic Systems: The Polish-Czech Example*. London: Routledge and Kegan Paul, 1953.

Ellman, Michael. *Soviet Planning Today: Proposals for an Optimally Functioning Economic System*. Cambridge, Eng.: Cambridge University Press, 1971.

Eorsi, Gyula, and Harmathy, Attila, eds. *Law and Economic Reform in Socialist Countries*. Budapest: Akademiai Kiado, 1971.

Fallenbuchl, Zbigniew M., ed. *Economic Development in the Soviet Union and Eastern Europe*. 2 vols. I. *Reforms, Technology, and Income Distribution*. II. *Sectoral Analysis*. New York: Praeger, 1975.

Feiwel, George R. *The Economics of a Socialist Enterprise: A Case Study of the Polish Firm*. New York: Praeger, 1967.
_____. *New Economic Patterns in Czechoslovakia*. New York: Praeger, 1968.
_____. *The Soviet Quest for Economic Efficiency*. New York: Praeger, 1967.
Friss, Istvan, ed. *Reform of the Economic Mechanism in Hungary*. Budapest: Akademiai Kiado, 1971.
Gamarnikow, Michael. *Economic Reforms in Eastern Europe*. Detroit: Wayne State University Press, 1968.
Granick, David. *Enterprise Guidance in Eastern Europe: A Comparison of Four Socialist Economies*. Princeton: Princeton University Press, 1975.
Grossman, Gregory, ed. *Value and Plan: Economic Calculation and Organization in Eastern Europe*. Berkeley: University of California Press, 1960.
Hangen, Welles. *The Muted Revolution*. New York: Alfred A. Knopf, 1966.
Hayek, F.A., ed. *Collectivist Economic Planning*. London: Routledge, 1935.
Hirszowicz, M., and Morawski, W. *Z Badan nad Spolecznym Uczestnictwem w Organizacii Przemyslowej*. Warsaw: Ksiazka i Wiedza, 1967.
Hohmann, Hans-Herman; Kaser, Michael; and Thalheim, Karl C. *The New Economic Systems of Eastern Europe*. Berkeley: University of California Press, 1975.
Horvat, Branko. *Towards a Theory of Planned Economy*. Beograd: Yugoslav Institute of Economic Research, 1964.
Kaser, Michael C. *Economic Development for Eastern Europe: Proceedings of a Conference Held by the International Economic Association*. New York: St. Martin's Press, 1968.
Kaser, Michael, and Zielinski, J. *Planning in East Europe: Industrial Management by the State*. London: The Bodley Head, 1970.
Katz, Abraham. *The Politics of Economic Reform in the Soviet Union*. New York: Praeger, 1972.
Keizer, William. *The Soviet Quest for Economic Rationality: The Conflict of Economic and Political Aims in the Soviet Economy 1953-1968*. Rotterdam: Rotterdam University Press, 1971.
Kirschen, E.S., ed. *Economic Policies Compared: West and East*. 2 vols. Amsterdam: North Holland/Elsevier Publishing Co., 1974.
Kordaszewski, J. *Placa Wedlug Pracy*. Warsaw: Ksiazka i Wiedza, 1963.
Kornai, Janos, *Overcentralization in Economic Administration*. London: Oxford University Press, 1959.
Lange, Oskar, ed. *Problems of Political Economy of Socialism*. 2nd ed. Warsaw: Ksiazka i Wiedza, 1959.
Lange, Oskar, and Taylor, Fred. *On the Economic Theory of Socialism*. New York: McGraw-Hill, 1965.
Lauter, G.P. *The Manager and Economic Reform in Hungary*. New York: Praeger, 1972.
Lavigne, Marie. *The Socialist Economies of the Soviet Union and Europe*. Trans. T.G. Waywell. White Plains, N.Y.: International Arts and Sciences Press, Inc., 1974.

Ludz, Peter C. *The Changing Party Elite in East Germany.* Boston: M.I.T. Press, 1972.

Marczewski, Jan. *Crisis in Socialist Planning: Eastern Europe and the USSR.* Trans. Noel Lindsay. New York: Praeger, 1974.

Marer, Paul. *Selected Comparisons of the Financial Systems of the USSR, Czechoslovakia, Hungary and Poland.* Washington, D.C.: U.S. Arms Control and Disarmament Agency, 1971.

Neuberger, Egon. *The Legacies of Central Planning.* Santa Monica: Rand Corp., 1968.

Oren, Nissan. *Revolution Administered: Agrarianism and Communism in Bulgaria.* Baltimore: Johns Hopkins Universty Press, 1973.

Pryor, Frederic L. *Property and Industrial Organization in Communist and Capitalist Nations.* Bloomington: Indiana University Press, 1973.

Richta, Radovan. *Civilization at the Crossroads.* White Plains, N.Y.: International Arts and Sciences Press, Inc., 1969.

Robinson, William F. *The Pattern of Reform in Hungary.* New York: Praeger, 1973.

Selucky, Radoslav. *Economic Reforms in Eastern Europe: Political Background and Economic Significance.* New York: Praeger, 1972.

Sik, Ota. *Plan and Market Under Socialism.* White Plains, N.Y.: International Arts and Sciences Press, Inc., 1967.

Sirc, Ljubo. *Economic Devolution in Eastern Europe.* New York: Praeger, 1969.

Skilling, H. Gordon. *Czechoslovakia's Interrupted Revolution.* Princeton: Princeton University Press, 1976.

Smolinski, Leon. *East European Influences on Soviet Economic Thought and Reforms.* Working Paper No. 6. Bloomington: Indiana University, International Development Research Center, 1971.

Spulber, Nicholas. *The Economies of Communist Eastern Europe.* New York: John Wiley and Sons, 1957._____. *Socialist Management and Planning.* Bloomington: Indiana University Press, 1971.

_____. *The State and Economic Development in Eastern Europe.* New York: Random House, 1966.

Thalheim, Karl C., and Hohmann, Hans-Hermann, eds. *Wirtschaftsreformen in Osteuropa.* Koln: Verlag Wissenschaft und Politik, 1968.

Timar, Matyas. *Reflections on the Economic Development of Hungary 1967-1973.* Budapest: Akademiai Kiado, 1975.

Toma, Peter, and Volgyes, Ivan. *Politics in Hungary.* San Francisco: W.H. Freeman and Co., 1977.

Triska, Jan F., and Johnson, Paul M. *Political Development and Political Change in Eastern Europe: A Comparative Study.* Denver: University of Denver Graduate School of International Studies, Monograph Series in World Affairs, 1975.

von Mises, Ludwig. *Socialism: An Economic and Sociological Analysis.* Trans. J. Kahane. London: Jonathan Cape, 1974.

Wellisz, Stanislaw. *The Economies of the Soviet Bloc*. New York: McGraw-Hill, 1964.

Wilczynski, J. *Socialist Economic Development and Reforms*. London: Macmillan, 1972.

Zaleski, Eugene. *Planning Reform in the Soviet Union, 1962-66*. Chapel Hill: North Carolina University Press, 1967.

Articles

Adam, Jan. "Systems of Wage Regulation in the Soviet Bloc." *Soviet Studies* XXVIII, No. 1 (1976), pp. 91-109.

————. "Wage Regulation in Czechoslovakia under the Economic Reform." *Jahrbuch der Wirtschaft Osteuropas*, 3. Munich: Gunter Olzog Verlag, 1972, pp. 209-230.

Allakhverdyan, D. "On the Economic Reforms in the European Socialist Countries." *Voprosy Ekonomiki*, No. 9 (1969), pp. 104-115.

Alton, T.P. "Polish Industrial Planning." *Journal of International Affairs* XX, No. 1 (1966), p. 94ff.

Balassa, Bela, and Bertrand, Thomas. "Growth Performance of East European Economies and Comparable Western European Countries." *American Economic Review* LX, No. 2 (May 1970), pp. 314-320.

Baylis, Thomas A. "Economic Reform as Ideology." *Comparative Politics* III, No. 2 (1971), pp. 211-229.

Beck, Carl. "Bureaucratic Conservatism and Innovation in Eastern Europe." *Comparative Political Studies* I, No. 2 (July 1968), pp. 275-294.

Berend, Ivan T. "The Historical Background of the Recent Economic Reforms in Eastern Europe." *East European Quarterly* II, No. 1 (March 1968), pp. 75-90.

Bergson, Abram. "Market Socialism Revisited." *Journal of Political Economy* LXXV, No. 5 (October 1967), pp. 655-673.

Bognar, Jozsef. "Economic Reform, Development and Stability in the Hungarian Economy." *New Hungarian Quarterly* XIII, No. 46 (1972), pp. 29-43.

————. "Initiative and Equilibrium: Major Political and Economic Issues in Hungary." *New Hungarian Quarterly* XI, No. 37 (1970), pp. 23-27.

Bolland, S. "Freedom of Decision Within the Framework of the Central Plan." *Eastern European Economics* XI, No. 1 (Fall 1972), pp. 3-17.

Bottcher, Manfred. "Where Do We Stand with Planning in the New Economic System." *Die Wirtschaft*, No. 48, 1965. Reprinted in trans. in *Eastern European Economics* VI, No. 3 (Spring 1968), pp. 50-54.

Brown, J.F. "Reforms in Bulgaria." *Problems of Communism* XV, No. 3 (May-June 1966), pp. 17-30.

Brus, Wlodzimierz. "The Development of the Socialist Economic System in Poland: Remarks on Some General Problems." *Hamburger Jahrbuch fur Wirtschafts- und Gesellschaftspolitik*, 10. Tubingen: J.C.B. Mohr, 1965, pp. 155-173.

_____. "On the Role of the Law of Value in Socialist Economy." *Oxford Economic Papers* IX, No. 2 (1957), pp. 209-221.

Brzeski, Andrzej. "Economic Reform in Poland: The Cautious Avant-Garde." *Quarterly Review of Economics and Business* VII, No. 3 (Autumn 1967), pp. 19-28.

_____. "'Intensification' of Economic Growth in Eastern Europe." *Jahrbuch der Wirtschaft Osteuropas*, 2. Munich: Gunter Olzog Verlag, 1971, pp. 269-290.

_____. "Poland as a Catalyst of Change in the Communist Economic System." *Polish Review* XVI, No. 2 (1971), pp. 3-24.

Chawluk, A. "Economic Policy and Economic Reform." *Soviet Studies* XXVI, No. 1 (January 1974), pp. 98-119.

Clecak, Peter. "Moral and Material Incentives." In R. Miliband and J. Saville, eds., *The Socialist Register, 1969*. London: Merlin Press, 1969, pp. 101-135.

Cohn, Stanley H. "The Soviet Path to Economic Growth: A Comparative Analysis." *Review of Income and Wealth*, Series 22, No. 1 (1976), pp. 49-59.

Csikos-Nagy, Bela. "Profit in Socialist Economy." *Economie Appliquee* XXV, No. 4 (1972), pp. 815-831.

Dellin, L.A. "Bulgarian Economic Reform — Advance and Retreat." *Problems of Communism* XIX, No. 5 (September-October 1970), pp. 44-52.

Doktor, K. "Research on Behavior and Opinions of Workers in a Polish Factory." *The Polish Sociological Bulletin*, No. 3-4 (1962), pp. 113-116.

Dreyer, J.S. "The Evolution of Marxist Attitudes Toward Marginalist Techniques." *History of Political Econmy* VI, No. 1 (1974), pp. 48-75.

Elliot, James R., and Scaperlanda, Anthony E. "East Germany's Liberman-Type Reforms in Perspective." *Quarterly Review of Economics and Business* VI, No. 3 (Autumn 1966), pp. 39-52.

Erlich, Alexander. "The Polish Economy After October: Background and Outlook." *American Economic Review* XLIX, No. 2 (May 1959), pp. 94-112.

_____. "'Eastern' Approaches to a Comparative Evaluation of Economic Systems." In Alexander Eckstein, ed., *Comparison of Economic Systems*. Berkeley: University of California Press, 1971.

Feiwel, George R. "Construction of a Long-Range Economic Plan: Kalecki's Polish Perspective Plan 1961-75." *Indian Economic Journal* XIX, No. 3 (October-December 1971), pp. 287-301.

Frank, Z., and Waelbroeck, J. "Soviet Economic Policy Since 1953: A Study of Its Structure and Changes." *Soviet Studies* XVII, No. 1 (July 1965), pp. 1-43.

Gamarnikow, Michael. "Economic Reform in Poland." *East Europe* XIV, No. 7 (1965), pp. 2-9.

_____. "Poland Returns to Economic Reform." *East Europe* XVIII, No. 11-12 (November-December 1969), pp. 11-18.

_____. "The Reforms: A Survey." *East Europe* XV, No. 1 (1966), pp. 13-23.

Gellner, Ernest. "The Pluralist Anti-Levelers of Prague." *Government and Opposition* VII, No. 1 (Winter 1972), pp. 20-37.

Glowczyk, Jan. "The Limits of Reform or a Reform Without Limits." *Zycie Gospodarcze*, September 7, 1970. Trans. and reprinted in Radio Free Europe

Research, *Polish Press Survey*, No. 2147, October 8, 1970.Goldman, Josef, and
Flek, J. "Economic Growth in Czechoslovakia." *Economics of Planning* VI,
No. 2 (1966), pp. 125-137.

Granick, David. "The Hungarian Economic Reform." *World Politics* XXV, No.
3 (April 1973), pp. 414-429.

Grossman, Gregory. "Economic Reforms: A Balance Sheet." *Problems of
Communism* XV, No. 6 (November-December 1966), pp. 43-55.

_____. "Economic Reform: The Interplay of Economics and Politics." In
R.V. Burks, eds., *The Future of Communism in Europe*. Detroit: Wayne State
University Press, 1968, pp. 103-140.

Harvey, Curtis E., and Hincke, John I., Jr. "Central Planning and Economic
Growth in a Mature Socialist Economy." *Jahrbuch der Wirtschaft Osteuropas*,
5. Munich: Gunter Olzog Verlag, 1974, pp. 345-360.

Hegedus, Andras, and Rozgonyi, Tamas. "Social Conflicts in Decisions on the
Enterprise Level." *Kozgazdasagi Szemle*, July-August 1967. Trans. in Radio
Free Europe Research, *Hungarian Press Survey*, No. 1871, November 27, 1967.

Hegedus, Andras, and Tardos, Marton. "Some Problems Concerning the Role and
Motivation of Enterprise Executives." *Kozgazdasagi Szemle*, No. 2, 1974.
Trans. and reprinted in *Eastern European Economics* XIII, No. 2 (Winter
1974-1975), pp. 90-108.

Held, Joseph. "Iron Out of Wood." *Problems of Communism* XV, No. 6
(November-December 1966), pp. 37-43.

Holesovsky, Vaclav. "Labor and the Economic Reforms in Czechoslovakia."
Amherst: University of Massachusetts Labor Relations and Research Center,
1968. (Mimeographed.)

Janossy, F. "Discrepancies in the Hungarian Economic Structure — How They
Came About and How They Can Be Overcome." *Acta Oeconomica* IV, No. 4
(1969), pp. 351-378.

Kaser, Michael. "Planned Economies Under Reform." In George Schopflin, ed.,
The Soviet Union and Eastern Europe. New York: Praeger, 1970, pp. 291-300.

Kaufman, Adam. "The Origin of the Political Economy of Socialism." *Soviet
Studies* IV, No. 3 (January 1953), pp. 243-272.

Keren, Michael. "Concentration and Devolution in East Germany's Reforms." In
Morris Bornstein, ed., *Plan and Market: Economic Reform in Eastern Europe*.
New Haven: Yale University Press, 1973, pp. 123-151.

_____. "The New Economic System in the GDR: An Obituary." *Soviet Studies*
XXV, No. 2 (April 1973), pp. 554-587.

Klatt, Werner. "The Politics of Economic Reform." *Survey*, No. 70-71 (1969),
pp. 154-168.

Kocanda, R., and P. Pelikan. "The Socialist Enterprise as Participant in the
Market." *Czechoslovak Economic Papers* IX (1967), pp. 49-64. Trans. from
Politicka ekonomie II (1967), pp. 93-103.

Kyn, Oldrich. "The Rise and Fall of Economic Reform in Czechoslovakia."
American Economic REview LX, No. 2 (1970), pp. 300-306.

Lakos, Sandor. "Questions of Social Equality." *New Hungarian Quarterly* XVI, No. 57 (1975), pp. 33-43.

Levcik, B. "Wages and Employment Problems in the New System of Planned Management in Czechoslovakia." *International Labor Review* XCV (April 1967), pp. 299-314.

Lindblom, Charles. "The Rediscovery of the Market." *The Public Interest*, No. 4 (1966), pp. 89-101.

Machonin, Pavel. "Social Stratification in Contemporary Czechoslovakia." *American Journal of Sociology* LXXV (March 1970), pp. 725-741.

Marek, Edward. "Workers' Participation in Planning and Management in Poland." *International Labor Review* CI, No. 3 (March 1970), pp. 271-290.

Miller, Dorothy, and Trend, Harry G. "Economic Reforms in East Germany." *Problems of Communism* XV, No. 2 (March-April 1966), pp. 29-36.

Mlynar, Zdenek. "Problems of Political Leadership and the New Economic System." *World Marxist Review* VIII, No. 12 (December 1965), pp. 75-82.

Montias, John M. "East European Economic Reforms." In Morris Bornstein, Ed., *Comparative Economic Systems: Models and Cases*. Rev. ed. Homewood, Ill.: Richard D. Irwin, Inc., 1969, pp. 324-336.

Moravcik, Ivo. "The Czechoslovak Economic Reform." *Canadian Slavonic Papers* X, No. 4 (Winter 1968), pp. 430-450.

Moravec, P. "Trade Unions in Eastern Europe." In George Schopflin, ed., *The Soviet Union and Eastern Europe*. New York: Praeger, 1970, pp. 331-335.

Najduchowska, H. "Dyrektorzy przedsiebiorstw przemyslowich." In Jan Szczepanski, ed., *Przemysl i Spoleczenstwo w Polsce Ludowej*. Wroclaw: Zaklad Narodowy im. Ossolinskich, 1969, pp. 79-103.

Naor, Valob. "How Dead is the GDR's New Economic System?" *Soviet Studies* XXV, No.1 4 (October 1973), pp. 276-281.

Nyers, Rezso. "Problems of Profitability and Income Distribution." *New Hungarian Quarterly*, No. 40 (Winter 1970), pp. 11-29, and No. 41 (Spring 1971), pp. 21-41._____. "Questions of Principle and Practice in Socialist Economic Integration." *Acta Oeconomica*, No. 2 (1969), pp. 119-154.

Olivera, J. "Cyclical Economic Growth Under Collectivism." *Kyklos* XIII, No. 2 (1960), pp. 229-255.

Pashev, Apostol. "The New System of Management — An Important Stage in the Development of the Bulgarian Economy." *Planovo stopanstvo i statistika*, No. 5, 1966. Reprinted in trans. in *Eastern European Economics* V, No. 3 (Spring 1967), pp. 3-8.

Portes, Richard D. "Economic Reforms in Hungary." *American Economic Review*, LX, No. 2 (May 1970), pp. 307-313.

Pravda, Alex. "Some Aspects of the Czechoslovak Economic Reform and the Working Class in 1968." *Soviet Studies* XXV, No. 1 (July 1973), pp. 102-124.

"Resolution of the Central Committee of the Communist Party of Czechoslovakia on the Principles of the New System of Planned Management." *Eastern European Economics*, No. 3 (1965), pp. 3-18.

Roberts, Paul Craig. "Oskar Lange's Theory of Socialist Planning." *Journal of Political Economy* LXXIX, No. 3 (May 1971), pp. 562-577.

Rychetnik, Ludek. "A Model of Postwar Economic Growth in Eastern Europe." *Jahrbuch der Wirtschaft Osteuropas*, 5. Munich: Gunter Olzog Verlag, 1974, pp. 195-218.

Schroeder, Gertrude E. "Soviet Economic 'Reforms': A Study in Contradictions." *Soviet Studies* XX, No. 1 (July 1968), pp. 1-21.

Smolinski, Leon. "Planning Reforms in Poland." *Kyklos* XXI, No. 3 (September 1968), pp. 498-514.

_____. "Reforms in Poland." *Problems of Communism* XV, No. 4 (July-August 1966), pp. 8-13.

Spittmann, Ilse. "East Germany: The Swinging Pendulum." *Problems of Communism* XVI, No. 4 (July-August 1967), pp. 14-20.

Sturmthal, Adolph. "Workers' Councils in Poland." *Industrial and Labor Relations Review* XIV (April 1961), pp. 370-396.

Treml, Vladimir G. "Interaction of Economic Thought and Economic Policy in the Soviet Union." *The History of Political Economy* I, No. 1 (Spring 1969), pp. 187-216.

_____. "The Politics of Libermanism." *Soviet Studies* XIX, No. 4 (April 1968), pp. 567-572.

Vitak, R. "Workers' Control in Czechoslovakia." In Jaroslav Vanek, ed., *Self-Management*. Baltimore: Penguin Books, Ltd., 1975.Wilczynski, J. "Profit Under Modern Socialism in Eastern Europe." *Australian Quarterly* II, No. 2 (June 1970), pp. 95-101.

Zielinski, Janusz G. "On the Theory of Economic Reforms and Their Optimal Sequence." *Economics of Planning* VIII, No. 3 (1968), pp. 195-215.

Government Documents

U.S. Congress. Joint Economic Committee. *Economic Developments in Countries of Eastern Europe — A Compendium of Papers*. Washington, D.C.: Government Printing Office, 1970.

U.S. Congress. Joint Economic Committee. *New Directions in the Soviet Economy*. Washington, D.C.: Government Printing Office, 1966.

U.S. Congress. Joint Economic Committee. *Reorientation and Commercial Relations of the Economies of Eastern Europe*. Washington, D.C.: Government Printing Office, 1974.

U.S. Congress. Joint Economic Committee. *East European Economies: Slow Growth in the 1980's* (2 vols.) Washington, DC: Government Printing Office, 1986.

U.S. Congress. Joint Economic Committee. *Gorbachev's Economic Plans*. Washington, DC: Government Printing Office, 1987.

INDEX